Rock Bock

Stephen Najda

In memory of Bish

The Editor's Note

This book is written in English and Scots.
It is set between Scotland and France so it also includes sentences in foreign language depending on the encounters made during numerous adventures.

Charlotte J. March

(Bish)

"My Way" by Jacko

'Shut the fuck up will yis...show sum respect!' Spiney whispered out so loudly that almost everyone in the room could hear.
Rep kinda fidgeted around, not wanting to be put down and especially not wanting to be put down by Spiney.
  'Today we are gathered to celebrate the life of Jacko. Humanists accept death as part of the natural order. We are here not to prejudge a person who has passed away, rather to illuminate sincerely and affectionately on the life of Jacko.'
  'A mean...whit the fuck is he goin' owan aboot?'
  'Shut it Rep!' Bish said annoyingly.
Some girl turned round and gave an annoying 'Shhh!'. Rep ignored her and continued, 'A mean...when does the real priest cum owan?'
  'He is the real priest ya fuckin' eggit, now shut it!'
  'A mean...whit kinda priest is he?
  'Shhh!' Rep ignored the girl and continued.
  'A mean...is he a catholic priest or a protestant priest?'
  'He's a humanist priest ya fuckin' tube!!! Now shut the fuck up!' Spiney butted in, whispering loudly.
  'Eh? Whit's a fuckin' humanist priest when he's at hame?'
  'Shhh!'
  'He's kinda like a non-religious priest,' Steevie interrupted.
Rep squinted his face as if to say—Do you think A'm stupid?—and continued his rant.
  'Eh? How cun yis get a non-religious priest... Eh? Smart arse!'
  'You know...it's kinda like...a heid-yin in a religion for non-religious folk who don't believe in religion.'

~ Rock Rock ~

Rep contorted his face even more.

'Shhh!!!'

Rep, Bish, Spiney and Steevie are sitting at the back of a crowded crematorium full of mourners, dressed up as punks, fidgeting and poking each other, not really wanting to be there, trying to be respectful and not obnoxious. Everyone else is quiet, except with a few sniffs and sobs, solemn in respect.

The Humanist minister continues,

'I ask you to stand for a moment of silent reflection. Before we return Jacko to the earth, there will be a short piece of music to reflect the character of Jacko and the life he lived. I ask you to exit after the music. There'll be no closing words.'

The room was silent except for a few sniffs and snobs from the crowd.

A dark velvet cloth draped over Jacko's coffin moved slightly.

'Fuck! A nearly shat meself there!'

Spiney glared at Rep.

'The coffin's movin'... Jacko's trying tae get oot!' Rep whispers out loudly.

'Shut the fuck up Rep will yis...it's Jacko getting' ready tae go intae the flames.'

'Shhh!'

'Fur fuck sake Rep, can yis no control ureself fur a minute.'

'Shhh!'

The room is silent again. The Humanist minister bows his head. A few noises came over the crematorium PA system.

The room is silent again. Suddenly, the sound of a squeaky male voice gurgles out over the PA system.

And now, the end is near.
And so A face the final curtain.

People in the crowd started to look around wondering what was going on.

'Fuck me! Is that Frank Sinatra A'm hearin' Singing "My Way"? Frank Sinatra at Jacko's funeral! That's fuckin' weird!' Rep whispers out loudly again.
The vocals continues:

> *You cunt, A'm not a queer.*
> *A'll state my case, of which A'm certain.*

Eyebrows raised and faces turned in the crematorium, wondering what was going on.
The four boys look at each other. Bish interrupts Rep before he starts ranting on gain, 'That's no Frank Sinatra.'
The music continues:

> *A've lived a life that's full o'shite.*
> *Travelled each and every nowhere.*
> *And more, much more than this,*
> *A did it my way.*

'Is that Sid Vicious I'm hearin?' Spiney asks Bish.
'That's no Sid Vicious; that's Jacko singin'.'
'Fuckin' Wacko Jacko up to his old tricks again!'
'Fuck me! That's spooky eh! Jacko singin' at his own funeral! Eh?!' Rep butts in.
'Shut it will yis!'
Jacko's rendition of "My Way" continues in a slow methodic tone:

> *Regrets, A've had a few*
> *Too many to tell yis.*
> *A did, what A had tae do, just tae fuck yis.*
> *A've taken every drug along the shite way.*

A planned each careful step on turds.
And more, much more than this
A did it my FUCKING WAY!!!

The tempo of the song picks up as Jacko's sound goes into full punk mode mimicking the Sid Vicious rendition of "My Way". The curtains parted and the coffin moves slowing into the void to the sound of "My Way" by Jacko.

There were times, A'm sure yis knew.
When there wus fuck, fuck-all else tae dae.
But through it all, when A was owan empty.
A threw it up or shot it up.
What's more, much more than this.
A did it ma WAAAYYY!!!

Malkied awe the fuckin way.
Owan a bender tae chase the dragon.
Sum say A'm as gallus as fuck.
A know yis laughed and snide.
Sum say A huvnae a scoobie.

And now the tears subside.
So A say goodbye tae ya, cos.
A don't like de fucking chips.
But A know fur certain, we'll meet in hell.

Fuck yis and fuck that
Every fucker is a fucking rat.
But all A want tae say is fuck yis all.
And fur de record, A killed the fuckin' rats
And did it my way, FUCKIN' WAAAYYY!!!
And now the end is near, and I face the final curtain.

A did it my FUCKIN' WAAAYYY!!!

The last few gurgled sounds from Jacko's voice blasts out of the PA. Spiney, Rep, Bish and Steevie are jiggling about, wanting to start dancing.
The curtains close. The music stops. People looked around, in shock and surprise, wondering what they had just heard, was it over or more to come. Not sure whether to clap or cry.
The boys look at each other.
　'Is that it finished?'
　'Cun we goes now?'
The four boys made their way outside of the crematorium to the car park. Bish stops in his tracks and freezes. The three others stop, wondering what Bish is up to. Bish suddenly springs into life, pogoing up and down, going mental, arms trashing about all over the place, giving it laldy.
Bish stops and pipes out.
　'Pure fuckin' dead brilliant! Beat that... Jacko whit a space cadet! That was some fuckin' ace finish frum Jacko there. Pure fuckin' magic... Ace send off... A did it my way...pure fuckin' magic! Dancing awe the way intae the flames. Fuck, the boy hud style... A face the final curtain...the curtains opened, und Jacko goes inate the flames. Fuckin' ace! The boy had somethin'...style!'
　'Spooky, eh? Recorded his owan funeral song...eh?' Rep butts in.
Spiney had to get a word in over Rep.
　'Fuckin' bampot, if yis ask me! Fuckin stupid cunt, fair und square, if yis ask me!'
And there was me.
　'Jacko was a fuckin' eggit...taken awe those drugs. Just did his heid in...malkied awe de way! As the boy said!'
Bish was impatient.

'Cumowan let's get tae the bikes und get oota here...'

'Good idea. Let's get goin' intae the hills. There's climbing tae be done. We can get sum vitols on the way, then get tae the 'Coe before it gets dark und get a good doss.'

But Rep wasn't up for that.

'Fuck that fur a laugh Captain Shitey Sensible! There's dancin' tae be dun the night. And we cun go uptae the 'Coe later.'

'It will just be like the last time, wandering aboot awe oor the place in the dark, goin' nowhere, just roon and roon in circles awe night. It will just be an epic like the last time.'

'Fuck oaf Captain Shitey Sensible, yur awais moaning yur heid oaf. If yis ure no moaning, yis ure fuckin' whingin' yur heid oaf. Yur as exciting as huvin' a dose o skits in de bath.'

'Hoy! Cunt! That's my line...'

Rep gives two fingers to Spiney.

'Fuck this fur a laugh. Cumoan, let's get oota here.'

'Naw cumoan, let's get goin' intae the hill's, there's climbin' tae be dun', Spiney said.

Rep butted in.

'No...cumoawn, there's a great disco owan the night..it'll be brilliant.'

Spiney starts taking the piss out of Rep, singing out some disco classics.

'A'm in the mood fur dancing, romancing, prancing, wanking...get yur spandex shorts owan and impress the Gary Glitter fans... Eh? Just think, yis will be the Dancing Queer... A mean Dancing Queen...or is it the Dancing Queer... A cun never work out what the lyric is sayin'.'

Rep was not amused.

'Shut yur pus! It will be brilliant.'

'Like fuck it will! The last time yis said it would be brilliant, the D.J. wus shite und yis started a fight and we got chucked oot.'

'Uch, well the DJ was shite…kept playin' awe this disco shitey stuff.'

'Get yur spandex owan, A'm in de mood fur dancing, romancing, prancing, wankin', A'm the dancin' Queer, roamacing, prancing, wankin'.'

'Fuck oaf! It will be brilliant. It's a different D.J the night… und he's playing punk.'

'Fuck oaf! It will be shite!'

'It will be brilliant!'

'It wus shite last time.'

'No it wusnae!'

'Aye it wus.'

'No it wusnae!'

'A remember it well…the Bay City Wankers? Shite-A-Lang, Shite-A-Lang and we sang with the gang, Do-Op-Doo-Wop-Dooby-Day.'

Spiney started to sing, and put in a stupid dance routine and a few wanking gestures for effect.

'Shite-A-Lang, Shite-A-Lang and we sang with the gang. Do-Op-Doo-Wop-Dooby-Day. We're dancin' in shite with oor blue suede shoes awe de night away. Shite-A-Lang, Shite-A-Lang and we sang with de gang. Do-Op-Doo-Wop-Dooby-Day.'

Rep was not very happy with Spiney's antics.

'A'm tellin' yis, there's punk owan!'

Spiney continued singing and dancing.

'Get ure tartan scarf owan! Ya Bay City Wanker. Shite-A-Lang, Shite-A-Lang and we sang with the gang. Do-Op-Doo-Wop-Dooby-Day!'

'Cumoan let's go tae the disco, there's plenty o time tae go up the hill later.'

'It will be another epic, like the last time.'

'The voice o Captain fuckin' Shitey Sensible whingin' again.'

'The disco will be shite!'

A slanging match ensued between Rep and Spieny.
'Fuck oaf it will be brilliant!'
'Fuck oaf it will be shite!'
'It will be magic!'
'It will be shite!'
'Cunt!'
'Arsehole!'
'Prick!'
'Knob-end!'
'Shite-hole!'
'Twat!'

Bish jumps onto his machine. With one big thrust of his boot, kick-starts it alive with a loud roar, black smoke belched out from the exhaust. Spiney and Rep continued exchanging profanities. Bish revs up his machine to drown out the squabbling. Revving was like waving a red rag to Spiney, and Bish knew it. Spiney stop arguing with Rep, jumps onto his machine and kicks it alive. Black smoke poured out the back as the machine backfired and spluttered to life.
Looks of "fucking idiots" from mourners in the crematorium car park.
Bish gave the nod to Rep. Rep jumped on the back of the machine and gave a "V" to Spiney for good measure. Spiney signals over to Steevie to get on the back of his machine. Bish and Spiney eyeball each other in a revving contest.
The starter flag was raised. The bikes revved to the max. Bish and Spiney drooped down over the handle bars, revving the engines hard. The flag dropped. Clutches out, gears engaged and we're off at the maximum rate of knots doing a wheelie down the road, with Steevie and Rep hanging on for dear life, and leaving a trail of smoke and a black rubber streak on the road.

The race was now on. It was head to head at full throttle. The unspoken rule, he who gets to Erskine Bridge first, dictates where we go. The bikes flew round corners and flat out along straights.

Bish got to the bridge first, took a right and headed into town; we're goin' to the disco. After all it was Friday night and there was dancin' to be done, and Bish knew that Spiney would follow.

Pure Fuckin' Mental

Dancing

We had to get out of the disco fast. Rep had been taking the piss out of some punk rockers. They had taken an instant disliking to him. Two punks kicked Rep to the ground. Spiney, Bish and I jumped on them, but this seemed to aggravate a whole bunch more like angry wasps roused from their nest. Spiney whacked one of them in the face, blood poured from his nose. The scene was becoming ugly: a couple of beer glasses were thrown in our direction. The three of us dragged Rep across the dance floor, up the stairs, out of the disco and onto the street. The bouncers at the door were trying to calm the situation. Rep was still full of fight.

'Cum owan ya fuckin' bastards!'

'Shut up Rep, ya tosser.' Bish was trying to calm Rep down.

'Square go! Take yis awe on! Fuckin' wankers!' Rep was straining at full voice to get the words out, saliva pouring down the side of his mouth.

Spiney was trying to restrain Rep with a half Nelson and drag him away.

Rep was still struggling to get back to the disco.

'Fuckin' wankers!'

The other three of us wanted to get away.

'Moan tae fuck. Let's get tae the bikes an' oota here!'

After all the fuss had died down and we were some distance from the disco, Rep's face was beaming a mile wide from ear to ear. He had lost all his front teeth in a previous encounter and didn't see any point in getting a new set to be knocked out again. Rep seemed to enjoy aggravating punk rockers, it was just part of the scene.

We made our way through the empty Glasgow streets to the bikes, still with dancing in our feet. It was a typical Glasgow autumn night, cold and wet. Sounds of The Jam, The Buzzcocks, The Sex Pistols, Siouxsie and the Banshees, Stiff Little Fingers, The Ruts, GenX, The Undertones and the like were ringing in our ears. One of us would suddenly stop, and then spring into action pogoing up and down, then all four of us would pogo up and down in the rain.

We got to the bikes. Steevie moaned away to Spiney.

'It awais ends up like this. Rep getting' us chucked oot.'

'A know, it's typical fuckin' Rep, awais up tae trouble.'

'It awais ends up like this...und we could be up in the 'Coe...und start climbing first thing in the morning...instead we're gonna huv another epic as usual.'

'A know, it's typical fuckin' Rep, awais getting' us in an epic.'

Rep was getting annoyed about being talked about and butted in his usual blunt manner.

'Stop fuckin' moaning will yis!'

Steevie continues.

'It's awais the same, getting chucked ootae a disco, 'cos Rep ends up fightin'...and the next thing, we'll end up wae an epic on the hill. It's awais the same story...'

'Awe...it's Captain Shitey fuckin' Sensible again... Stop fuckin' whingin' will yis, it's awais moan moan moan...moan aboot this, moan aboot that, whinge aboot this, whinge aboot that. Cun yis no geeus peace fur fuck sake!'

'We hud tae rescue yis the disco...next time we'll just leave yis tae get yur heid kicked in.'

'Yis can dae wae sum facial adjustments...give yis sum

improvements eh?'
Bish joined in, seeing Rep was having difficulty putting his helmet on.

'Rep cunnae help it. Yis yur just a Bay City Roller urn't yis?'
Rep fiddling about with his bike helmet.

'Awa'n bile yur fuckin' heids in a bucket o shite!'
Rep had no time for any banter and kept fiddled about with his hair. He had mixed tomato ketchup and wallpaper glue in his hair to make spikes, but had forgotten about the need for a helmet. Bish was hassling Rep for taking such a long time to put his helmet on. Rep was more concerned about carefully folding back his spikes, so that they would pop up once the helmet was off, or so he hoped. Rep had self-pierced a safety pin through his right eyebrow to look cool. But the safety pin made it problematical to put the helmet on. Rep carefully negotiated the helmet past his safety pin.
Bish was becoming impatient.

'Cum owan tae fuck, let's get owan the road!'
Spiney jumped on his bike and kicked it to a start. The silence of the night was broken with a deafening roar. Large plumes of black smoke erupted from the exhaust. The bike coughed and spluttered as Spiney gave more throttle. A smell of two-stroke oil permeated the air.
Bish was getting more animated with Rep's antics.

'Hurry up will yis. Get owan the back!'
Then... We were off—at full throttle—leaving a large cloud of blue smoke and a large black streak of rubber on the road. This was Spiney's trademark. A reminder of where he had just been. Bish's machine came to life a few seconds later.
The race was now on.
It was past midnight and we had survived the disco to go climbing. The race was to get to Glencoe and the doss before

Bish and Rep and get a good night's kip. This was a typical Friday night: go dancing, and then drive like lunatics at some small hour into the mountains and go climbing first thing in the morning.

We drove through the streets of Glasgow at speed, jumping lights and sneaking down one-way streets the wrong way.
Glasgow was left behind, and soon Spiney and Bish were driving like madmen along Loch Lomond, following the twisty loch-side road, weaving in and out of every bay and point.
Bish and Rep managed to get out in front. Bish's machine was faster on the straight. His body was draped over the petrol tank; chin sticking out, teeth in a permanent grin, a bracing smile against the wind and cold, helmet hanging from his chin, more off than on. Rep, riding pillion, was sat upright pinned by the wind against two large rucksacks strapped to the back of the bike, eyes forced tightly shut by the speed, or fright.
Spiney and I were behind. Spiney was supreme on the bends; each corner had to be taken at maximum speed, sparks flying from the foot-peg as it carved out a large groove in the tarmac. Spiney wore goggles like some First World War flying ace, which gave him an intense, suicidal manic look. I was on the back with eyes closed going round bends. I gave up looking at the road going flying past, only a few inches from my knee. Then Spiney would lean the bike harder into the corner. Spiney's secret was to drive the full width of the road on the assumption that you could see any oncoming car's headlights. However, this assumption did not take into account other things on the road like rabbits, pot-holes, fallen trees, etc.

On the road

Nothing else mattered except climbing. The machines were

a means to an end—to go climbing. There was no money, so we improvised and 'Bitzers' were created out of trashed bikes found in dumps, broken down and carefully reassembled for maximum performance—to go climbing—faster.

Occasionally disaster struck. The road to Glencoe was a history of crashes. Almost every corner was well known from bitter experience.
I remember missing the corner for the bridge over the River Dochart on my new machine. There was some oil on the road and instead of going round the corner and over the bridge, I went straight on, hit the bridge and went over the handle bars. I was lucky not to have ended up in the river below. The front wheel was mangled and forks buckled. I had to take the front wheel off and reshape it with some rocks borrowed from a nearby stane dyke. It took me an age to drive the last few miles to Glencoe in second gear, battered and bruised, the bike bobbling up and down at each revolution of the slightly squared front wheel and the handlebars pointing at a strange angle to the direction of the bike.

Then there was the time Spiney ran out of petrol in Crianlarich. I was riding pillion. We managed to persuade a local from the pub to give us some petrol. He was totally pissed and managed to pour more petrol over us than went into the petrol tank.
Spiney wanted to leave in his usual spectacular style, but there must have been an air bubble or some water in the fuel since nothing much happened except for a few coughs and splutters from the engine. Spiney gave full power on the throttle to clear the engine.
Not much happened. Then, suddenly, the bike took off in a spectacular wheely down the road, both of us hanging on.

However, it was a bit too spectacular: the front of the bike went high into the air, threw me off the back and crashed onto Spiney's left knee. A very impressive motor-biking display for people dining in the restaurant overlooking the road.

The bike was fine, but Spiney's leg was in a bad way, blood everywhere. I bandaged him up as best I could and put a bit of wood, as a splint, down his leg to stop his bones crunching. I hadn't learned to drive a bike at that time so we improvised. We rigged up a sling around the petrol tank so that Spiney's left leg could rest horizontally, sticking out the front of the bike. He could operate the clutch with his right hand while I operated the gear change with my left foot from the back of the bike. We drove all the way to Fort William that night. Next day it was obvious that Spiney had to go to hospital: there was to be no climbing that weekend. We drove back down to Glasgow, late at night, with Spiney's leg in plaster, in a sling around the petrol tank and sticking straight out beyond the headlight of the machine, like some goose-stepping Nazi storm-trooper, suddenly frozen by *rigor mortis* to the side of the bike.

Then there was the time when Bish got a puncture in his front tyre going round one of the fast Glencoe corners in a race with Spiney. Bish went over the handlebars and bounced on his chin for quite a distance along the road. The standing joke was that's where Bish got his smile. The bike was fine, but Bish was covered in blood and ended up in hospital. The crash stopped Bish from climbing for a day or two.

Then there was the time in the snow: Spiney was making a determined effort to get to Glencoe in the middle of a blizzard at night. I was on the back of the bike. There was so much snow everywhere that it was difficult to work out what was road and what was not. He was driving in second gear (careful not to get wheel spin) with his feet out near the road surface to provide extra stability in case the bike went into a slide. We drove past an occasional abandoned car or truck left at the side of the road.

Coming down to a bridge, I could feel Spiney struggling with the bike. He was trying to turn the bike into a corner and over a bridge, but instead we were going straight on. I could make out a muffled, 'Fuuuck!!!' from Spiney before we disappeared through a gap in the fence and down a steep embankment. I fell off the back of the bike, bounced down the embankment and came to a stop in a large snowdrift. I saw Spiney following his bike further down the embankment. I realised that the snowdrift that stopped me was actually a car covered with snow, and that there were several other cars at the bottom of the embankment, all abandoned, each with a varying thickness of snow cover.

Spiney was pinned down under the bike, cursing and swearing. I waded through the deep snow and dragged the bike off him. The front mudguard had been forced inside itself, had seized the front wheel and punctured the tyre.

We scrambled up the snow covered embankment to the fence that had been ripped out, and tried to free one of the fence posts to use as a lever, but could not disentangle a post from the bundle of fence wire. Instead, the two of us had to drag the bike through the deep snow and halfway up the embankment to bash away at the front mudguard with a fence post that was still connected to the big bundle of coiled up wire. I would hold the bike in position on the slope and Spiney would bash away. After a couple of bashes with the fence post, the bike would topple over and slide back down the embankment. It had to be pushed up again and Spiney would hold the machine while I bashed away. Eventually, the front wheel was released.

Spiney tried to kick-start the bike, but could only manage a pa-

thetic sickly cough from the engine. The two of us had several attempts pushing and dragging the bike up the embankment. Each time we almost managed it, but each time the bike tumbled back down to the bottom and we ended up on our faces. We gave up and left the bike where it lay. The two of us wandered into the blizzard, like walking snowmen, looking for a doss, but couldn't find anywhere to sleep, so we came back to the bike and spent the night in one of the abandoned cars.
Next day a passing snowplough stopped and helped drag the bike out of the ditch.
The road to Glencoe was closed that day. That weekend's climbing was abandoned.

Then there was the time when I was on the back of Bish's machine when the chain came off and went round my ankle…

Then there was the time when I crashed…

And then there was the time…

Somehow we managed to survive the motorbikes to go climbing.

The petrol pump

Spiney stopped in Tarbet, a small village on the west shore of Loch Lomond. It was raining heavily. There was a 24-hour petrol machine there. We needed more petrol to get to Glencoe, but the machine wasn't working. It didn't want to take our wet pound note. Spiney fiddled about with the pound note.
   'Fuckin' thing!'
We pushed and thumped the pump.
   'Gee it a guid kick.'

Spiney tried to kick the petrol pump but misjudged his kick, slipped on the wet ground and ended on his backside.
'Shite!'
'Ha! Ha! Ha!'
'Let's see that wan again!'
'Ha! Ha! Ha!'
'Smart arse eh?
'We'll no make the Coe the night.'
'Why the hell didn't yae put more juice in when we wur in the toon?'
I said the obvious.
Spiney came out with some excuse of wanting to go faster on the straits, improve handling round corners, distribute the weight more evenly, stop wear on his front tyre...
What he was trying to say was that he forgot.
'Shhh...' Spiney changed the subject.
Spiney had overtaken Bish on one of the tight loch-side bends a few miles back.
'A cun hear Bish cuming... We'll huv tae stop him.'
The two of us stood in the middle of the road, listening to the noise of the bike getting louder. Spiney muttered something about how Bish's timing was out. Spiney knew about bikes and engines and things like that. He had built several machines from bits and pieces given to him or found on scrap heaps.
Bish flew past, between Spiney and I, at a great rate of knots. The tail brake-light came on and bounced about as Bish put on the anchors, Rep desperately gripping onto the back frame, to try to stop himself going over Bish and the handlebars. There was a strong smell of burning brake pads and rubber. They turned round and came over to us.
Bish snapped at Spiney, annoyed that he had to stop.
'Whit the fuck's up? Is someone deid?'
'Oot'a juice.'

'Why the fuck didn't yae fill it up in Glasga, ya tosser!'
'A hud tae get owan the road first.'
'Fuckin' eejit.'
'Tough shit, we're off tae the Coe… Y'ull huv tae wait fur petrol. See ya owan the hill raamorrow. Byeee…' Bish gave a wave and Rep gave a "V".
'Too bad, we've the music and the gas and the food…so yae can fuck off if yis want and freeze yur balls oaf!'
That was the start of an argument in the middle of the road and in front of Tarbet Hotel. It was early in the morning. Volumes of abuse were being thrown around.
'Fuck yis off tae the Coe then!'
'We're off tae the Cobbler instead, wankers!'
'But the Cobbler is shite.'
'Its awewis pishin' doon there.'
'We goat soaked the last time we wur there.'
'Whit the fuck dae yae think the 'Coe will be like…fuckin' Benidorm!?
'A cun just see it noo, wae awe these birds walking doon the Buachaille, way their bikinis owan, tits bouncin' aboot, suppin' on their Martinis.'
'Just like fuckin' Butlins man! A hope yae huv yur penguin suit.'
'Fuck off! The rock's shite on the Cobbler. It's awewis dead slippy in the wet.'
'Naw it's no!'
'Aye it's!'
'It's yur fault fur wanting to go dancin'.'
'Naw it's no!'
'Aye it's!'
'Naw it's no!!!'
'Aye it is!!!'

The argument changed from a shouting match to squabbling. Bish and Rep wanted to head up to the 'Coe by themselves. Spiney and I would then have to doss somewhere nearby for the night and follow in the morning. Alternatively we all could go to the Cobbler instead, go onto the hill tonight, sleep under a large boulder and go climbing in the morning. The Cobbler was chosen. It was not far away.

As a calming experience, as often happened after a major decision had been taken, Bish's cassette recorder came out.
Sex Pistols "Anarchy in the U.K." was loaded into the machine. Full Volume. The music blasted out.
All four of us pogoed up and down to the rhythm of the music, shouting our heads off and bumping into each other. Then, Rep was on the road, wriggling about in a puddle of water doing the worm. Towards the end of the song, I realised that lights were coming on in the hotel.
    'Shite! Let's get oota here.'
The four of us jumped back on the bikes. The bikes were started: engines revved up; lots of noise; smoke pouring out of the back; gear engaged, clutch out. Then we were off leaving two large black rubber streaks down the road.

The race was on to get to Succoth, a small forestry village just round the loch head from Arrochar. We planned to leave the bikes there and go into the hill. It wasn't far from Tarbet, but Spiney was trying to do the ton and catch up with Bish. Spiney's tall frame was draped over the petrol tank, I was lying over his back to try and improve the aerodynamics and get more speed out of the bike. The trees at the side of the road were flying past, just a blur. We drove through Arrochar in a few seconds.
Bish and Rep reached Succoth first, got off the main road and

started unloading the rucksacks from Bish's bike. The rain was now much heavier, but we raced to get the bikes unpacked and get onto the hill. There wasn't much thought about the rain. Getting wet was all part of the game.

Within a minute or so of stopping the bikes, a blue flashing light appeared round the loch-side; somebody must have called the police, or we had woken them up passing through Arrochar. The police didn't see us and drove past at speed. We carried on unpacking.

A few minutes later, the police came back down the road slowly, after giving up the chase. They saw us and drove over. Bish and Rep were closest to the main road. The police car stopped by them. The cop in the passenger seat wound his window down a little, to avoid getting wet. Bish went over to speak to them. Rain was dripping off his face.

'Terrible night officer...Is someone lost?'

'What have you lads been up to?' asked the cop in the passenger seat.

'Just off the hill officer.' Bish speaking in a very deliberate, posh accent, turned around, indicated that we were just packing up the rucksacks.

'The weather's too bad, nobody in their right mind would be on the hill the night.'

There was a suspicious look from the cop. Bish's posh accent wasn't very convincing, but he carried on regardless.

'We're going to camp the night in the wood over there, out of the way.'

'We're looking for two bikers speeding.' The cop in the driver's seat interrupted.

'We saw two bikes flying past a few moments ago, nice machines,' replied Bish Could huv been Germans, must huv been doin' at least the ton.'

'Crazy in this weather,' Rep said. Bish agreed.

There was a silence.
Spiney reached over his bike in the pretext of turning on the fuel, but disconnected a H.T. lead and tried to start the engine. There were a few splutters, nothing happened.
He tried again, and again, the engine turned over, but didn't start.
Spiney went over to the police car and asked:
　'D'yae huv any WD40? Ma bike never starts in the wet.'
No reply.
The cop wound up his window and they drove on.
Luckily they didn't get out to check the bikes, because the engines were glowing red hot. As a precaution we drove around with permanently dirty number plates.
We moved our bikes further down a forestry commission road to be less conspicuous and carried on unpacking.
Rep came out with:
　'A told yis wae shouldnae huv played "God Save the Queen". It's banned by the BBC!'
Nobody replied.

Lost

All four of us were soon on the hill, carrying large packs. Four head torches in the dark racing up the hill. It would take a couple of hours to get to our boulder doss. The rain turned to snow. Soon, we were in a blizzard, struggling to walk into the wind. The race to the doss took second place. Trying to find out which direction to go now took priority. Nobody had taken a compass bearing because of the rush to get in the hill and since everybody reckoned they knew the mountain well.
　'Shouldnae de burn be on the left?' My nose numb and jaw frozen as I tried to make my voice heard over the howling wind.

'It does'nae feel right wae the land going up tae the left.'
There was a silence. Everybody else had probably realised we were lost some time ago, but were too proud to admit it in the rush to get up the hill.

We were somewhere on or near the Cobbler, at night, in the middle of a blizzard, and had no hope of finding our doss for the night. Distance, direction, movement and balance were all fused by the driving snow and the darkness; we may have advanced half a mile, or just a few yards—it was difficult to judge. We were walking directly into the biting wind, then it would quickly change direction; then we would have an argument whether we were walking in a straight line or round in circles. It was difficult walking, across large boulder fields, the snow and darkness making everything look flat. Every few steps, the snow crust would give way and a leg would disappear between rocks. It was exhausting work, fighting every step.
We had been walking for a couple of hours with no real idea of where we were going.
In the distance, I was convinced that I could see someone walking and shouted out.
    'Halloo there!'
Spiney and Bish were wondering what was going on.
I tried to convince them.
    'Look, there's someone oor there.'
They looked...but couldn't see anything.
    'Whit the fuck ure yae owan...the bendy juice? There's nuthin there There's just a pile o boulders.'
A few steps forward and I realised that my tired mind had been playing tricks. A little later, I was convinced that I could see a cat sitting in the distance. I squinted my eyes into the driving wind and snow to double-check. This time, I didn't say

anything. A few more steps forward quenched my imagination. My cat turned into a rock sticking out of the snow.
After some time, cliffs appeared all around, gullies disappeared into the night, mist swirled around dark pinnacles. We didn't know if we were on the south peak or north peak of the Cobbler or maybe even on a different mountain.
Spiney announced:
'A know where we ure noo. It's no far tae go.'
Everyone looked at each other, unconvinced of Spiney's certainty.
Bish interrupted:
'A know where we ure noo as weel. We wis here holf an oor before!'
'Naw we wurnae.'
'Yes we wus.'
'Naw we wurnae.'

Too tired to start another argument, we started walking again, bracing ourselves into the blizzard.
A little later Spiney came up with a great idea.
'Let's climb up tae the top.'
He was pointing to a steep system of chimneys going up into the darkness.
'Then we'll know where we ure.'
Impeccable logic, nobody could argue against that.
'Looks a piece a pish—nae fuckin' bother.'
Everybody else was too tired to disagree.

We climbed up to the bottom of the chimney. It was sloping left to right with a large chock-stone jammed about 60-70 feet up. Spiney reckoned that there was a hole large enough to squeeze through between the back of the chimney and chock-stone. We started to get organised. Our rucksacks were opened to get our climbing gear and within a few seconds were full of spin-drift. It was a struggle with the cold and the dark, trying to put our climbing gear on, fingers frozen. Trying to tie knots in our old frozen hawser rope, stiff as wire. We had just bought new climbing harnesses, so we felt like real climbers, but had only one rope between four and a couple pieces of protection; it was all we could afford. I set up a belay. Spiney headed up the chimney without his rucksack. The light from his head-torch disappeared into the darkness and wind and snow. All three of us down below were stamping our feet to keep warm, then some more spin drift would come down and cover us in a freezing shower.

'Hurry up! Hurry up, fur fuck's sake!' was the cry every five minutes, but we knew the words would be lost in the darkness.

At last, there were a couple of strong tugs on the rope. I untied the belay and tied on Bish and Rep's rucksacks at the end of the rope for Spiney to pull up. The rucksacks started their slow ascent. They got as far as the chock-stone, then they got stuck.

Rep was becoming impatient waiting.

'Fuck this, A'm off up, and soloed up to the chock-stone.'

Bish followed Rep. The two of them struggled to release the rucksacks and turn them around so that they would fit through the hole. The two rucksacks, Bish and Rep disappeared from view.

After what seemed like an eternity, the rope came back down. To speed things up, I decided to climb with my rucksack on my back and tied Spiney's to the rope in front on me.

I was climbing with an old pair of second-hand crampons with no front points and two old masonry claw hammers adapted as ice axes. The climbing gear was useless. My crampons scratched away on the rock looking for something to stand on, the claw hammers scrapped against icy rock and the heavy rucksack on my back swayed about in the blustery wind. I was making my way up the chimney but feeling very insecure at each step.

I struggled up to the chock stone. I pushed Spiney's rucksack in front of me partly through the hole between the chimney and the chock-stone, but it got stuck. Then I tried to squeeze myself past the jammed rucksack, but I only managed to get myself stuck. I couldn't move up. I tried to push harder, but then lost my footing. I was jammed with feet dangling in air. I started to panic, searching for hand and footholds. My crampons scratched against the rock to find a foothold. My claw hammers bounced off rock as I tried to get a placement. Bits of frozen heather were ripped out trying to find something to hold onto. Nothing felt secure.

If only my rucksack was a bit smaller, I could squeeze through. After an enormous effort, I contorted my body into a position where I could just release the straps on my rucksack, but with a gust of wind my foam mattress disappeared into the darkness. Losing my foam mattress wasn't the plan, but with a smaller rucksack, I could just about squeeze past the chockstone. At the belay, Spiney gave me a lot of hassle for taking such a long time. Bish and Rep couldn't be bothered waiting and had continued to the top.

Eventually Spiney and I reached the north peak summit of The Cobbler almost at dawn. At last we knew where we were. The snow had stopped falling and there was a bit of blue sky appearing in the far distance.

From the summit we quickly descended to find our doss. Bish and Rep were already there, crashed out underneath a large boulder. Spiney and I unpacked quickly and soon all four of us were fast asleep. We were all knackered, after a long night of dancing, motorbiking, wandering about in a blizzard, and climbing in the dark.

≈

I was awoken by The Jam blasting out of the tape recorder at full volume.
 'Shut that fuckin' thing doon!' was a cry from the corner.
There were plenty of groans.
 'Cumoawn. get y'ure arse intae gear!'
Bish was trying to encourage people to move.
 'D'ere's blue sky oot d'ere und d'ere's dry rock, A'm off rocking! See ya later!'
There were more groans.

Bish was right; it was a magic day and not a breath of wind. Soon sounds of punk rock reverberated around the amphitheatre of vertical rock as Bish played his cassette recorder somewhere on the mountain.

Pure Fuckin' Mental

There was blue sky without a cloud to be seen and the air felt warm. Last night's storm seemed almost like a bad dream. Snow still lay in the shadows and gullies, but most had disappeared in the bright sunshine. The rock was drying quickly. We hadn't brought much gear for rock climbing. Spiney announced he was off to solo some of the easier climbs and disappeared up the hill. I followed a bit later and climbed about on the large boulders and bits of crag that were scattered around, half hoping to find my foam mattress that had disappeared into the night. I never found it.

At the end of the day, I soloed up one of the V. Diffs on the north peak of The Cobbler and lay on the summit of the north peak admiring the view and watching the sun go down. There was an occasional shout or punk rock line echoing around the mountain from Bish or Spiney somewhere on the south peak. Drowsy in my slumber, I thought I heard a faint 'help'. After last night and not much sleep it was easy to convince myself that my imagination was running wild again. A few moments later there was a more definite cry for help.

I got up from my slumber and tried to figure out where the sound was coming from. I went over to the edge of the cliff, lay on my stomach, inched towards the edge and looked over. All I could see was 150ft vertically straight down to the bottom of the cliff. There's something frighteningly unreal about looking over the edge of a cliff: it's almost like a hypnotic trance willing you over, to slowly slide off the edge and float down to the bottom, a Medusa tempting fate.

'Hallooo!' I shouted over the edge.

A few seconds later, a distant desperate sounding voice replied:

'Gee'us a hon fur fuck sake!'

I was still trying to work out where the voice was coming from.

'It's me. A'm stuck.'

'Is that you Rep? Where the fuck ure yae?'

'Oor her! A'm owan the edge o the peak,' a voice of desperation replied.

I could hear that Rep was totally gripped, with a certain anxiety in his voice.

'Gee'us a hon for fuck's sake!'

I moved further along the cliff and looked over again. There was still no sign of him. I moved further along the edge of the cliff, looking down the vertical precipice, trying to find Rep. However, there was a problem, the north summit comes to a sharp pointed overhanging nose and I was beginning to run out of mountain. I started to feel nervous about my own situation and didn't fancy going much further along the top of the cliff. Then I noticed eight fingers curled round the edge of the cliff, almost right at the end of the overhanging nose. It was Rep. He was totally gripped, unable to pull himself over.

'Holy shite! How the hell did yae get there Rep?'

'Nae time fur questions just gee'us yur hon fur Christ sake!'

I went on my stomach again and looked over the edge. I could see Rep's head and a pair of terrified eyes. I got a fright when I first saw him. His spikey hair had all gone flat and the stuff he had put in his hair last night had run down his face. It looked as if Rep had been scalped or garrotted around the head, with globules of congealed blood running down from his forehead. I could see Rep's "bloody" anxious face, with pin, then a lot of exposure down to the rocks below.

There was panic in his voice.

'Gee'us yu're hon for fuck sake!'

In times like this you don't ask questions. I squatted down and found a hold for my left hand for support. With my right hand I grabbed his right wrist. He grabbed my wrist. I pulled and heaved at his arm. In a single movement Rep unceremoniously appeared over the edge.

We both lay on the ground laughing. Rep was laughing in relief that he was out of his situation. I was laughing that the both of us didn't end up at the bottom of the hill, dead!

It was starting to get dark.

The two of us made our way back down to the doss for the evening.

Underneath the boulder everybody was chatting away, tucked up in sleeping bags, about where they had been and what they had climbed. Spiney was cooking dinner. And Bish played bits of punk rock from his cassette recorder and the story of how Rep got stuck on the north peak got told over and over again.

'Whit wur you trying tae dae?'
Rep came out with all this stuff about heading up an easy V. Diff, then getting lost.

'There's no V. Diff's owan that part o the rock, ya daft bastard.'
Rep trying to sound as if he knew where he was, 'Look it's here in the guide book.'
Bish wasn't convinced.

'Yu're owan the wrong part o the fuckin' mountain, ya eejit!'

'No, A wusnae!'

'Yes – yae fuckin' well were! That's were Club Crack is – it's an extreme. Y'a tube!'

'No, A fuckin' wus'nae!'

'Yes, you fuckin' wus!'

'Fuck up, youse! A wis away tae de right o Club Crack'

'Fuck knows where yae wur – yae wur right owan the lip o that big overhang.'

'That wis pure fuckin' mental! Yoo cood o'topped yur'sel, ya bampot!'

'Bet yae wudnae doo that trouser filler again.'

'Bet yae A cood, piece a' piss, nae fuckin' bother.'

'Yeh, yeh... Yae wur right oot owan the edge o that big overhang, y'ure just a fuckin' space cadet!'

'A'm tellin' yae, yae wur fuckin' gripped oot'a y'ure skull, yae wis spaced oot'a y'ure brain.'

'Naw A wusnae.'

'Yes yae wus.'

'Naw A wusnae.'

'Yes yae wus.'

I interrupted the conversation between Bish and Rep.
'Fuckin' basket case, yae wur! Just lookin' doon at yae, wis geenin' mae the wullies.'
Spiney joined in the argument.
'A saw de brown stuff steamin' doon the hill and A wus owan the other side o the hill.'
'Y'ure just a mental bastard.'
'Fuck up youse!'

Bish played some more snippets of punk rock, then Spiney served up dinner. It was a brown horrible mess on the plate. Spiney had put an extra special dod of earth into Rep's dinner; nobody had noticed.
Everyone was hungrily munching away, when suddenly Rep got up and started coughing violently and throwing up.
'Ya fuckin' cunt! Wit de fuck wis in d'at? It's fuckin' bowfin!'
Spiney rolled about in laughter.
Rep realised the plot.
'Ya bastard!'
Rep took a dollop of food and threw it at Spiney.
Bish tried to calm the situation.
'Quiet doon there boys!'
'A huv just carried awe d'at food up de hill. Noo eat it!'
'A'm tryin tae, but that big bastard hus put sum shite in ma dinner.'
Spiney was still laughing his head off.
'Naw a didnae. It's awe that shite yur talkin' that made yae throw up!'
'Fuck off!'

Things went quiet again and everybody started munching away.
Rep was a brilliant climber. Everybody liked to give him a

hard time and slag him off when he got stuck on the hill. More often than not one of us would solo a route, get stuck and have to be rescued by the others. This time it was Rep.

After dinner and suppin' on a brew the stories started to come out, each trying to out-do each other in bragging rights. Spiney started.

'Remember the time we wis climbin' owan that railway viaduct in the toon and this ambulance stopped and the bloke told us tae get doon. "Get tae fuck doon frum there," this punter sais. "Get tae fuck," A sais, but this punter insists on rescuing us. Then the next thing wis that he turned owan his flashin' lights and siren and widnae turn them off till we goat doon! Whit a fuckin' tosser!'

Then it was my story.

'At least yae hud an ambulance there tae take away de bits. A wis doon at Dumbarton Rock soloin' this route. It looked a piece a pish but A goat totally gripped half way up. A hud tae pull up owan this dod o grass and it came oot just when A wis aboot tae pull up owan't it. Totally shat mesel, A did – thought A wus doon the hill! Though A wus mince!'

Then Bish.

'That wis nuthin, A remember the time A wis at Dumbarton rock on Windjammer, just aboot tae pull oor the top when this heid appeared lookin' doon at mae, nearly gave me a fuckin' hairy, it did – thought A wis doon the fuckin' hill at a faster rate o knots. Reckoned de punter wis aboot tae top himsel or sumthin'. A sais, "fuck off! Yur no jumpin' here, ma pal's doon below." He looked at mae as if he just shat his pants and took oaf like there wis nae taemorraw!'

'Well, did he jump?'

'Fuck knows. He must o disappeared back oor the castle wall.' If it wasn't stories about climbing it was stories about biking.

There was my story.

'A wis owan ma way back hame frum the Whangie and A wis just startin' tae overtake this big artic. A hud tae really hammer the engine. It wus screemin' like a wild cat trying tae get roond this big truck, revin' the engine like fuck, lying oor the petrol tank, trying tae get the thing tae go that wee bit faster. A wis almost in line wae the driver's cab when this other truck appeared cumin the other way. A thought A wis mince. A just hudtae go fur de gap, straight doon the white line; it wus nearly curtains fur mae.'

When it came to bikes Spiney, the master biker, always had to make a comment on how bad everyone else's driving skills were.

'Serves yae right. It takes skill, no a lack o brains tae overtake.'

I continued.

'A member the time A wis chasing yae up tae Neilston quarry tae get a bit o rockin' dun. Cudnae keep up. Anyway, there wis this bit A thought A wis catching up, but A totally missed this fuckin' corner and ended up goin' straight through this hedge and landed in a field o coos, up tae de eyeballs in keak, A wis. There wis awe these coos just lookin' at mae as if A wis a total plonker.'

'We'll y'ure a total plonker!' Spiney rolled over in laughter.

'Fuck off! A goat cuvered in keak, A did.'

'Well, it'll no make much difference, yur brain is full o shite anyway.'

'Fuck off!'

'A remember that time owan the dams road when yae wur beltin' roon that magic bend. Daein' mental speeds when yae hit awe these leaves owan the road. That wus spectacular, thought yae wis fuckin' history. Yae wur lucky tae fly oor that stane dyke rather than get impregnated intae it.'

'The front end o ma bike goat a bit mangled then.'

'Yae wis lucky that it wis only yur bike and no yur brains!' Bish cut in and went all serious about Jacko.

'Talkin' aboot brains... Amazin' whit happened tae Jacko, jumpin' oaf like that...total fuckin' mess it wus...brains splattered all oor the place.'

'Uch, he wis doped up tae the eyeballs wae sum shite. He wis awais takin' sumthin'. Whit a daft cunt he wis.'

'He wid awais tell mae, yur oaf yur fuckin' heid daein' that climbin' stuff.

'A wid awais tell him, it's you it's oaf yur fuckin' heid takin' awe that shite...then he wid go oawn aboot this arty stuff and how he wanted tae get a different view...piss artist if yis ask mae.

'Piss artist A yustae call him... Piss fuckin' artist.'

'He wanted tae become famous like David Bowie...fuckin' Star Man? Fuckin' Space Cadet if yis ask me.'

'Naw, A heard that he wanted tae become like Sid Vicious.'

'Sid Vicious? Well he became like Sid Vicious – fuckin' deid wae drugs!'

'Naw, he wus more like Sid...but without the Vicious bit... more like Sid Wanker.'

'Mibbe that wus his problem?'

'Mind yis, that was sum song at his funeral. Did yis see everyone looking around wondering whit the fuck was goin' owan. Ace eh? "My Way" by Space Cadet fuckin' Jacko...and the coffin goes intae the flames; that's class. Yis know what A mean, fuckin' class!'

Each of us had our own theory on why Jacko died.

'A heard it wis no the drugs it wis suicide. A heard he wis smiling awe the way doon.'

'That's crap, You name it Jacko hud it...just did his heid in it did...he wis awais doped up tae the eyeballs...didnae know night frum day.'

'Naw, naw, naw...that's awe shite. A hurd he wis smiling 'cos he wis oaf the drugs and dinnae wantae go back owan again.'

'Uch well... At least that's wan less fur MacTin tae go oawn aboot.'

MacTin was our geography teacher. "Barrhead scum" he used to call us. He would pace up and down the classroom, back stiff as a board, and with a nervous twitch in the eye, he would broadcast out.

'Barrhead scum... A taught yur faithers! They were scum... and you're scum!'

You could not argue with MacTin, he was right, we were scum, but then there was some real scum, and then there was Jacko.

Bish continued.

'Jacko left a note in his pockat. A don't like de chips...it said. A don't like the fuckin' chips! Cun yae believe it. A don't like the fuckin' chips!'

Rep broke the silence.

'Well d'at wis Jacko fur yis, awais a bit mental if yis ask mae.'

But Spiney had the last word.

'Anyway yis will no huvtae worry aboot Jacko anymare, his heid bust open like a dropped jar o strawberry jam.'

The conversation about Jacko was getting a bit serious and depressing. Jacko was an enigma. Nobody could figure out Jacko when he was alive. He was always trying to be different. Nobody could figure out Jacko when he was dead. The only thing consistent about Jacko was that he was smiling as he jumped.

Spiney livened up the conversation.

'Remember the time when we wis cycling doon this big

hill way Wee Shugisy und that daft Kenny whit dayae ma call him, belting doon this hill we wur…and just at the bottum… there wis this cattle grid, naebudy realised it wus there. Wee Shugisy ploughed in and wus totally minced, fuckin' chibbed awe his face in he did, lip awe bust tae fuck, bits o teeth lying aboot whit a fuckin' mess. Spittin' teeth oot awe oor the place he wus.'

'Yu'll huv tae tell us aboot yur teeth, Bish. It's a classic. A cunnae stop laughing everytime yis tell it…pure fuckin' classic!'

'It wis no fuckin' joke! A wis on this route at Loudon Hill, just aboot tae clip intae this runner—cudnae quite stretch up high enough wae de rope—so A put the rope in ma mooth tae geeus a bit more o a stretch. Then, A just lost it. A just popped oota this jammin' crack and A wis goin' doon the hill at a faster rate o knots. The next thing A member wis awe this blood pourin' oota ma mooth. A cudnae finger oot whit hud happened.'

'Well whit happened?'

'A forgot tae shout when A fell oaf and the rope ripped awe ma fuckin' teeth oot!'

'Fuck sake! That's a classic. A cudnae think that one up if A tried…'

'Uch well, at least yu'll save a bit on toothpaste!'

The stories continued into the night. Eventually, the four of us settled down for the night lying in our sleeping bags, underneath the large boulder.

A strong odour soon permeated through the air. Somebody had farted. It was a big one.

'Awe fur fuck sake!'

'Who de fuck wis that?'

Everyone looked at Spiney. He was smiling and said nothing.

'Awe Jesis, it's you und yur fuckin' beans.'

'Its awais you und ure fuckin' beans.'
'It's the last time yur dayin' the cookin! It awais ends up, way yae farting!'
The four of us again settled down for a night's sleep under the boulder, lying side by side.

Rain

I awoke suddenly, my head soaking wet. It was sometime in the morning; it was dark and raining torrents. The wind had changed direction and was blowing rain straight into our doss. The four of us were starting to get very wet. Soon everything was soaking; the sleeping bags, clothes, the lot. In fact, we would have been dryer if we had simply jumped into one of the deep pools in the nearby burn. Nobody could be bothered moving from under the boulder until first light, so we just lay there silently, soaking wet, and feeling totally miserable.

I stared up at the darkness and thought about MacTin stomping up and down the classroom shouting his head off,'Barrhead scum!' Maybe MacTin was right? Maybe we were just plukey scum with no hope and no future?
MacTin had a funny peculiar facial twitch, accompanied by a speech impediment. The story was that it was a war wound. Every time he said 'scum', it was more like s-s-s, a few twitches of his right eye, then...Kum!...exploded out. It was good material for everyone to take the piss. We all tried 's-s-s' a couple of exaggerated twitches of the eye, followed by a Hitler salute timed for the 'Kum!' Jacko got caught once in the classroom by MacTin for doing his impression and got belted. He sat at the back of the room and cried.
MacTin's class was the only time the four of us and Jacko were in the same room together at school. The four of us would sit at

the front, laughing and never taking anything seriously; Jacko would sit at the back, very quiet, staring into space. There was something very familiar about Jacko since we all grew up together, yet there was something very different. He was always trying to be different. When we said black, he would say white. When we were into punk, Jacko was into David Bowie; when we were gripped in the mountains, Jacko was doped out of his head; when we were out playing football, Jacko was round the back of the gym puffing on a fag. However, there was mutual respect. Greetings usually consisted of: 'Hauw's it gauw there ya poofter.'

Followed by an instant reply, 'Fuck off cunts!' before the conversation started.

A big drip of cold water landed on my head every few seconds from the rock ceiling above. I tried to ignore it and started thinking how I managed to end up sleeping under a boulder. It was all because of Bish. Bish was always boiling over with enthusiasm, he could never keep still, he was always on the move, once he had something in his head there was no letting go, he would just go on and on. Bish dragged all of us into the hills.

'Cumoawn, better in the hill than awe that shite back hame,' he would say to get us moving.

Bish had a point; who needs all that shite when you can climb? First it was the local crags, Neilston Quarry, Loudon Hill, Dumbarton Rock. We would cycle for hours to a crag, do a climb, then cycle for hours back home. Once hooked, there was no stopping us; every weekend or holiday we were away in the hills; every night we were planning the next trip or training for the next climb.

There was no thought, why? It just seemed the natural thing to do, and once started, we couldn't stop. It was something I couldn't understand; getting scared shitless halfway up a cliff, reaching the top, and then wanting to go back again for more just to get scared shitless again. It didn't make any sense. But then you would do a climb, pushing close to the edge, at the limit of your ability and, suddenly, everything made sense. A sense of being alive.

I shuffled a bit to the side in my sleeping bag to avoid the drips on my head, but bumped into Bish.

'Cun yae no stay still there! A'm tryin' tae get sum doss.'

I settled down again, but a rock was sticking into my back and I had to move again.

'Fur fuck sake! Cun yae no stay still fur two minutes?'

I shuffled around a bit more and settled down again. There were a few more grunts and groans. Then all went silent.

We wanted to get into the Highlands and do bigger climbs. Spiney built the motorbikes to get us there. If something needed fixed, Spiney would fix it. He was always fixing things or making things. Anything of interest that passed his way, he would use it or keep it.

The previous winter had been cold and Spiney and I played about on some small icefalls. This year Spiney just wanted to climb big ice. Ice climbing is a mad game. With rock you are reasonably sure what you are holding on to, but with ice you are never sure. Climbing ice can be a scary business.

'Yae huv tae switch oaf yur brain when climbing ice,' Spiney always used to say.

It's funny because Rep used to tell Jacko, 'Yur brain must be switched oaf tae take d'at shite.'

Rep was fearless, straight in there no questions asked. Rep was a natural-born climber and provocateur. He was always pushing himself on the rock and pushing himself into confrontation. He set the standard that the rest of us tried to follow. But then, the three of us often had to pull Rep out of trouble.

The four of us just wanted to climb harder and longer climbs. Nothing else seemed to matter. There was an unspoken competition between the four of us to climb the most outrageous climb or difficult piece of rock. More often than not it was just a chaotic, disorganised, shambolic mess, getting lost on the mountain, stuck halfway up a climb, a bike crash, forgetting to bring the food, getting chased by the police. It was all part of the scene – all the carry on and nonsense trying to get into the mountains for a good day's climbing.
Spiney bumped into me.
    'Move over will yae.'
    'Fuck oaf, there's a big rock owan ma back.'
    'The rain is pourin' doon ma arse here.'
    'Its time yae hud a bath anyway, yae smell boufin', ya scabby git.'
    'Shuuut, there's sum folk tryin' tae sleep here...'
All went quiet again.

There was no money to buy expensive climbing gear so we improvised and often soloed climbs. Soloing is a mad game; one mistake and your dead. No questions asked. One slip and your off. There is no second chance. There is no going back. One fucking slip and you are dead. But the only thing you can think of is to hold on, to stay alive, to feel the rush, the excitement of overcoming the odds, getting to the top and staying alive.
I thought of Jacko. I could see Jacko fall through the air. I could see Jacko's body crunching against stone. I could see Jacko's skull crack open and the blood gush out. I could see the brains on the ground. Next time it could be me...or Spiney...or Rep... or Bish lying at the bottom of a cliff...dead with head smashed open, blood all over the place.
    'Aaahhh!'
One of Spiney's sneezes was coming up.

'Oh No!'

The rest of us cowered away, preparing for the worst. It wasn't one of your average sneezes. It was one that was amplified a hundred times for maximum affect.

'CCChhhooo!!!'

'Fur fuck sake! cun yae no keep yur mooth shut?'

We settled down again.

I lay awake under the boulder, listening to the wind and rain. Occasionally, a big wave of rain would come in, blown in by a strong gust of wind. I covered my head as best I could with a polybag. My shoulders and backside were in puddles of water. My sleeping bag was paper thin, and I had no mat. I was cold and shivered away.

Poor Jacko, he was just one sad bastard who was into drugs in a big way. Even in class, with MacTin ranting and raving away, Jacko would sometimes sit like an angel at the back with a bit of glue in his cupped hand, sniffing away, stoned out of his head.

Maybe Jacko wanted to feel the rush, the excitement, the risk; like us on the mountain? Maybe he wanted to cheat death, laugh at death. Maybe that's what life is all about – just staying alive and cheating death? But...why take drugs when you can climb?

A big drip of water from the rock ceiling above landed every few seconds on my sleeping bag. I tried to get out of the way and shuffled a bit to the side, bumping into Spiney and Bish.

'Cun yae no keep still fur Christ sake!?'

'Shhh. A'm tryin' tae sleep.'

'Ma arse is freezin'...move oor a bit will yae?'

'Naw.'

'Fuck off!'
'Will yae two shut the fuck up!?'
'Cum owan move a bit eh?'
'Whit dae yae mean move over? A'm holf oot the boulder as it is. A'm gettin' soaked.'
'Yur getting' soaked... A'm fuckin' drenched!'
'There's a fuckin' river flowing doon ma back here.'
'Tuf shit.'
'Shut de fuck up will yis!'

After a few moans all went quiet again.

I tried to get some sleep, but ended up thinking about MacTin again. The class usually ended with MacTin going on about how we would all end up somewhere between prison and the dole.

'A taught yur faithers, they were s-s-skum and you're s-s-sum!'

Maybe MacTin had a point? Maybe fate has already written the future and there is no way to change, so what is the point in trying. There didn't seem to be many choices in life. There is a certain inevitability about life that keeps repeating itself, going round and round in an endless loop with no way out.

The only thing that made any sense was to climb, nothing else mattered except for that bit of rock in front of you. I couldn't understand where the drive was coming from. It was insane. There was no logic in it.

Jacko used to say, 'A take sum stuff 'cos it makes mae feel good.' I couldn't say, 'Climbing makes me feel good,' because most of the time it didn't; it was just misery lying under boulders getting wet and cold. But, there was something fundamental inside driving you on, there was something magical, something

special about the mountains that made you go back again and again.
Maybe Jacko had found the same with drugs?
Too many questions with no answers were going through my head.
I drifted into some sort of sleep.

≈

The first grey sky of dawn started to appear. I got out the stove and tried to make a brew, but everything was soaked. I rummaged about in my rucksack for some food for breakfast. Last night I had made up some sandwiches with the last of the bread and the scrapings from the pot. I pulled out a plastic bag that contained breakfast, but now the bag was full of water. I poured out what was left of the sandwiches.
Spiney shouted over.
    'Hay, how aboot sumthin' tae eat?'
    'Sorry breakfast hus dissolved and been washed away.'
    'Whit huv yae dun wae ma pieces? Huv yae thrown them oot?'
    'Pieces...it wis mare like soup. Yae cun lick the grund oor there if yae want.'

We lay there feeling hungry and depressed.
    'Any buddy else wae sum vitols? A'm starvin'...' asked Bish. Nobody answered. There was nothing left to eat. It was miserable as we lay there under the boulder. The rain was still coming down in sheets.

It was a slow morning; all thought of climbing was out.
Bish got his tapes out to get us moving. He slotted one into his music machine. This time it was Eddie and the Hot Rods. The

batteries were low and the dampness made the tape squeak as it went round. A feeble sound came out.

Halfway through the song Bish suddenly sprang to life and said, 'Let's set up a punk band.'

There was a deafening silence of disbelief. A few seconds passed.

Bish repeated himself, 'Let's set up a punk band!'

Bish was serious. We all looked at each other.

'Fuck oaf Bish, we cannae play anything!'

Bish came back with an instant reply.

'That's whit it's all aboot, ya daft bastards!'

Everyone looked at each other, not really understanding what Bish was going on about.

We packed up our wet clothes and wet sleeping bags and put them into wet rucksacks. The rucksacks were heavy with all the wet gear. It had turned cold again and the rain was now falling as sleet.

Once packed, we headed down the hill in gusting wind and horizontal rain. Bish went on and on about starting up a punk band all the way down the hill. Everyone ignored him, pretending they couldn't hear because of the wind.

'We shud set up a band yae know. It'll be dead easy, a'm tellin' yis.'

'Whit was that Bish... Nice weather eh?'

'The four o us will make a dead good band. A cun just see us noo, playin' at the Apolla in Glasga in frontae millions.'

'A bit chilly this wind... Eh Bish?'

'Dae yae still huv that auld guitar? Yae cud be up there playin' in a band.'

'Looks like it cood start snawin' again there Bish.'

'A cun just see us now owan Top o'de Tops.'

'Hus nobody tolds yis that punk is dead?'

We got to the bikes and loaded up the rucksacks. Bish's bike started first time; Spiney kicked away at the kick-start, but his machine wouldn't start.

'Fuckin' thing never starts in the wet! Geeus a bump start, eh?' Spiney and I pushed his bike down the road. Spiney jumped on, a few pathetic sounds came out of the engine, but the bike slowly came to a halt. Breathless, I gave up pushing.

A few deep breaths later, I tried pushing the bike again, but the bike came to a halt with a dead engine. Spiney started kicking away again at the kick-start.

Bish drove up a few yards to Spiney and started ranting and raving about setting up a punk band again.

'Did yae see the Sex Pistols swearing at that bloke on telly. A think they're just shite, a bunch o wankers. Noo, if we set up a band.'

'Bish, will yae shut yur puss, and geeus a hond wae the bike.'

'Aye, sure...but A still think we shud get a band goin' soon.'

'Cun yae geeus a tow, tae get us goin' fur Christ sake!'

'Aye sure...dae yae still huv that guitar yae ustae huv?'

'Aye, A do...und A'm gontae wrap it roond yur fuckin' neck if yae don't geeus A tow.'

Spiney tied a piece of cord to the back of Bish's bike.

Bish was still yapping on about a band.

'A know where A cood get yae a better wan.'

'OK Bish start towin' us slowly, will yae.'

'We cood get...'

'Will yae geeus a tow fur fuck sake!'

'Oh! Aye!'

Bish pulled away, dragging Spiney's bike.

Spiney tried to start the engine in second gear, but the engine kept backfiring and produced a lot of smoke.

Bish tried a second attempt, a bit faster this time, but again

the bike still did not want to start.
Spiney leaned over and attempted to dry one of the H.T. leads. There was a loud 'Aaaggghhh!'
As an electric shock ran up his wet right arm, Spiney fell over, pulled the bike down on the road, and simultaneously dragged Bish's bike over. Bish and Spiney unceremoniously crashed onto the road.
Rep and I ran over, laughing our heads off.
 'That wus magic!'
 'Ha! Ha! Ha! That wus sum style there, slidin' along owan yur arse.'
There was a smell of petrol everywhere.
Rep and I got the bikes upright. Bish and Spiney were on the ground cursing and swearing, blaming each other for crashing.
 'It wus yur fault fur pullin' mae oor.'
 'Naw, it wusnae!'
 'Aye, it wus.'
 'If yae hud been pullin' faster A widnae o tried tae dry mae plugs.'
Spiney got back on his bike and kicked away to get the thing going. The bike started to sound more promising. Bish got back on his bike. It started first time. Rep jumped on the back and they disappeared down the road.
They reappeared a few moments later for a laugh.
 'Yur yis no goin' hame de night? See yis...'
And Rep joined in.
 'Byeee fuckers!' followed by an emphatic "V".

They disappeared again down the road at full speed, leaving a smell of two-stroke in the air.
Eventually the bike started. Spiney gave it full throttle. The bike coughed and spluttered to get going. Smoke was everywhere.

'Cummon let's get oota here...jump owan de back.'
I jumped on between Spiney and the packed rucksacks. The bike backfired a few more times, and a big belch of black smoke appeared out the back. The engine misfired a few more times. Then were off at full power, flying down the road chasing after Bish and Rep in the rush to get back home.

Devils Delight

BCT

Next day at school, Bish was still going on about setting up a band. Everybody thought it would be a passing fad. He was really into the punk rock scene and listened to John Peel on Radio One every night. Bish had an amazing collection of tapes that he played on an old, trashed cassette recorder. The cassette recorder was covered in different coloured graffiti: Anarchy in the U.K., The Clash, This is Punk Rock baby, etc written all over it. The cassette recorder went everywhere with him, and he would often come running over and play selected bits of John Peel from the night before.

'Fuckin' dead brilliant this bit is!'
Everybody would humour Bish.
'Yeh, really great Bish.'
'Just listen tae this track, pure dead magic!'
'Yeh, yeh... Fantastic.'
Nobody could hold Bish's enthusiasm back.
'Just hear that bit wae de guitar; pure mental stuff!'
'Yeh, it's really dead good Bish.'
'We cood dae that better, if we hud a band.'
'Sure thing Bish.'
'A'm tellin' yis; we shood set-up a band.'
'Hus no one told yis that punk is deid?'
'Punk will never die.'
'Yeh, yeh...'

≈

Bish's cassette recorder would also appear on climbs. Halfway up a cliff, the cassette recorder would come out and punk rock would blast across the mountain. The cassette recorder would come out when you were leading a climb and just about to do some desperate moves, palms sweating and fingers shaking in holds. A reassuring shout down to Bish,

'This bit's mental, keep a tight hold fur fuck sake!'
It would result in a shout from down below.

'Hold owan a minute. A'm just replaying the last track', or something like,

'Cun yae hear that sound – pure fuckin' magic tae ma ears.'
The cassette recorder would come out when we were trying to follow some desperate moves that Bish had just led, and suddenly the sound of punk music would blast out overhead; it was time to get worried. Bish was more interested in his music than holding onto the end of the rope.

≈

Weeks later, Bish was still going on about setting up a band. The rest of the team started going along with it, more to keep Bish happy than anything else.

≈

The band started to get put together in Spiney's garage over mega tea-drinking sessions. The garage was our organisation centre. It was where all our climbing trips were planned, and bikes were put together. The garage was full of junk of all shapes and sizes, covering the floor, the walls and hanging from the ceiling. Bits of boats, bicycles, engines, sails, motorbikes, garden things, rope, wood and a wide selection of other weird and wonderful things. Spiney was always taking machines apart and re-assembling them into new "Bitzers" to improve the handling or speed. Bits of bikes came from skips and dumps. In a few weeks a new machine would appear out of a heap of junk, then a few weeks later it would disappear, to be resurrected later in a new form. Long winter nights were spent assembling and dismantling motorbikes, discussing future climbing trips and trying to organise the band.

The band appeared out of the chaos of the garage. A space was cleared in one corner, which meant piling junk even higher in another corner. An old trashed guitar, a burnt out amplifier, a poxy speaker and a mike that occasionally worked were borrowed from a friend. Once everything had been plugged in and set up, we stood around feeling that we had achieved something, but not really sure what to do next. A sense of excitement was tempered by our naivety. We all looked at each other wondering what to do next – how to make the music.

Bish was born a punk. The band was his idea and he would have to be lead singer. Bish would also supply some of the lighting and electrical stuff. He had a large collection of flashing lights hanging all over his bedroom. Nobody asked why.
Rep borrowed his brother's drums. A couple of cymbals were made from some old steel drums lying behind the garage.
Spiney could play a few chords on the guitar; he would play lead guitar.
I couldn't play anything and tried to strum along with Spiney on his old, beaten up bass guitar with two strings.

There was a lot of discussion on what to play. We started trying to rip off some Sex Pistols, then some Clash stuff, but it didn't work very well.
Spiney thought we could do better ourselves.
    'That stuff is a bunch o' wank. It dusnae mean anythin, it's awe just shite.'
Bish was a bit more constructive.
    'We need sum songs fur oorselves. We need words tae hit

the public.'
Quickly followed by Spiney, 'Yeh, make them think!'
Then Rep joined in, 'That's right! Get them between the fuckin' eyeballs!'
Everybody looked at me. Since I couldn't play anything and couldn't think of a quick reply to get out of it, I was left to come up with some songs for the group.

'Yeh. OK... A'll try und think up sumthin'.'
I went away that night with Spiney's bass guitar to practise a chord and wondering how to write a song.

≈

The next few weeks were wet. That restricted our climbing sessions to the local crags. There would be a race on the motorbikes to get to the crag first and have a couple of hours climbing. More often than not it would rain, but we would climb on. Inevitably, one of us would get a fright on a climb and somebody would have to run round to the top of the cliff and drop a rope down. After the climbing there would be a race back to the garage for a music session at the end of the day – and an occasional crash, usually trying to keep up with Spiney.
I still had no idea about how to come up with a song for the band.

≈

The garage sessions usually involved Spiney strummin' away on his guitar, completely out of tune, then Rep joining in, bashing about on the drums, completely out of rhythm with Spiney. This was the cause of arguments that bounced back and forward.

'Stop that fuckin' racket, will yae!'

'Stop moanin' will yae!'
'Keep in time, fur fuck's sake!'
'Shut y'ure fuckin' wheesht!'
'Geeus a break fur fuck sake!'
'Shut yur puss!'
'A'll shut yur puss fur yae!'
'Just try it yae big shite!'

Bish would usually quieten things down by shouting at the top of his voice down the mike 'Whaaa!!!' and causing ear piercing feedback in the amplifier.

There were still no songs for Bish to sing. He had to get by with one liners pinched from other songs he could remember from the John Peel show the night before. He did not try to sing along with the guitar or drums.
    'Babyalon is burning in anxiety...'
    'It's a White riot...'
    'I can't stop to mess around, like a brand new rose in town...'
Then everything would come to a stop and we spent hours trying to figure out how to put the words to the guitar or guitar to drum or drum to guitar. Nothing made any sense. Maybe this was what punk was all about?

There wasn't much room in the garage for Bish to fully express himself. On one occasion Bish was trying his new dance technique, spun round, tripped over something and went headfirst into a precariously balanced pile of junk. All sorts of rubbish rained down on his head, with an almighty clatter. The rest of us ran for cover.
Bish lay motionless. Two feet were visible from under the pile of rubble. Spiney and I took a foot each and pulled Bish out.

'A need sum songs tae sing,' was all he had to say.

≈

I had been thinking for some time about how to write a song for Bish. The problem was where to start and what to write about. I watched telly for a couple of days for ideas, staring endlessly at the box. Sentimental crappy love songs were right out the window. There was some Country and Western I thought about turning into punk because it looked so ridiculous. Top of the Pops was depressing manufactured music.

I started to think about Rep getting gripped on the Cobbler and Jacko jumping off. Jacko's death really bothered me. It wasn't the fact that he was dead. It was the fact that he was smiling as he jumped. What was he thinking before he jumped? What was he thinking in that fraction of time as he stepped over the edge? What was he thinking as he fell through the air?

Every time I got gripped half way up a cliff, mind frozen in fear, body shaking with exhaustion, sweat pouring from every pore, every muscle straining in the extreme. The only thought is to hold on; the last thought is to jump.
How could Jacko so casually step off the edge with a smile on his face? Where was his fear?
I could see Jacko's smile as he stepped over the edge to his death. I could see fear in Rep's eyes, as he held on for dear life to the edge of the cliff. Somehow, the two situations appeared similar, but the reactions seemed extreme. What was the difference?
One second between life and death...
Why did Jacko jump off with a smile on his face?
One second...to pop a pill and fly through the air.
Next time on the mountain, a slip and one of us could be flying through the air. The end is the same.

One second...to lose your grip and fall down a cliff.
Is that the only difference between life and death? One fucking second?
I could picture Jacko flying through the air with a big smile on his face. I could see Jacko at the bottom, head smashed open, eyes popped out of their sockets and his big goofy teeth sticking out from the blood and brains.

I started writing down a few words.

> *Take a happy drug*
> *To find a sad tomorrow.*
> *It's a fool's paradise.*
> *Adam's temptation fate.*
> *Madness or maybe a natural state,*
> *gives a fear of living.*
> *That disturbs the brain,*
> *One second and it will be all away.*

I was convinced that there had to be some connection between the adrenaline rush in the mountains and Jacko's craving for drugs. But like Jacko, there was a paradox, a commonality, yet also a complete opposite. I started to write.
 'What is the chemical that controls your mind? Or is it your mind that controls your chemical?'
Piss artist was what we called Jacko when he was alive.
 'A need drugs tae make mae creative,' Jacko would say.
That was usually met with disillusion and ridicule.
 'That's a bunch o wank, yur just a piece o shite. Yur a junkie, Jacko, fair und square.'
After he died, the word was that he would have become the next David Bowie.
Here was also a paradox I couldn't understand, between Jacko's self-destructive manner and his search for creativity.

Somehow Jacko's depressed mind seemed to go hand-in-hand with the creativity. But, that didn't make much sense; what is the point of being creative if you are going to kill yourself?

I wrote some more.

> *Need a drug to confuse reality?*
> *To help the creative process flow?*
> *Good idea to kill myself,*
> *Before I become a star.*

The misery and adrenaline we found on the mountains, the pleasure and self-destruction of Jacko seemed to balance his depression and creativity; there appeared to be connections, but also opposites. Nothing seemed to fit. Nothing made any sense. It was like three points on a triangle, but only two of the points could be connected at any time.
The first few words of a song appeared. It wasn't much, but it was a start. The song was called "Flying", in memory of Jacko. I liked the lyrics and gave them to Bish to memorise for our next session. The next problem was how to make the music.

≈

Not much later we were all back in the garage to try our first song. The instruments were plugged in and the amp turned on. Bish picked up the mike and started singing into it. It was the first time we'd heard Bish sing more than one line. He had a voice, but you could hear that it was not working right. Bish complained of having a cold, but Rep reminded him of how much he had drunk the previous night.
It was the first time we tried to put the words to music or music to words. Nobody was sure how or where to start. Spiney was strummin' away some country and blues stuff. Rep start-

ed off slowly with Spiney, then ended up playing so fast that he broke a drum stick. Bish forgot the words to the song. I had to write them down again.

Spiney on the guitar and Rep on the drums managed to work something out, but then we couldn't get the words to fit the music. The ancient amplifier system broke down in a puff of smoke and needed repair. I was total crap on the guitar and couldn't manage to play one chord for more than a few seconds. Nothing was going right. We gave up in despair for the night. Our first attempt at the song was a total disaster.

A second attempt, the following night, was not much better.

A third attempt left us totally depressed. Setting up a band was going to be a lot harder than we thought. We were getting nowhere fast. The idea of the band was quietly drifting away into a memory. Bish didn't say anything. It was unusual for Bish to be so quiet.

≈

One night, planning our next climbing trip and listening to various punk cassettes, Bish was looking through a pile of maps and at the same time kept asking me to find pieces of music on his cassette recorder. I was winding a selection of tapes forwards and backwards trying to find the specific track that Bish wanted to hear, when I came up with the idea of pinching bits and pieces of recorded music and playing them backwards or forwards at different speeds or stretching the tape to get a whole new sound. All the sound bits could then be recorded continuously onto Spiney's ancient reel-to-reel tape recorder. The pre-recorded music could provide a backing sound to the band.

Spiney's ancient reel-to-reel tape recorder was our saviour. It solved the rhythm problem and also gave us some interesting music to play around. The only problem was that the tape recorder always had a habit of stopping every 10 minutes or so for no apparent reason.

Late nights were spent making up new sounds and putting it on tape. Spiney worked on his guitar skills, Rep learned the beat for the drums from his brother and Bish would try singing in front of a mirror to get his act right. I would try to keep in tune with the bass guitar and put some more songs together.

≈

There had not been a practice session for some time, but that gave each of us time to polish up our acts. I managed to write a few more verses to "Flying" and gave them to Bish to memorise.

≈

We were back in the garage all ready to go.
Bish started off.

> *A'm just hangin' ontae a piece o rock.*
> *A'm just holdin' on tae re-a-li-tyyy.*
> *Fuck, fuck, A'm just holdin' on, on, on, tae re-a-li-tyyy.*
> *A'm gripped oot'a ma fuckin' skull.*
> *Nowhere tae go but up, what de F-U-C-K!*
>
> *Take a Haaapyyy Drug. Whaaa!*
> *tae find a sad Tomorrooow. Undeeer!*
> *It's a fools Parrra Dise. Ohooo!*
> *Adams Temptation. Apple Fate. EHHH!*
>
> *If yae don't like de – CHIPS!!!*
> *yae cun alwais com – PLAIN!!!*
> *One second tae pop a – PILL!!!*
> *If yae think yur in – SAIN!!!*

Spiney had stopped playing the guitar. Rep was barely hitting the drums. The three of us all stared at Bish as he was going through his routine as if in a trance, possessed by the music, an inner persona was appearing. We all stood back, stunned in silence and looked at each other.
Bish was absolutely brilliant.

> *A quick fix – and forrrget de wooorld,*
> *all the ills and problems – dat okuuur.*
> *Take a chemical – tae delude yur braaaiiin,*
> *Try and run – but yae cunnae run-run-ruuunaaaway.*

Bish was still carrying on by himself, unaware that everybody had stopped playing and were looking at him.

> *Madness or maybe, a natural state!*
> *Gives a fear o living*
> *Dat disturbs de braaaiiin,*
> *one second and it'll be awe – away!*
>
> *Whit is de – CHEMICAL!*
> *Dat controls yur – MIND!*
> *Or is it yur – MIND!*
> *Dat controls yur – CHEMICAL!!!*
>
> *Need a drug tae confuse – REALITY.*
> *Tae help de creative processsm – FLOW.*
> *Good idea tae kill – MASEL*
> *Before A becum a – STAAAR!!!*

Bish stopped. He composed himself for a moment and asked.
  'Wis that alright?'
  'That was fuckin' amazin'.' Spiney replied.
  'Ure the words alright, Bish?' I asked.

'Just fine. A changed them a wee bit tae get ma voice box roo'nd sum bits.'

'Let's dae it again and put a guitar bit in between a couple o the verses, and then we can all join in on the backing vocals with the RE-A-LI-TY bit.' I suggested.

'Rock Rock Rock!' Bish piped out.

'Spiney and Rep on the drums cun dae their stuff at the start.'

'Rock Rock Rock!'

'OK, let's get goin' one more time...one, two, three.'

'Rock Rock Rock!'

'Will yis stop sayin' that, und start bein' serious.'

'OK, here we go, one more time...one, two, three.'

I turned on the tape recorder at a piece of pre-recorded music and brought Bish in.

That night was spent working on the song, on the vocals, moving sounds around, taking bits out and adding new bits to the tape. Eventually we were happy with the song. A script was worked out on paper, when the tape recorder was to be switched on, when Bish would sing, and when the backing instruments would play.

There was a sense of satisfaction that at last something was starting to work. A sound was beginning to appear.

≈

Nobody had thought about what kind of style the band should have. In fact we already had our own style, a subculture of our own invention. Hardened punks made room for us. They took a step back, trying to figure us out. We were something beyond the traditional punk. We didn't "dress up" like "conventional" punks. It was more of dressing down.

There were no Mohican haircuts or bondage trousers full of

zips – except for Rep – that was good material to slag him off and was totally useless for the hills. Instead, we wore clothes that had been in the mountains, hanging in shreds off our bodies, and then had fixed a dozen motorbikes, dripping with oil and grease.

Occasionally, there was an effort to get "dressed up" for the dancing. Usually Rep would appear with a new look and everyone else would follow. He was always one step ahead of fashion.

There was a phase of sticking our heads in a peat bog to look "earthy" on the dance floor that was very popular with the girls.

Then there was the "blue period" after one very wet day on the hill; Rep found his body had been stained blue for days by the dye in his jumper. We all ran around with blue body and face paint after that.

Once that became passé, Rep appeared with his Tartan Army kilt that had been used for the previous Scotland World Cup campaign. There was a toilet chain attached from the bottom of the kilt up to a dog collar round his neck. He had covered his groin area with luminous stuff from one of these mountain tube things. When the UV lights on the disco were turned on, he would pull the chain to lift his kilt, and run about on the dance floor exposing his luminous parts. Nobody else had the guts to be such an exhibitionist.

Then there was the "open flesh wound" period. The "open wound" period happened after Spiney and I had bike crashes within a few days of each other. Spiney broke his leg after the petrol-spilling incident, followed shortly by myself crashing under a car on my way home after a wild party.

I flew round a corner too fast, lost control of the bike and ended trapped under a car. The crash took the skin off my left side; stones from the road were embedded in my ripped flesh from the bottom of my foot to the top of my head.

Spiney's plaster cast had come off after he fell in a river and part of the broken bone was exposed. He didn't go back to hospital to get a new cast. Instead, we went dancing with our injuries. It looked great but was a bit painful. We got a lot of sympathy and decided an injury could be a good policy for getting girls.

Instead of having to wait for an accident or going through the pain of self-inflicting an injury, we spent many happy hours constructing wounds made up from various animal bones, chicken skin, guts, a first-aid kit and some other bits and pieces. Deep slash across the face with forehead hanging off, or there was protruding bone from fractured arm, or my favourite was stones stuck to congealed blood.

It was quite effective. On one occasion, a passing ambulance stopped Spiney, insisting on treating his impaled-wooden-spike-to-lower-abdomen wound. On another occasion, two concerned police officers tried to arrest Spiney for grievous bodily harm after seeing my deep-slash-across-the-face wound. It took a lot of convincing that it wasn't real and we were actually off dancing.

The next problem was what to call the band. We were loosely called the Borrheid Cream Team or BCT for short, as a rip off of the various cream teams that appeared in the climbing press. The name lived on; the band was called BCT, a bit like a poor man's version of the more famous punk band XTC. The BCT label was reinvented to stand for Balls, Cunts & Tits, for shock value, in case anyone asked what it meant.

≈

Spiney was getting better and better on the guitar, wriggling about on the floor doing the worm, trying to play the guitar at the same time, then rolling over on his back and continuing to play, all sorts of weird sounds coming out of the guitar.

Rep was hitting the drums so hard and fast that a pile of broken drumsticks appeared beside the drum kit.

Bish was becoming more and more impressive on vocals. A series of growls, squeals, grunts, whistles, hoots and shouts complemented his singing ability. Sometimes, in his dance routine it looked like he was having an epileptic fit; jumping up and down, doing a series of turns, wriggles and twitches on the floor. Sometimes when not singing he would spend long periods of silence looking diagonally up at the ceiling, mouth open, saliva pouring out.

I was still a disaster on the guitar and was relegated to going through the actions with the guitar unplugged. I decided to concentrate on writing some more songs rather than playing the guitar.

≈

I was starting to get into the swing of writing songs.

A song came out of Bish. "Rock Rock Rock" often appeared in Bish's conversation, sounding a bit like a croaking frog, just before he was about to start climbing or when he was stuck half way up a cliff or getting psyched up for singing. For some reason I couldn't get "Rock! Rock! Rock!" out of my head. I started writing a song that I called "Rock Rock Rock" as sort of symbolising the mixture of punk rock and rock climbing. It didn't have many words, but the title sounded good.

I continued to add bits and pieces to the songs, finding new bits of music, chopping old bits off. Many late nights were spent in the garage, perfecting the sound with the rest of the band. The music was starting to work. By Christmas we had two and a bit songs in our repertoire. A sound of pure energy, aggression and revolt all rolled into one was beginning to appear.

≈

The Christmas holidays were coming up and the ice-climbing season was about to start. Our music sessions started to get mixed with prolonged discussions about new climbs. We were looking forward to a good winter climbing. The band took second place for the moment.

Spiney and I planned to climb some of the big grade V ice climbs on the north face of Ben Nevis. Neither of us had climbed anything as difficult as a grade V ice climb before. There was something special about a grade V ice climb – a big psychological barrier for us to overcome – something to prove to ourselves. Our main objective was Point Five gully on the north face of the Ben. In the early days, many big names had tried to get up it and failed. The first ascent took five days to complete using siege tactics. Point Five gully had a big reputation as a difficult and unprotected climb. I nervously read my Iain Clough climbing guidebook for Ben Nevis and Glencoe. The guidebook warned in big, bold letters that this part of the north face was suitable only for the most experienced ice climbers.

Spiney and I had just bought some new ice climbing gear. Point Five gully seemed a good place to start.

Into the hills (a few days before the New Year)

Well, our first attempt on Point Five gully came to nothing. There had been a wild storm blowing all day, we got lost and spent hours trying to find Point Five. Then, Spiney got stuck on the crux of Point Five gully and spent hours trying to climb back down. I stood frozen at the belay waiting for Spiney to come down. That night our tent ridgepole snapped in the gusting wind and the tent almost disappeared into the night. It was a complete washout and we also didn't manage to climb our first grade V ice climb. We packed up in the darkness and headed back down to Fort William. The rest of the night was spent in a gravel skip.

With the tent out of action the plan was to go over to the Cairngorm, walk into Shelter Stone for a couple of days ice climbing and then meet the rest of the gang in Aviemore for Hogmanay. We parked our bikes in the Cairngorm ski station car park and headed into the hills with large rucksacks. It was a great day after the blizzard on the Ben; blue skies and snow everywhere. The walk over the Cairngorm Plateau and into Shelter Stone was one of those extraordinary days. A fantastic day you never forget. Clear and crisp, not a breath of wind, everything was frozen solid, great fields of ice running in all directions over the Cairngorm Plateau. Crampons crunching into the ice as we walked.

Spiney and I made our way across the plateau and descended down between Hell's Lum and Stag Rocks. Huge cascades of ice poured out from Hell's Lum. We had been into Shelter Stone before in summer, but in winter it was a different world. The huge frozen faces of Shelter Stone Crag and Cairn Etchachan dominated the whole glen. Loch Avon far below was frozen over. A thick blanket of snow lay everywhere.

We were going to stay at the Shelter Stone boulder. The boulder is easy to identify in summer, but under such deep snow it was more difficult to find amongst the many other boulders, which had fallen from the neighbouring Shelter Stone Crag at sometime in the distant past.

The Shelter Stone boulder is one of the largest and has a small cave underneath. You have to crawl through a narrow entrance and into a larger chamber. In summer, it is quite comfortable inside and can hold up to six people with just about enough room to sit up. In winter we were in for a bit of a shock. Snow had piled up around the base of the boulder and we couldn't find the entrance.

'Where the fuck is the way in?' Spiney asked in desperation, trying to clear some of the snow away from the base of the boulder.

'Let's start digging over here.'

We managed to find the entrance after some excavation, but it became obvious that the Shelter Stone had filled up with hard-packed snow and ice. It was beginning to get dark. We had no tent, it had been left with the bikes. Either we kept digging and made some room inside the Shelter Stone or we would have to bivouac the night outside.

It was now dark, the head-torches were on and we were still hacking away at the ice and snow trying to clear some space. The cave had filled up with snow and ice to only a few inches beneath the rock ceiling. Spiney was on his belly chipping away at the ice. I collected the debris and chucked it outside. Then we changed round and I would hack at the ice; with lots of swearing, and lots of sparks flying when the axe missed ice and hit rock.

Eventually after several hours we had hacked away about two or three feet of ice; enough space for the two of us to get our sleeping bags rolled out.

'Phew! That's it. Let's call it a day. Let's get unpacked and get a brew on.'

We were lying on a scoop of ice that felt more like an ice coffin inside the cave, with our faces only a foot or two from the rock ceiling. Within a few minutes condensation started to drip from the rock ceiling and soon we were getting wet. The brew went on and the condensation got worse. Soon the sleeping bags were wet. We had something to eat and then settled down for a freezing night in wet sleeping bags. It was pure misery.

Late in the night I suddenly woke up when a mouse ran over my face. I sat up quickly and whacked my head against the granite ceiling. Spiney woke up wondering what was happening and also whacked his head against the rock. I could feel a lump on my forehead and blood running from a wound. After that we slept with helmets on.

Chancer

It was bitterly cold in the morning. Everything was frozen solid in our ice cave. I lay in my sleeping bag, stiff as a board, and watched my breath condense in the cold air. Neither of us wanted to move from the relative warmth of our wet sleeping bags and move into the freezing morning air. Both our heads had been cut and bruised from hitting the granite ceiling in the night. After great effort, I put a few ice chips into a pot and started a brew. The pot balanced precariously on the stove, about to fall over at any second. Soon the condensation from the heat of the stove started to drip from the rock ceiling and we were getting wet again. Some lukewarm tea was made; we gulped it down to feel some warmth come back. The brew gave us some incentive to get moving.

Getting out of a wet sleeping bag and into clothes that had frozen in the night, trying to get frozen feet into frozen boots, tying frozen laces with frozen fingers: it was miserable. I crawled out of the icy cave and ran about jumping up and down to get the blood circulating again and get some feeling back into my fingers and toes.

It was a great day: clear blue sky and very cold.

Spiney was inside trying to get some breakfast going. The

smell of fried bacon soon permeated the air. I dragged the rucksacks out to get the climbing gear organised. By the time breakfast was finished and we were ready for the hill.

The plan for today was to climb on Hell's Lum Crag. Our first objective was to climb a route called "The Chancer". The Chancer is about 450 feet high on steep ice at the left side of Hell's Lum. It was marked as a grade V ice route. We still hadn't done a grade V and were keen to try.
The two of us walked up to Hell's Lum to find the climb. The guidebook said to traverse in from Hell's Lum Gully to climb the upper ice flow. However, a more direct route straight up an icicle looked more interesting. The icicle had formed over the lip of an overhang and was completely free standing.
Our new climbing harness and front point crampons were put on, and our new "Terrodactyl" ice axe and ice hammer slotted into their holsters. We roped up and climbed up to the base of the icicle. I put in a peg belay on a rock wall to the right of the icicle. Spiney came up to the belay, moved across to the bottom of the icicle, and put a sling round the base to use for protection in case he fell off. The icicle wasn't very wide; just a bit wider than a body. Spiney tapped his ice axes into the vertical ice and then kicked in the front points of his crampons. He started off very tentatively, not sure if the icicle could take his weight. Spiney was heavier than I was, so I was happy for him to try first. Off he went up the icicle with slow deliberate cautious moves; tapping in his iceaxes and kicking in the front points of his crampons. Soon he was at the top of the icicle and disappeared over the next bulge. It was a good lead. The icicle held Spiney's weight.
The rope slowly moved through my hands. After some time the rope was almost finished. I shouted up to Spiney that all the rope had been used, but probably he could not hear my

shouts. The rope was still moving so I untied the belay to give Spiney more rope and started to traverse into the bottom of the icicle. I waited at the bottom of the icicle for Spiney to set up a belay. He seemed to take forever and I was starting to feel cold.

Eventually, a faint voice from up above shouted down, 'Climb.' I moved quickly onto the icicle, took off the sling and started to climb up. It was the first time I had been on such steep ice and I was finding it hard work. Fumbling about trying to get the ice axes to stay in, frantically kicking front points to hold on ice.

At last I managed to get to the top of the icicle, a gibbering wreck, strained muscles quivering with fatigue, breathless and totally knackered. I was happy to see a long run out on less steep ice up to the belay. I climbed up to Spiney at the belay. I led the next pitch over steep ice bulges, up to the bottom of a large ice wall, and then moved off to the right to set-up a belay on a rock wall. I brought Spiney up to the belay.

The next pitch looked very steep, with bulging ice everywhere. It looked like the crux of the climb. Spiney eyed the pitch. I was happy it was not my turn to lead after my struggles below on the icicle. Spiney traversed into the base of the large ice wall and placed an ice screw at the bottom for protection. He started climbing, each ice axe and each crampon front point being carefully placed. I stood watching from the belay, feeding out rope as he moved. He was making good progress up the ice wall. I was impressed; he was moving on steep ice with confidence. Half way up the ice wall, precariously balanced on the crampon front points, he stopped on the vertical ice to place another ice screw for protection. It is not easy to place an ice screw standing on vertical ice, but he managed it. Spiney clipped a carabiner into the ice-screw and then tried to feed the rope into the carabiner with his right hand. He held the loose rope in his teeth before pulling up some more rope with his right hand. Just at the moment when he reached up and tried to clip the rope into the carabiner, he dropped it, and in the process unbalanced himself.

What happened next was like a slow motion replay. His body pivoted back, both his ice axes popped out of the ice as he fell backwards, the front points of the crampons stayed in the ice. Spiney came off backwards with an impressive swallow dive, arms wide apart. He was in full flight for a second or two, then… Splat!

He landed spread-eagled on his back, head downhill about 60-70 feet below where he had fallen off. Spiney had landed with such force that he disappeared beneath a crust of snow; a bit like one of those cartoon characters falling off the end of a cliff and creating a big body shape imprint on the ground. The rope ran through my woollen mitts, but I quickly stopped Spiney's fall. The belay held, otherwise the both of us would have been down the mountain.

Spiney came to a stop. There were a few moments when there was no movement.

I shouted down, 'Ure yae OK?'

There was no reply. Spiney liked to be dramatic in these kinds of situations.

'Ure yae OK?'

I could see some movement from down below.

There was a grumbled moan, 'Yea, OK.'

'Huv yae broken anything?'

'No, think A'm OK,' replied a shaken voice.

'That wis a spectacular!'

'Glad yae wur impressed,' Spiney started to extract himself from the crater he had just created in the snow.

'At least yae shouted when yae peeled oaf and no like a Bish special, pullin' awe his front teeth oot!'

Spiney slowly got himself together, dusted himself down, then slowly front pointed up to the runner in the icewall that had held him.

'U're yae goin' tae huv another shot?'

'Fuck off!' was the instant reply.

'Dae yae want a shot, yursel?'

'No way. It's getting dark. We'll huv tae get oot'a here soon.'

Spiney climbed up to the ice-screw he had placed and took it out, then traversed over to the belay. We abseiled off the belay peg, down to Hell's Lum Gully, then climbed up the gully. At the top we had to cut through a huge cornice to reach the plateau. It was dark when we arrived on the plateau. Neither of us had remembered to bring a torch; it didn't seem necessary when we left in the morning. There was almost a full moon and we could just about navigate by moonlight over the plateau. However, trying to find the Shelter Stone boulder from all the others was no easy task in moonlight; then, finding the entrance to the cave in the dark was even more hassle; then, finding a headtorch stashed away in some iced up corner was even more fun in the pitch darkness, crawling about, heads hitting against the rock ceiling.

At last a beam of light came on from a headtorch and we could get organised for the evening. It was soon freezing cold, the condensation from our breath was starting to drip from the rock ceiling again. I got straight into my sleeping bag to get some warmth. It was frozen solid due to the dampness from the previous night. Both of us wriggled about in the bags for some time to warm up and to try to defrost the sleeping bags. Soon the brew was on and some dinner cooking. The condensation started dripping off the ceiling again, soaking the sleeping bags.

We had something to eat and settled down for the night. It was going to be another cold, wet miserable night and we failed again to get up our first grade V ice climb.

I started singing "Flying"...and trying to imitate Bish.

> *A'm just hangin ontae a piece o rock.*
> *A'm just holdin' owan tae reality.*
> *I'm gripped oota ma fuckin' skull*
> *Naewhere tae go, but up, whit the fuck!*

'That wis a Jacko special yae did today! So whit wus it like flying through the air, und survived tae tell the tale? Did yae see yur life pass before yae?'
Spiney was quite philosophical.
'It's more like owan second yu're there the next second yur no. Next time yae cun jump oaf, und A'll hold owan tae yae, und yae cun tell mae whit it wus like.'
I was still curious about Jacko.
'Dae yae know whit wus goin' through Jacko's heid when he jumped?'
'A dinnae no... he must o hud a thing aboot sumthin'.'
'Dae yae think it's true he wus laughin' as he jumped?'
'That's whit everybuddy sais the same thing... He wis laughin as he went oor... A saw him at the bottom... His face awe gone...nae nose...nae fuckin' teeth. His back was awe bust tae fuck... His arse wus almost in his heid. His heid wus bust open, blood everywhere. He wus still groanin' when A got there. He wusnae quite deid. Amazin' eh?!'
'He wus just sum space cadet...fuckin' doped up tae de eyeballs. A dinnae no if A cud step oor the edge like that. A just keep holdin' owan when A'm gripped oota ma heid. Takes sum bottle...dus'int it.'

'A dinno he wus just one daft cunt; his heid wis awe messed up. A dinno if it wus awe those drugs he wus takin' or whether the drugs were tae calm him doon... Fuck knows...'

The conversation when a bit quiet.
I started again.

'His folk were awe up set...just ordinary folk... He wus just like owan o us.'

'Uch, he wus a real chancer. A hurd he'd been nickin' dosh fur years und the polis wur awais doon at his door, but sumhow he managed tae keep gawin'. A suppose he hud tae pay fur awe that shite he wus takin' or sumthin'.'

'Whit the fuck made him step oor that edge?'

'He wus cumin' oot wae awe this bullshit aboot wantin' tae dae sumthin' different.'

'Yur mooth is awe broon. A sais tae him.'

'Mibbae he wus a poof? A heard sumbuddy say he wus a poof.'

'A don't think so, that's no whit the birds say.'

'Mibbae he wus just simply bored tae fuck?'
Spiney started to be philosophical again.

'Awe yae cun dae today is tae stare intae a TV box or get pissed. There's no much else tae look forward tae.'

'Goan ure the good old adventure days when yae wid end up in sum cannibal's stew pot in darkest Africa, or eaten by a tiger, or been chopped up fightin' the natives or sumthin.'

'Nooo, the future is a nuclear wasteland or stare intae a TV box or a Jacko special...take yur choice? Anyway who cares, let's get sum doss.'
Spiney went out like a light. I tried to sleep, but Spiney started to snore and kept me awake. I stared up into the darkness and thought about what Spiney had said.

In the past, there was adventure exploring new lands, fighting wars, or leading the hunt. But now the adventure has gone, there's nowhere left to explore, wars are fought at the press of a button and nature has been tamed by technology. Maybe that's what Jacko was looking for, a new challenge...a new adventure?

I put on my headtorch, got out a pen and paper, and started to write with frozen fingers.

> *A new technology must be alright,*
> *available only for the jet-set.*
> *Famine in Africa is fine,*
> *to watch on my TV set.*
> *Plague in Asia won't infect me,*
> *lying on my sofa bed.*
> *War beamed into my living room,*
> *no worries to dodge the flying lead.*
> *Slave to my machine,*
> *pollution is my right.*
> *An information age,*
> *but no one understands.*
> *Lost in a sea of technology,*
> *reach out for a helping hand.*
> *No hope of a life belt,*
> *helpless against the force of progress.*

Stripped down to the bare essentials, may be it is simply man against nature? But in the modern world, nature has been tamed by man and the only adventure left is an artificial chemical. A drug you can buy. It's a modern convenience. But, maybe, if we push nature too much, it will push back?

*Mother nature acting in best interest,
against a man-made dying-planet fate.
Kill the land and extinct the sea,
a problem I cannot see.
A slow death of stress,
or was it suffocation by car exhaust.*

I gave up and tried to get some sleep, freezing in the cold and damp. It was going to be another night of pure misery.

Devil's Delight

Getting up the following morning was again difficult. The outside of the sleeping bag was frozen again from condensation that had dripped off the ceiling. I started to get a brew organised; shivering in the cold of the morning I put some ice chips into a disgusting, unwashed pot. The stove went on and both of us had our hands around the gas burner, trying to capture any lost heat to warm frozen fingers. Everything that was near us was soon soaking wet; the food, the sleeping bags, clothing. Everything that was further away was frozen solid. A cup of cold tea, with residue of last nights curry mixed in with some baked beans got us started for the day.

Movement was a real labour; trying to put frozen socks onto frozen feet; trying to put frozen feet into frozen leather boots. Once the boots and clothing were on it was time for a quick exit and jog outside to get warmed up.

There was a change in the weather today. The blue sky had gone. Instead there were dark, ominous, menacing clouds racing over the Cairngorm Plateau. The base of Hell's Lum Crag was barely visible. Shelter Stone Crag behind us looked very dark and oppressive. Today, we were going to try a climb called Devil's Delight, another grade V climb, straight up the highest part of Hell's Lum; 550 feet high. It was more of a mixed climb on rock and ice, rather than continuous ice like The Chancer.

It was another late start by the time we got organised and set off up the hill to find Devil's Delight. The cloud was now down almost at the Shelter Stone and it started snowing heavily, soon we were in a blizzard. We got to the base of Hell's Lum and contoured around the bottom of the cliff to find the start of the climb. The guidebook description was to climb up a gully, then a corner and crack, but it was difficult to identify where the climb started; one bit of the cliff seemed much the same as the other. The two of us stood at the bottom of the cliff, in the middle of a storm, looking up and trying to figure out where the route went.
Eventually Spiney announced, 'A'm goan up here.'
   'Where?'
   'Up here.'
Spiney was pointing at a very steep wall with a tiny ice runnel coming down.
   'That just looks ridiculous. Yur yae sure this is the right way up?'
   'Fuck knows! We'll be here awe day lookin' fur the route, so A'm goin' up here.'
Spiney had a habit of not following the guidebook, but going straight up the first piece of ice that took his fancy.
I set up a belay at the bottom of the cliff. The first pitch was straight up a steep slab. Spiney checked his climbing gear, and then set off up the steep slab. There was a thin ribbon veneer of ice coming down from above. The runnel of ice disappeared into the cloud and mist above. It looked like a difficult and unprotected climb. Spiney started to move up the slab. Yesterday's fall didn't seem to have dented his confidence too much. Spiney set off with slow deliberate movements of each

ice axe and crampon front points being placed. The ice was very thin. I could hear metal against rock at every swing of ice axe or kick of crampon. There was a continuous stream of ice knocked down from above as Spiney made progress up the ice runnel. Soon there was nothing but a vague outline of Spiney above, disappearing into the mist.

Then everything seemed to go quiet. The sound of metal against rock had stopped. The rope stopped moving through my hands. The ice being knocked down from above had stopped.

It seemed quiet for a long time. Looking up, I could see that Spiney had come to a difficult section. From down below there was no obvious way to go. It looked desperate. Spiney hadn't put in any runners. I was hoping that there wasn't going to be another spectacular because it would really be a spectacular fall this time.

The rope started to move very tentatively then stop. Then move again slightly then stop. He was taking for ever to get over this section. I was standing on the belay getting very cold. At last, the rope started to move faster again. Good, Spiney must be over the difficult section now, I convinced myself.

'Rope Finished!' I shouted up in my loudest voice.
There was a distant reply:
'Start climbing. Don't fall off!' Spiney hadn't found a belay yet and was still climbing.

There was no rope left; I undid the belay knot and started off nervously since I knew the climb was totally unprotected, but relieved to get my blood circulating again.

The climbing was very thin. I could see through the thin verglass to the rock underneath. The front points of my crampons and ice axes were hitting rock at each placement. However, the ice seemed thick enough to hold my weight. There was a shout from above. Spiney had found a belay. I stopped and rested as best I could.

I was a lot happier when Spiney announced from up above that he was belayed. I looked up. The ice was getting thinner higher up. I set off again. I started climbing confidently, feeling secure. However, soon the ice was becoming so thin, the feeling changed to not really knowing why I was able to stay on. I had no confidence in any of the ice axe placements. My crampons were scraping away on rock underneath the thin ice veneer, trying to find some security. The ice was getting thinner and narrower. It was obvious that it was impossible to continue climbing up this little cascade of ice. My right leg started to shake uncontrollably. I transferred more weight to my left leg, but I was nervous that my left leg would pop out or start shaking as well. My arms were straining to hold on to the axes. A cold sweat was breaking out on my brow.

'How the hell did yae get up here?' I shouted out.

'Get as high as yae can on the first ice runnel then transfer left onto the next', was the shout from above.

'Fucking hell! This is ridiculous!'

Well I may as well go for it since Spiney is holding on to me.

I shouted up, 'Hope yae huv a good belay?'

There was no reply. It was a confidence booster to say that he didn't have a good belay so don't fall off!

I managed another move higher. The ice was so thin I didn't really understand how it could take my weight. I could see another tiny ice runnel about 10-12 feet up to my left, just too far to reach in one stretch. It must be what Spiney was talking about. I tried to move to the left and reached up with my left ice axe. At full stretch, I found a wee ripple in the rock sufficient to hold the tip of my axe, but I couldn't trust it to hold my weight. I moved my right ice axe to where my left one had been on the ice runnel. I moved my right foot to just above my left knee and tried to find something for my crampon front points to bite into. I took as much of my weight onto the two ice axes as I dared, pulled up and then stretched out with my left foot, scraping against the rock trying to find something that would support my weight. My heart was pumping away. The adrenaline was going at maximum. I felt I could be off at any second. My right leg was shaking uncontrollably again. The muscles in my arms were taut with fatigue holding on to the ice axes. Sweat started running from the palms of my hands down my wrists. I felt in a very precarious and insecure position.

I found something for my left crampon to hold onto and put some weight on it. It seemed to hold. Then I transferred my right leg from the ice runnel, scratching around on the granite to find a ripple in the rock that would hold my front points. The front points gripped onto something, but I had no confidence in the foot placement. It was a very committing move.

I took out the right hand ice axe and crossed it over my left, reached up to a little tuft of heather and whacked the ice axe into some frozen turf. It felt more secure. I transferred my weight onto my right axe and pushed out with my left foot looking for a hold. In a quick movement, I pulled up on the ice axes and put my weight on my left crampon. The crampon front points slipped: I thought I was off, but the two axe placements held me. My feet peddled about to find something for my crampons to grip onto. My left crampon gripped onto something, but it didn't feel very secure.

I was standing with my left foot on one tiny hold with leg muscles quivering with fatigue and my right leg dangling in free space. I tried to free the right hand axe, but I couldn't get it out. I was fumbling about trying to twist and lever the axe out, trying not to unbalance myself. It was a long reach and I knew if I lost my balance, I would be down the hill and Spiney soon after. Eventually, I managed to work it free. Another couple of placements and I was over the difficult bit. The climbing became a bit easier above. I got up to the belay a bit shaky, my heart still beating like a sledgehammer against my rib cage.

'Shite, that wis mental; took sum bottle tae lead that one.'

'Yeah, it wis a bit thin.'

I had a breather at the belay and asked which way was up.

'It's up here,' Spiney was pointing to a crack in a vertical wall. There was an overhang to get over half way up the wall. I surveyed the route above.

'Y'ure jokin'!'

The wall disappeared into the mist above. The crack didn't look as difficult as the last pitch, but it didn't look easy either.

'Y'ull get up that nae bother!'

I wasn't so convinced. After psyching myself up, I started to move off up the crack. It was just about wide enough to jam my arm in. I moved up a couple of moves using a combination of jamming with one hand and finding ice axe placements at the back of the crack with the other. The crack became thinner and thinner the higher I moved up.

I continued to struggle up. The crack started to fade out. I hammered in a good peg for protection.

I continued to move up again. The rock was pushing me out and to the right. I leaned sideways as far as I could to the right, stretching every muscle in my body to reach a small handhold. I felt almost on the point of swinging off.

I reached the hold. I stretched across with my right foot to reach a tiny foothold, in a wide bridging movement, my crampons grating away on the granite. The crampon seemed to hold. In one movement, I transferred my body weight to the right foot, pushing away with my left hand for balance. My left leg was left hanging. With that movement I was in a position just about level with the overhang. I reached down with my right hand to grab my ice axe that was dangling from a wrist loop, and whacked the ice axe into a good piece of ice over the overhang. It felt like a solid placement. I pushed away with my left hand, hoping the right hand ice axe would not pop out, reached up and whacked the left ice axe in above the right one. I took all the weight on my arms and heaved myself up and over the overhang, in a very awkward manoeuvre, crampons scratching away on the granite trying to find footholds.

It didn't look very elegant, but I was over.

I found a placement for my right crampon, stood up on the front points, took out the right hand ice axe, reached up at full stretch and whacked the ice axe into some ice at the back of a crack. There was not much ice for the second ice axe, so I scraped away some snow to reveal a reasonable hold to get my fingers around. I pulled up again.

By this time, the sweat was pouring off my brow, and the storm blowing around seemed a hundred miles away.

It looked a bit easier above. I continued up a system of grooves. It was great ice climbing. There was good ice at the back of the groove so I could move fast. I stopped after a full run-out of rope, set up a belay and started to bring up Spiney. Looking down, the rock face plunged into mist; above it rose, sheer, into wild grey cloud. I had no idea how long the pitch had taken to lead.

Spiney came up to the belay and we had a discussion where to go next. The day was getting on. It looked easier to traverse to the side, but Spiney wanted to continue straight up.

He took off up a crack in the wall just above the belay. The rope moved slowly through my hands. It looked difficult climbing. Spiney disappeared from view round a corner. I fed out the rope as Spiney made his way up.

After some time the rope came to a stop. Then it would creep slowly through my hands. Then the rope would stop again. Progress was slow.

We were high up on the cliff, in the middle of a storm, the wind blowing snow and ice straight off the plateau and down the face of the cliff, and now it was getting dark. There was no shelter from the wind. I shuffled about on the belay to find the most comfortable position.

'Get A Move Owan! It's Gettin' Dark!' I shouted up at the top of my voice.
I was getting anxious about the time.

'A'm almost up,' came a distant almost unintelligible voice in the wind.
A few seconds later the rope went tight and slid through my hands. Spiney had fallen off. I managed to quickly stop the fall. For some time there was no movement in the rope. I could hear nothing except the hollowing of the wind and the occasional sound of steel against granite. The wind was blowing chunks of ice off the plateau and blasting onto my face. I had lost all sensation in my nose and cheeks. I was feeling very cold.
The rope went tight.
Spiney had fallen off again.
After what seemed like an eternity, there was some movement in the rope.
I was shouting up every few minutes, more to try and keep warm than in hope of a reply.

'Whit's Happ En Ing?'
I started to sing "Flying" to myself.

> A'm just hangin' ontae a piece o rock
> A'm just holdin' on tae reality.
> A'm gripped oot'a ma fuckin' skull...

Eventually I got a faint reply:
'Hold owan orange. A'm comin' doon a bit.'
I held tight onto the orange rope. I started to feed the orange

rope slowly through my descendeur and pulled the slack in on black.

I could make out a dark silhouette of Spiney above in the mist. There was another faint shout:

'A'm belayed. Up yae cum.'

I set off up the crack that Spiney had just climbed. It was steep difficult climbing. I moved up the ice-choked crack as quickly as I could. Eventually, I arrived at the belay.

The light had almost gone. The two of us were hanging from a single peg almost at the top of the cliff. If the peg pulled, both of us would be down the hill. I put in another small chock as back up, but had no confidence in the protection. The storm was blowing wild and it was almost dark, the situation felt very abstract, almost as if you could untie from the belay and walk away into the mist.

I asked what the problem was.

'Trying tae mantelshelf just couldnae get any placements. A fell off twice. It's getting too dark tae see anything now.'

'A just couldnae find any decent placements fur ma axes. A've scraped awe the snaw away and there's just nothin' tae hold ontae. Another couple of feet and A'll be awright. Yae cun belay me up there and A cun climb owan yur back and get oor de mantelshelf.'

'Ure yae serious? Yur no climbing owan ma back wae those fuckin' crampons.'

'A've a better idea, yae cun take de belay and A'll stand owan yur back!'

There was some indecision whether to go up or down.

'We'll huv tae get movin' otherwise we'll be here awe night.'

Spiney made the decision.

'We'll huvtae go doon the hill! A don't think A cun get up

before it gets pitch dark,' he shouted over the wind.
It was not a good decision, but there were no other better options. We reckoned three long abseils to the bottom.
As the two of us hung from the belay, Spiney rummaged around in my rucksack for my head-torch and I organised the abseil. This time we had remembered to bring our head-torches.
Spiney fumbled away in my rucksack to find my torch.

'Hold still fur fuck sake, A cunnae find the fuckin' torch!' Eventually Spiney found the head-torch, put it on my helmet, turned it on and took over setting up the abseil. I rummaged about in Spiney's sack trying to find his headtorch, put it on his helmet and turned it on. A faint light appeared. Then within a few seconds the light faded to nothing. There was only one head-torch working.

Untying frozen knots with frozen fingers, suspended from a piton at the top of the cliff, with a storm blowing and in the dark was not the way we had planned the climb.

Abseiling is a dangerous game at the best of times, but abseiling in the dark, in the middle of a storm and not really sure of the next belay, is not recommended. A mistake could be disastrous. I was going to abseil first. I asked Spiney to check the rope work.

I always have a certain amount of apprehension just before an abseil; will the anchor point hold?

My imagination ran riot. I could see Jacko smile as he tumbled through the air in slow motion and asked myself if I would be smiling if the piton pulled out. I could see Jacko's buck teeth sticking out from the blood and guts. Maybe it will be me this time?

The other chock I had put in was more of a psychological belay. If the piton pulled, I was sure it wouldn't hold, and both of us would be off, flying down the mountain.

I checked the rope work for the last time, clipped in a descendeur, abseiled off the peg belay and slid into the darkness. After a long abseil I set up a belay at the bottom of the rope and signalled for Spiney to come down. Spiney would take the dodgy chock out and abseil off the single piton.

We had worked out a system with the head-torches: three flashes equal to OK to descend. I had the only head-torch that worked so I abseiled first with the head-torch and Spiney would have to fumble about in the dark to get down.

Another couple of dodgy abseils saw us at the bottom of the cliff. We still hadn't climbed our first grade V ice climb.

30 minutes later we were back at the Shelter Stone doss.

We were looking forward to another night of misery in the cave with wet sleeping bags.

The following day was Hogmanay and we had arranged to meet Rep and Bish in Aviemore. This was our last night under the Shelter Stone boulder. We brewed up and had the last of our food. I had made the mistake of making a brew and not doing the cooking instead. Spiney had a habit of mixing everything altogether in one unwashed pot, and serving up a disgusting mess. Spiney served up the dinner.

'This stuff is bouf'in.'

'Shut yur whesht, y'ure stumuck willnae know the difference.'

'It's really bogin', doubt if it will reach ma stomach.'

A bottle of whisky miraculously appeared from a stash in the corner.

'This will sort yur stumuck oot!'

We ate and drank into the evening.

I started writing some more bits to the song.

'Whit's that yur writin'?'

'A'uv been inspired by yur cookin' tae write sum mare songs.'

With frozen fingers, I scribbled away with an old mangled pen on wet paper.

Mother nature acting in best interest,
Against a man-made dying planet fate.

Spiney snatched the paper from my hand and read my scribbling.
'Whits that goat tae dae wae ma cookin'.'
'Its simple, it's a fucked up mess.'
'Well that's de last time A'm daein' the cookin'.'
'Promise.'
A few more slugs of whiskey were downed.
'I wrote a bit more o flyin' last night... Cumowan, let's huv a sing-song.'
I sang through the words trying to imitate Bish. Spiney joined in with the percussion on a can of beans and trying to make a dum-dum-dum sound of a bass guitar.

Whit's the che-m-ical!
That cunt rols-yur-mind!

Spiney joined in with some more dub-dub-dub and a bit of lead guitar deh-deh-deh and a bit of drum chui-chui-chui sound. A few more slugs of whiskey were downed.

Or is't-yur-mind!
That cunt-rols-yur chem-ical!

I scribbled down some more words and both of us sang out aloud in our semi-drunken state. More often than not the pen wouldn't work or my head torch would go out.
The two of us sang out loudly at the tops of our voices, lying in our sleeping bags underneath the boulder, and arguing how the words would fit to the music, Spiney imitating playing the guitar and I hitting a can of beans for some beat.

Smile und fly-through the air!
Like a bird-tae close-tae the sun.
Smile fur owan secund-o-flight.
Und follow the golden path-tae heaven!

Spiney was getting carried away with the guitar and hacked his head against the granite ceiling. There were a few moans and groans.
Then we continued. A'm just hangin' owan tae a piece o rock!

We sang through the song several times until hoarse, and the bottle of whisky was finished. The whisky and singing brought some warmth back.

The conversation was back on Jacko.
   'Remember years ago when we wus playin' fitba up at the garages und Jacko wus stoned oota his heid. We wus playin' when Jacko staggered oot frum behind wan o the garages und collapsed owan the grun. He wus lyin' in this puddle o water rolled up like a baw in the middle o oor game, so we picked him up tae the side und used him as a goalpost... A cunnae huv been more than twelve at the time. Left the cunt lyin' there aifter oor game hud finished we did.'
   'A cunnae remember that.'
   'Mibbe yae wusnae wae us when that happened.'
Spiney kept the conversation going.
   'A remember, A asked Jacko no that long ago. "Dae yae know whit de fuck yur takin'?" "Naw, A'm experimentin, the daft cunt sais. A like tryin' different stuff tae see whit it dus." "Dae yae know whit yur fuckin' dayin'?" A asks. "Dae yae know whit yur dayin' when yur dayin that climbin' stuff?" the cunt sais. Completely bamboozled me it did. A wusnae sure whit tae say. De cunt wis awais like dat. Shifty bastard as he wus.

Awais hud sumthin' up his sleeve. Awais hud tae huv the last word he did. A sais tae the cunt, "Wae awe that shite in yur boady, yu'll no see twenty." "Uch, yu'll faw oaf a cliff und dee before mae." "Well at least A'm no walkin' aboot hoof deid like yae," A sais. "A'm in control," he sais. "A know whit A'm daein'," he sais. "Like fuck." A sais...'

'Jacko wis just the same as us.'

'A dinnaeno, Jacko couldnae fit in. Sumtimes he looked so fragile like he cood shatter intae a million bits; othertimes he wus so deep he wid stare right through yae. It wus scary, he wus sufferin' awe de time. He wus wan troubled boy. "Why ure we here?" He sais tae mae once. "At school yae mean?" A sais. "Naw here," he sais, "earth, owan de planet." A sais, "A dinnaeno, yae tell me?" Then the cunt walks away...'

'Well, he wus goin' owan aboot life after death und awe that stuff wae me tae. Dae yae think there's life aifter yur deid?'

Spiney starts philosophising again.

'Fuck knows! When yur deid yur deid. A don't know why yur so worried aboot Jacko. A wid worry much more aboot gettin' a SS20 owan yur heid. Sum cunt is gonnae press the wrong button und we're awe gonae get blown tae fuck... If its no a nuclear war, it'll be sum deadly virus or sum bug that'll wipe us awe oot. Yu'll be wan o the lucky wan's, und faw oaf a cliff anyway... Better fawin' oaf a cliff, than getting a Russian SS20 owan ure heid or daein' a Jacko special doped up tae de eyeballs. When yur deid, yur fuckin' deid... Now, let's get sum doss.'

The two of us settled down for some sleep. However, after a few minutes the warmth of the whisky started to disappear. It was going to be another cold, night of pure misery.

I stared up into the darkness. Spiney was already starting to snore; he always seemed to drop off quickly. I started thinking about our conversation. Spiney had a point; the rest of the world seemed insane, some cunt could press the button and it would be the end.

I could see the cunt about to press the button. I could see the smile on his face. It was Jacko's smile.

One second we're here…next second we're all nuclear dust.

Jacko seemed mad. The world seemed mad. Maybe the world was on a self-destructive path of no return, like Jacko, and there's nothing you can do about it. For all the high points in humanity: science, art, society, there was a Jacko madness that could destroy everything.

I remembered after a day's rock climbing at the Quadrocks near Largs. I saw a nuclear submarine sail down the Clyde and the Hunterson nuclear power station in the same view. It had never dawned on me before, that a nuclear weapon arsenal and a nuclear power station were all located a few miles from where I lived. Spiney's prophecy could happen, may be 'we're awe gonae get blown tae fuck'.

I started writing.

> *There's a nuclear bomb in my back garden,*
> *I have no shield against a cancer threat.*
> *What can I do to protect my child.*
> *The law is made to keep me down.*
> *My eastern friend I cannot see,*
> *But I know nuclear bombs from heaven*
> *Will land on my head*
> *Do they believe the same as me?*

BCT to the Rescue

I woke up with a sore head and feeling terrible. I was not sure if it was last night's dinner or the whisky. There was a grumbled out of Spiney.

'O fuck! Ma heid! O fuck! Ma heid!'

It was light outside. I got out of my wet sleeping bag and was soon shivering with cold. After a lot of effort the brew went on. We drank a cup of disgusting lukewarm tea, with bits of dried food floating around, finished the last few scraps of food, and got organised for the long walk out to the bikes. Outside it was another cold day. The cloud was down low and there was a light mist floating around. We were in no rush. Casually we got all our stuff together for the pad out.

The two of us slowly plodded towards Lurcher's, a pass between Hell's Lum and Stag Rocks, without much purpose and much chatting. It was a grim day. At Shelter Stone it was relatively calm, since it was in the lee of the wind, but we knew to expect a wild wind on the plateau. However, we knew the way well and were confident that we could cross the plateau in any conditions, a single compass bearing from the top of Lurcher's to Coire na Ciste and then down to the car park by the ski lifts. On the way to Lurcher's, it appeared to be getting dark.

'It's no a bit dark isn't it. Whit time is it?'

'Dunno, ma watch is at the bottom o' the sack.'

We hiked on a bit further.

Soon it was obvious that it was dusk.

'Shite. We must o dossed a bit too much after that bottle o whisky last night.'

'It's that whisky, it dus ma heid in!'

By the time we reached the top of the pass it was dark and the full force of the wind hit us. A cold Arctic wind coming down from the north blasted straight into our faces.

The wind was so strong, that sometimes it stopped us in our tracks and we had to sit down with our backs to the wind and wait for it to drop a little. Other times, we leaned so hard into the wind that if it dropped a little we would overbalance and topple over. Any exposed flesh was blasted by flying ice. Progress was slow, walking into the blizzard, but steadily we made our way across the plateau.

We had been walking for a good hour on the plateau, maybe longer – it was difficult to judge.

I was sure I could hear something in the howling wind. Was it a whistle? Surely it can't be a whistle; nobody with any sense would be on the plateau tonight.

It must be my imagination running wild again.

I forgot about the whistle and pressed on into the wind. A few minutes passed... I thought I heard the whistle again.

'Dae yae hear a whistle?' I had to shout over the howling wind. The wind was so loud and my jaw was so frozen that it was difficult to say more than a few words.

'Whit wis that!?' Spiney shouted in my ear.

'A whistle,' pointing in the direction I thought the sound was coming from.

'Rubbish.'

A few more minutes passed...

'That's definitely a whistle,' straining to work out what direction the sound was coming from.

Spiney didn't disagree this time.

'Whit shall we dae?'

'We could be in trouble oorselves owan a night like this if we're no careful.'

'Fuckin' eejits! Who dae they expect tae rescue them owan the plateau the night?'

We had a quick debate about whether we should leave our compass bearing and investigate or carry on and report it to the mountain rescue. We decided to investigate and moved off our bearing in the direction of the sound. A few minutes later we changed direction, and then again a different direction, following the sound in the shifting wind. We followed the sound of the whistle for some time. It appeared to be getting louder. We stopped and shouted out together,

'Ure Yae OK?' and again, 'Ure Yae OK?'
We listened as best we could. There was a faint reply in the distance.

'They're over there,' I pointed to a small clump of stones in the distance.
I could make out four figures huddled together in the distance, sitting on their rucksacks, behind a wee clump of rocks. They were lucky to find some shelter from the wind on the plateau. When they realised that someone had answered their distress call, three of them jumped up and greeted us. They looked very cold, but very happy to see us.

'Can you get us out of here?' an English voice asked.

'Whit the fuck ure yae daeing here?' Spiney asked.
One of them told us that they had been climbing on Coire an t-Sneachda, got lost trying to get back to the car-park, spent last night and all day on the plateau behind this wee outcrop not much higher than two to three feet. The outcrop was perched very close to an edge. I don't know if the English party realised how close they were to a large cornice and a very large cliff. A few steps and someone could easily disappear over the edge. I reckoned they must be on top of Stag Rocks.
I noticed that the fourth person was still crouched down behind the rock. He was not looking very well with his head in his hands.

'He's exhausted,' an English voice said.

I went down to speak to him. He looked glazed and I couldn't get much sense out of him. He didn't want to move. I reckoned that he had hypothermia and I went back over to the other group.

'Y'ure pal is dying. He'll no survive the night.'

Spiney and I had a chat about the best course of action. We got the group organised and set a new compass bearing from where we thought we were. One of the English had a watch. It was almost seven o'clock. My estimate of time had been completely out. One of the English party had some glucose tablets. I gave them to the punter with hypothermia.

Six of us headed into the dark. We were moving very slowly. Spiney was up front leading the party and carrying the weakest person's rucksack. I was at the back helping the weakest member of the party try and walk. He was stumbling about all over the place. When he fell over, I got him to his feet and got him walking again. After half an hour or so, Spiney and I would change places and I would lead. We were making very slow progress. The rough bearing we had taken would take us into Coire Cas and we reckoned that it should not take us much more than 2 hours.

We had been walking in the storm for three hours. The terrain around us did not look familiar. We were expecting to walk up a shallow valley with gentle slopes on our left and right. Instead, we had gone up a steep slope and down another. Doubt started to creep in about where we were. Three hours walking turned into four. We were lost. I was worried that we were heading towards the cliffs of Coire na t-Sneachda or even back to Hell's Lum. Every five or ten minutes, we were convinced that a cornice was coming up and we were about to walk over an edge of a cliff. One of us would go ahead and probe the snow. Progress was painfully slow.

Spiney and I discussed our options: keep moving, all six of us bivouacking the night out or one of us going for the mountain rescue and the other staying with the party. We discussed about the weakest member of the party, whether to put him inside one of our sleeping bags and leave him, carry him or drag him in a polythene bag. Two others of the English party were now looking very weak and I was starting to be concerned about them. We decided to keep moving and gain height and hope that we could identify the summit and have an idea of where we were. By this time, one of the English climbers and I had to drag his friend up the mountain.

Eventually, we arrived at the summit of Cairngorm at some hour early in the morning, much to the relief of everyone. There is a big cairn on the summit with a weather station inside. We banged on the door. Surprisingly, there was somebody inside. He got on his radio to the emergency services. Apparently, the mountain rescue had been out looking for the four English climbers all day, but had given up at nightfall. We were fed copious cups of hot sugary tea. It was amazing to see the change in everyone: out of the wind, a bit of warmth and a hot cup of tea.

All six of us set off down the hill for the car park. Once out of the cloud, we could see blue flashing lights from the police and ambulance in the distance. At the car park the English party said thanks before they were put into an ambulance. The police and ambulance disappeared from the car park. All was quiet except for the wind. The two of us stood in the car park by ourselves. Everything was shut and not a soul was to be seen. The bikes were still where we left them, but the blizzard had buried them under snow. We spent a bit of time half-heartedly trying to get the bikes out of the snow. We gave up and headed to the toilets for a doss. The hand dryer was useful to get hands warm again. Wet sleeping bags were rolled out on the ground, we crawled inside the bags and were soon asleep.

Hogmanay

A couple of tourists woke us up in the morning, they were very surprised to see two bodies in sleeping bags blocking their way to the urinals. Embarrassed, they disappeared without stopping.

'Time tae go. Let's get oot'a here.'

It was early morning and the first skiers had arrived. The bikes were dug out from under a snowdrift again. After a bit of effort the bikes started and we headed down to Aviemore.

Today was Hogmanay. Rep, Bish and the rest of the crowd were coming up from Glasgow for the Hogmanay party.

In Aviemore, the first priority was to get a good breakfast. We headed for the biggest, cheapest and hottest breakfast in Aviemore.

The warmth of the tea room and full stomachs made us feel drowsy. We spread ourselves out, unpacking our wet gear and trying to dry it as best we could. The windows started to steam up with all our wet gear. A damp, fusty smell of sweaty clothes soon permeated the café. We tried to make our tea last as long as we could. There was a group of well dressed ladies chatting incessantly in the corner. They had polythene bags of full of shopping piled up around the table. The bags kept falling over and all the stuff tumbled out on the floor. A nearby T.V. was blasting out a chat, game, soap show. The ladies were watching TV, drinking tea and chatting away at the same time. There was an occasional glance over at us, then a look away in disgust. They were talking about us.

It gave me an idea about a song for the band. I started to scribble down a few words on a discarded copy of The Daily Record.

Society expects us to conform, spend and throw away.

*Consumerism gone wild, materialism is the order of today.
We are living in a soft age, in a protected state.
Chance the dollar, it's the drug to swallow.*

I called it "Capitalist Consumer Chaos".

We met Bish and Rep at 2 o'clock at the train station as planned and checked out the town for possible doss sites. The only suitable doss we found was under a large open road bridge over the river Spey about a mile out of town. There was not much protection against the elements unless the rain/snow fell straight down; otherwise any wind and rain would blow straight through, but it was better than the Shelter Stone. Also it was very close to the train line, so every hour or so, there would be an almighty noise, as a train would pass by. We cooked up some dried food, got our dancing gear on and stashed our rucksacks. Bish brought his tape recorder and started to play some tapes to get us in the mood. It was going to be a long night.
With a bit of luck we would manage to crash a party and get some free food and booze and if we were really lucky manage a doss in a hotel cupboard or under a table or somewhere else inconspicuous.

All four of us headed into town dressed for the evening in T-shirts and jeans, and sliding about in sand shoes. Snow was lying on the ground and a cold wind blew.
We got to the centre. There was a big crowd gathering for the Hogmanay celebrations. Bish spied a Christmas tree lit up with lights and disappeared underneath the branches. The lights went off, then came back on a few minutes later. Bish had rigged up a circuit breaker to have some control of the lights and also some power for his tape recorder. The band went into its routine.

Bish shouted his head off singing "Flying" while the rest of us mimed playing the instruments. Spiney was on the ground wriggling away. Rep was doing swallow dives into a pile of snow. Four or five people came over to see what was going on. Bish tried his flashing Christmas tree show; however the concert came to an abrupt end. Something fused and all the lights went up in a puff of smoke. There was a strong smell of burning plastic. Bish's tape recorder was all right.
We gave up with the Christmas tree show and moved back into the crowd for the bells.
In the crowd we all parted company and disappeared in different directions, cheering and shouting, jumping up and down. A few seconds before midnight, the public address system broadcast a count down to the New Year. This was an incentive for Rep to shin up one of the flagpoles in the centre of the square.
Rep was starting to get into the mood of the evening swinging back and forward at the very top of the flagpole. The police were at the bottom trying to persuade Rep to come down. Rep was hanging on for dear life as he was swinging back and forward in danger of snapping the pole or being launched like a stone from a sling shot through the second storey window of a neighbouring hotel. Everybody around was half-closing their eyes in anticipation of the pole snapping. Eventually, the local constabulary persuaded him to come down, and he was dragged away.
The night went on. Excessive amounts of booze were consumed. The rest of the team had disappeared. It had been a long festive night. I managed to find a doss in a laundry cupboard for the night. I fell asleep, propped up against a pile of linen.

≈

The door opened. I fell out on the ground in a half-dazed state with a big pile of laundry falling around me.

'Ahhh!!!'

There was an almighty shriek from a cleaning lady.

'Not so loud fur God sake!'

'Don't worry A'm no deid.'

I got up and tried to get orientated. My head was splitting from the night before.

'Which way is oot?' I asked.

The cleaning lady was still in a bit of a state, she didn't say anything, but pointed nervously.

'Ta very much.'

'I'm a hotel inspector...'

'And a very nice place yae huv here...

'And A huv tae be goin... A huv tae inspect de big hotel next tae de train station next.'

I made my way out of what appeared to be a hotel and slowly wandered back to the bridge to find the rest of the team. The other three were there with some very sorry looking faces. Today was a rest day to recover from Hogmanay. The afternoon was spent in a teashop staring into a mug of tea. Nobody said very much. That night we dossed underneath the bridge.

Aviemore was our first live, open-air concert, in front of an audience of about 4 or 5 people. It wasn't much, but it was a start.

Lucy

Girls

It was the New Year and we were back at school. It was the first time we had been together since Aviemore to discuss our first "concert". Spiney and I reckoned that there was something missing in the band – there was no girl.
There was a big discussion about finding a girl for the band.
    'How aboot wee Sarah frum the bottom scheme?'
Bish would have none of it.
    'Fuck off! Y'ure just wan'tae shag hur.'
    'Wee Linda frum the chemistry class; she'd be smashin' she's goat big tits.'
    'Whit the fuck ure her tits goat tae dae wae it?'
    'We could put an ad intae the paper.'
    'We're no huvin a girl in the band. Did the Beatles or the Rollin' Stones huv any birds? No! So we're huvin' nun.'
When it came to music Bish seemed to know what he was talking about.

≈

The girl issue lingered on for weeks.
Spiney and I schemed together and put an ad into the local paper – we didn't tell Bish. The ad read: 'Girl singer for progressive punk band wanted'.
There were three replies.
The two of us were working one evening on a bike. There was a knock on the garage door. Spiney went over and opened it. A Goth was standing there, jet black hair, face white as a sheet with thick black make-up, dressed in a big black dress and black doc martins.

The girl didn't have a chance to speak.
Spiney said, 'Sorry, the funeral is next door,' and shut the door.
Another girl appeared later that evening who looked more hopeful. She had spiked green hair and big star make-up things around her eyes.

'Cun yae sing?' I asked.

The wee girl stood like a statue and started whining and screaming away in a piercing high pitched voice.

'Weee... Uuuhhh...'

Spiney and I looked at each other in unison and said, 'Sorry,' pushed her outside and closed the door.

The following night we were back in the garage working on a bike. There was another knock at the garage door.
A well-dressed girl with a ponytail stood at the entrance. She had an acoustic guitar strapped to her back.
We looked at each other wondering if she would be right for the band.
Spiney asked, 'Cun yae sing?'
The girl starts off with the guitar, singing with full voice and a big smile.

'Ha-lle-lue-ya the fields are brimming full of joy. Ha-lle-lue-ya heaven will come to earth and the angels will rejoice.'
Spiney interrupted.

'Hold owan a minute dear, wu're looking fur someone tae sing in a punk band, no a Mormon convention. Wae need someone tae shake their tits aboot and take their nickers oaf like.'
The girl looked shocked. She quickly disappeared.
Spiney closed the door and we started working on the bike again.

'Sum people...' Shaking his head, 'Whit the fuck dae they think punk is?'

Bish was right, a girl in the band was a bad idea.

≈ *Rock Rock* ≈

≈

An alternative solution to the girl problem was found.
Spiney had been out on a bike-bit scavenging expedition and found an old shop dummy dumped in a skip. The two of us went back on his motorbike to collect the dummy.

'A totally shat mesel when A saw the heid. A wis pullin' this bike frame oot'a this skip and suddenly a fuckin' heid popped oot! Fuckin' bricked it, A did. Shat ma keks, A did. Thought sumbudy hud dumped a deid boady in there. A almost phoned the polis! Anyway, here she is!'

Spiney pointed to a dummy's bald head and arm sticking out from the garbage. The two of us pulled the upper torso out from the skip. The legs were missing. We had to rummage about in the skip for the legs. The dummy was assembled and looked in pretty good condition. It was covered with old wallpaper and garden trimmings. We cleaned it as best we could.
The next problem was to get it back home. It is not easy to get two people and a life-sized dummy on a motorbike.
I thought about putting the dummy across the petrol tank with legs strapped out in front. That wasn't practical; it interfered too much with Spiney's driving. Another solution had to be found. Spiney strapped the dummy to my back with bits of string, with arms around my neck and feet around my waist. All three of us set off back home through the centre of town. Heads turned as the three of us drove through the streets of Glasgow. At each red light, there was always some punter ready to make a wisecrack.

'Halloo Darlin'. Cun yae gee me a ride as weel!?'
'Hae, Jim. Cun yae nae aford a blow up one?'
'Where's the gang bang, pal?'
'Cun A bring ma doll along as well?'

We got the dummy back to the garage and started to work on it. I cut off the breasts and hollowed out the upper torso, big enough to take Spiney's tape-to-tape recorder. I then re-assembled the chest with the tape recorder inside and glued the breasts onto each of the tape reels. At normal play speed, the breasts would rotate at a therapeutic two or three times a second. In fast forward or reverse the breasts would spin into a blur and cause a humming sound. I made a flesh coloured fibreglass plate to cover the rest of the tape recorder.

≈

The band assembled in the garage one night for a session.
    'Right Bish, we huv a new member fur the group.'
    'New member?'
    'Aye, she's smashin'.'
    'Who the fuck is dis? Barabra fuckin' Striesland?'
Bish wasn't happy.
    'She's cummin' along fur the session the night.'
    'Well… Yis cun go und fuck yourselves, 'cos A'm no goinae be there.'
    'Yes yae will…'cos she's here already.'
    'Where?'
    'She's standin' behind yae.'
Bish turns round.
    'Where?'
    'Under the polybag.'
    'Whit?'
Bish starts to unravel the polybag.
    'Whit the fuck is this?'
The latest member of the band was unveiled to Bish and Rep.
    'Isn't she just smashin', eh?'
    'Oh ma goad!'

Bish almost keeled over in shock, amazement and laughter.

'Ha! Ha! Ha! Where the hell did yae find that? Ha! Ha! Ha! A'll huv tae make sum flashin' lights fur hur tit's. Oh! Jesis!'

It was a good practise session that night. At the end of the session, we named our lead singer Lushes Lucy, Lucy for short. Lucy was the star of the band.

Suspenders

It was decided Lucy would look better with some clothes.
The four of us went up to Glasgow to buy some ladies' underwear for Lucy. It took four of us to pluck up enough courage to go near a trendy women's shop and buy some sexy underwear. I was pushed into the shop. I looked back to see three faces pressed against the shop window.
I approached the counter nervously.
There was a youngish girl standing behind the counter. She was very well dressed and wore a lot of make-up. There was nobody else in the shop that I could see.

'Ah, excuse me misses, A'm lookin' fur sum underwear fur ma maa, A mean ma sister. Bras and stockings and stuff like that. Sumthin' sexy, yae know.'

I was red as beetroot and nearly shaking. The girl behind the counter could see I was very embarrassed. She had probably seen all types in her shop before, with all stories, but not so many plukey, vagrant schoolboys.

'Yes sir, we have a full range of ladies' lingerie. What does your sister like?'

'Dunno, sumthin' sexy. Hmmm...small and frilly?'
'What size is she?'
It took me a few seconds to work out a reply.
'Big.'

Indicating with my hands that she was about the same size as the assistant, but then I realised that the girl was a bit overweight and might take offence.

'A mean, a wee bit bigger than yae.'

The assistant took the lead and showed me some of the range in stock.

'This one is very popular.'

'Whit's that?'

'Stockings with matching suspender belt.'

'How much is it?'

'£15.'

'Ah, it's a bit over ma price range. Dae yae huv anythin' cheaper?'

'Yes sir, this one comes in at a very reasonable £10.'

'Dae yae huv anythin' cheaper than that? Second hon stuff?' I asked in hope, 'Whit aboot used stuff?'

The assistant looked a bit shocked. She probably had never been asked that question before.

'How much do you want to spend?'

'A've goat two quid here and ah've goat another sixteen pence in ma poakit.'

There was almost a sigh of desperation from the assistant. She thought about it for some moments.

'I may have some damaged stock that I can sell.'

She disappeared under the counter and appeared with an old tattered box full of bits and pieces.

'I'll give you this one for £2.'

I picked it up and gave it a good inspection. I had no idea what it was and asked.

'Whit is it?'

'It's a suspender belt.'

'Done! Mmmh... How dus it work?'

'I'm sure your sister will know.'

'A'm no sure she does.'

The girl was not sure if I was taking the piss or not. I could see she was trying to figure me out.

'This bit goes round the waist and these bits attach the stockings.'

'Oh, yes, of course,' trying to sound as if I knew all along. I spied an old trashed wig lying behind the counter.

'U'r yae goin' tae throw that wig oot? Cun A huv it fur m'a sister as well?'

The lady put it in a bag without saying anything and gave it to me in an abrupt manner, happy to get rid of me. I paid my two pounds and walked out of the shop, proud of my achievement. As soon as the shop door closed, I was instantly questioned.

'Whit huv yae goat?'

I brought the suspender belt out of the bag and dangled it in front of everyone.

'Whit the fuck's that?'

'It's a suspender belt y'a eejit. Somethin' tae attach stockin's tae d'yae no know anythin! It's awe they've goat fur two quid.'

I was trying to sound convincing. There was no reply. Everybody looked at each other. Eventually Rep broke the silence.

'Y'uve been dun, two fuckin' quid fur a wee bit o string!'

That was the end of the clothing budget, so a pair of trashed tights found in a bin and an old pair of Y-fronts had to do for the rest of the sexy lingerie. The tights were cut to shape and connected to the suspender belt. The wig was glued down and blue tinsel from an old Christmas tree was added to her hair in plaits. The Y-fronts went on. For completeness, a toilet chain was acquired to use as a necklace, the wooden handle dangled in front like a pendant.

Lucy was looking great. She was set for the stage.

≈ *Stephen Najda* ≈

The birthday party

Bish's birthday was coming up. So it was a good excuse to have a party and get the band out in front of an audience. This would be our first test at playing live music.
A problem suddenly arose, it was going to cost money to rent some floor space; nobody had thought about money before. The money problem stopped us in our tracks for a few moments. The four of us looked at each other—what do we do?
Bish suddenly came out with a brilliant idea of charging people to get in. There was a look of disbelief that Bish was actually suggesting that somebody might pay to watch the band. Bish was full of confidence that we could make enough money to pay for a room and maybe a little extra as well.

Glasgow was searched high and low for a good venue: in other words, the cheapest place in town that would take a noisy band. A tiny shitty room was found at the student union.

≈

At last our big day came. We were all hyped up about playing to a live audience. Everybody looked anxious except Bish. He looked cool as ice and totally unconcerned.
The band was set up on a raised floor in a corner of the room. Bish tested the mic and amplifier. He went into his usual 'rock, rock, rock!' routine, causing high-pitched feedback from the amp, and resulting in everybody shouting volleys of abuse at Bish.
    'Shut-The-Fuck-Up!'
    'Ma brains ure like fuckin' mince!'
Spiney strummed away on his guitar to get the thing in tune. I could never understand why he always had to spend hours

tuning the guitar because it all sounded the same to me. Rep bashed away at his drums for a couple of minutes. He was under strict instructions not to hit the drums too hard and break any part of the kit. I set up Lucy beside the drums, checked the tape recorder was working and set the tape at the correct place. I had a stop watch to time the length of each piece of recorded music. I wrapped up Lucy in a Glasgow Corporation bin bag so she could be unveiled to the audience at the last minute before the start of the show.

The plan was to do our full repertoire of four songs, have a quick break, and then to repeat them again for the second half of the gig.

Spiney stayed with the instruments while the other three of us went out to find a suitable audience. Bish had printed out some leaflets advertising the gig.

BCT PUNK ROCK TONITE was printed across the front in bold typescript; a big arrow pointing to wipe arse here was written on the back. Each leaflet had been crushed into a tight ball, then flattened out, to give a used look. The three of us handed out the leaflets to an assortment of students and anybody else that looked the part. When we got back, Spiney was still strummin' away on the guitar, still trying to get it in tune.

It was eight o'clock. Time for the gig to begin. I opened the door. A group of friends and some unknowns were outside. Everybody paid something to get in. The going rate was £1, but anything would do. Soon I had over £14 pounds in my pocket.

The night started with a disco of some conventional punk music using Bish's tape recorder rigged up to the amplifier: Siouxsie and the Banshees, The Damned, The Adverts, Ramones, The Slits, The Undertones, X Ray Spec, Generation X, Sham 69, and the like, blasted out. The sound system was a bit

rough, but it was OK for dancing.
There were about 20 in the crowd, jumping up and down, going wild to the music. Spiney and Rep joined in the disco and had cleared a space in the centre of the floor for themselves. Bish and I joined in wriggling about on the floor doing the worm.
All these traditional punks stood around looking at the four of us, trying to figure out what was happening.
The disco went on for over an hour. By this time there were now more than 30 people crammed into the tiny room and I had over 20 pounds in my pocket.
The taped music stopped. It was now our turn.
We moved into position on the small stage. Spiney picked up his guitar. Rep sat behind the drums. I took position beside Lucy and picked up the bass guitar. Bish put on a pair of dark glasses with square white rims. Bish had painted "B" on the left eye, "T" on the right eye of the glasses and glued on a "C" on his forehead. Bish picked up the micro phone and shouted:

'Halloo Everyone! This is the Borrheid Cream Team – B! C! T! – Balls! Cunts! And! Tits! Wu're hear tae make a noise. So yae cun fuck off if yae don't like it!'
The audience is jumping up and down, pressing against the stage. I unveil Lucy. A big cheer erupted from the crowd.
Bish turns round and says, 'One, two, three.'
I turn Lucy on. The first track is "Flying". Music blasts out. The walls reverberate with sound. There's 27 seconds of music from Lucy, then Bish joins in.

> A'm just hangin' owan tae a piece o rock
> A'm just holdin on tae re-a-li-tyyy
> Fuck, fuck, A'm just holdin' on, on, on, to re-a-li-tyyy.
> A'm gripped oot'a ma fuckin' – Skuuull!
> Nowhere tae go but up, what the f-u-c-k.

Bish goes into a dance routine for a few moments. Then comes back to the mic to sing.

> *Just wan second tae... Go!*

Spiney and I join in on backing vocals:

> *Ma boady wants tae Go! Go!*

Bish sings solo again.

> *A just wanna be A B-oring Bastard!*

Spiney and I join in.

> *Boring Bastard! Boring Bastard!*

The tempo picks up and Rep is bashing hell out of the drums. There is a bit of sound from Lucy. Bish is dancing about the floor and starts giving the V-sign to everyone in the crowd. He then starts signing.

> *Take a haaapyyy drug. Whaaa!*
> *Tae find a sad tomorooow. Undeeer!*
> *It's a fools Paraaadise. Ohooo!*
> *Adams temptation. Apple fate. Ehhh!*

Lucy does her solo. Bish tries to give a quick moon to the crowd, but doesn't have enough time to get his trousers off and almost falls backwards off the stage. I hold on Lucy's tit for a few seconds to let Bish get back on stage. Spiney plays a solo bit on the guitar until Bish is back on his feet.
Bish starts signing again.

Just wan second tae... Go!
Ma boady wants tae Go! Go!
A just wanna be A boring bastard!
Boring Bastard! Boring Bastard!

If yae don't like the – CHIPS!!!
Yae cun alwais com – PLAIN!!!
One second tae pop a – PILL!!!!
If yae think yur in – SAIN!!!

Bish does a jig on the floor, trips and almost goes head first into the crowd, but manages to compose himself before the next line. I whisper over to Bish, 'Ure yae OK?'
Bish turns round, gives the thumbs up and starts singing into the mic again.

Just wan second tae... Go!

Spiney and I join in on backing vocals.

Ma boady wants tae... Go! Go!'

A just wanna be A boring bastard!

Spiney and I join in.

Boring Bastard! Boring Bastard!

Lucy does her solo bit. Bish is pogoing up and down on the floor, trying to jump as high as he could.
Bish is back at the mic and sings again.

A quick fix...and forget the wooorld,

> all the ills and problems...that occuuur.
> Take a chemical...tae delude yur brain,
> Try and run...but yae cunnae run-run-runaway.

Lucy plays by herself. Bish spins and drops to the floor, and starts spinning on his back.
Bish bounces back up to the mic and sings.

> Just wan second tae... Go!

Spiney and I join in on backing vocals.

> Ma boady wants tae... Go! Go!

Bish drops to the floor, pulls the microphone down and shouts.

> A just wanna be A boring bastard!

Spiney and I join in.

> Boring Bastard! Boring Bastard!

Lucy does her solo. Bish is back on his feet going round and round. He stops and sings.

> Only excitement in – LIFE!!!
> Jacko's style was a – FRIGHT!!!
> Sad bastard, just another – BOADY!!!
> on the pile o Human – SHITE!!!

Lucy plays her part. Bish suddenly stops and stares motionless up to the ceiling. He shouts into the mic.

Just wan second tae... Go!

Spiney and I join in on backing vocals.

Ma boady wants tae.. Go! Go!

A just wanna be A boring bastard!
Boring Bastard! Boring Bastard!

Lucy does her bit. Bish does a Nazi goose step across the stage giving a salute. He sings.

Madness or maybe...a natural state,
gives a fear o living
That disturbs...the brain,
one second and it'll be awe...away.

Bish does a Nazi goose step across the stage in the opposite direction. His left fingers in a 'moustache' over his upper lip, his right hand over his groin, jerking off. He starts singing again.

Just wan second tae... Go!
'Ma boady wants tae... Go! Go!
'A just wanna be A boring bastard!
'Boring Bastard! Boring Bastard!

Bish goes into a dance routine alongside Lucy as she sings. He then goes back to the mic and sings.

Whit is the – CHEMICAL,
that controls – yur MIND?
Or is it yur – MIND,
That controls yur – CHEMICAL?

Lucy does her solo. Bish starts dancing, jiggling about on the floor like some floppy doll, then springing up every now and then. He sings again.

> *Just wan second tae... Go!*
> *Ma boady wants tae... Go! Go!*
> *A just wanna be A boring bastard!*
> *Boring Bastard! Boring Bastard!*

Lucy sings. Bish drops the mic, stands in front of the audience with his finger up his nose, flicking snots into the crowd. He calmly walks back, picks up the mic and sings.

> *Need a drug tae confuse – REALITY.*
> *Tae help the krrreative process flow.*
> *Good idea tae kiiill mysel*
> *Before A becum a starrr.*

Bish is jumping up and down, spitting into the crowd. He comes back to the mic to sing.

> *Just wan second tae... Go!*
> *Ma boady wants tae... Go! Go!*
> *A just wanna be A boring bastard!*
> *Boring Bastard! Boring Bastard!*

Bish tries to put the mic into the stand, but drops it on the ground and has to go looking for it on the ground. He gets it back on the stand before the start of the next verse.
He carries on singing.

> *SMILE! And fly through the air,*
> *Like a bird too close tae the – SUN.*

> SMILE! For one second o flight,
> and follow the golden path tae – HEAVEN!!!

Lucy plays. Bish starts pogoing again as if trying to head a football, then goes back to the mic and sings.

> Just wan second tae... Go!
> Ma boady wants tae... Go! Go!
> A just wanna be A boring bastard!
> Boring Bastard! Boring Bastard!

Lucy dos her solo piece. Bish stops and stares into the crowd, then suddenly starts singing again.

> But A'm still here hangin' owan tae a piece o rock,
> A'm just holdin on tae re-a-li-tyyy.
> Fuck, fuck. A'm just holdin' on, on, on to re-a-li-tyyy.
> A'm gripped oot'a ma fuckin' – Skuuull.
> Nowhere tae go but up, what the f-u-c-k.

All four of us are up front with Bish to sing.

> Just wan second tae... Go!
> Ma boady wants tae... Go! Go!
> A just wanna be A boring bastard!
> Boring Bastard! Boring Bastard!
> Boring Bastard! Boring bastard!
> Boring bastard! Boring bastard!

We move straight onto the next song "Rock Rock".

Bish starts off in his usual way shouting, 'Rock, rock, rock,' into the mic before he starts the song. The sound is like Bish's brain getting sucked down into his voice box, out his throat and splattered into the microphone.

> The r-r-right huv nae r-r-right tae dictate.
> The r-r-revolution hus the r-r-right tae r-r-rock,
> rock, rock, rock, rock, rock, rock!

Bish is getting carried away with the occasion and put in a few more rock, rocks than I was expecting. I grab Lucy's tit to stop the tape recorder going round for a few seconds, then release it when Bish goes onto the next line.

> R-r-rock the E-sta-blish-ment.
> The r-r-right huv nae r-r-right tae dictate
> The r-r-revolution hus the r-r-right tae rock
> Rock, rock, rock, rock, rock, rock!

Spiney and I come in on chorus.

> Rock the establishment.

Bish is swinging the mic stand around and around before he starts singing.

> All yae cun dae is tae s-s-slag me off.
> Solve yur ain pr-r-r-oblem. Mate!
> Don't wanna dr-r-rug tae sedate ma br-r-rain.
> Need tae get spaced oot owan a r-r-rock face.
> Rock, rock, rock, rock, rock, rock!

> Rock the establishment.

A crowd of punks with long spikey orange hair, wearing cut-up tartan trousers covered in zips, come up to the front of the stage and start spitting at Bish.

> *Don't question ma life – Why?*
> *What's yur mistake, ya – Hide?*
> *If A lose ma grip and – Die.*
> *Don't remember me, but Par-r-rty.*
> *Rock, rock, rock, rock, rock, rock!*
> *Rock the establishment.*

The punks are still giving Bish a hard time. Bish stops dancing. He picks up a nearby pint glass, sprays it across the front of the audience and starts singing.

> *People say A'm – Cr-r-razy!*
> *A say it's a dead – Cer-r-rt!*
> *Who am A tae turn the tide,*
> *against the force o fate.*
> *Rock, rock, rock, rock, rock, rock!*
>
> *Rock the establishment.*

Bish starts dancing away. One of the punks in the audience is starting to get a bit angry and grabs Bish. It looks as if a fight could start. Rep goes straight in to sort things out. The drums go flying in all directions.
   'Cumowan ya bunch o wankers!'
Rep goes for the punk that grabbed Bish. Some of his mates jump on Rep. I hold onto Lucy's tit to stop her. Spiney keeps playing the guitar as if nothing is happening.
There are a few scuffles, and pushing and shoving.
   'Fuck oaf will yis!'
Some of the audience join in to help Bish and Rep. The couple of punks realise that they are heavily out-numbered and back

off. Bish gets back on stage. Rep is still up front shouting his head off.

'Fuck oaf yae bunch o wankers!'

'Cumoawn Rep back tae the drums.'

Rep gets back on stage and gets his drums organised.

Bish gives a 'One, two, three...'

I let Lucy's tit go and the band continue as if nothing has happened.

> Simply furgotten in a pile o – Shite!
> A diamond yae cunnae hide.
> Look at me through yur lookin'glass,
> don't like whit yae see?
> Rock, rock, rock, rock, rock, rock!
>
> Rock the establishment.

Bish spins around in circles before he starts singing again.

> Don't ask mae why A want tae climb,
> in yur fucked up state o mind.
> Tell mae A know – Nuthin',
> and A'll tell yae – yur – R-r-right!

Somebody throws some sort of fish net over the audience and traps five or six people inside. A couple manage to get out, but the rest are being dragged about on the floor like a catch of fish. Bish jumps off the stage and jumps on top of the net full of bodies. He gets dragged about for a few seconds, then jumps back on the stage to sing.

> Don't ask mae why A go owan the hill.
> Only place tae find peace o mind and will.

> *Look oot frum ma windae,*
> *don't like the world A see.*
> *Rock, rock, rock, rock, rock, rock!*
> *Rock the establishment.*

Three or four people are still being dragged about in the net, arms and legs hanging out. Bish jumps off the stage and onto the back of the net full of bodies. The net rips open, the bodies fall out and everyone gets back on their feet again, dancing away. Bish gets back on stage to sing.

> *Blunt ma ambition and bottle ma spirit,*
> *tae keep mae in ma place.*
> *Don't ask why A'm a – Waste o Space,*
> *A'm tryin' tae escape the human – Shite!*
> *Rock, rock, rock, rock, rock, rock!*

> *Rock the establishment.*

Lucy suddenly stops mid-track. Bish looks round anxiously. I gave Lucy a slap on the back. She starts playing again. Bish continues to sing.

> *A just wanna be an accountant,*
> *Mr Sensible and huv a hoose.*
> *Live a life o boredom,*
> *And die in ma council estate.*
> *Rock, rock, rock, rock, rock, rock!*

> *Rock the establishment.*

Next song is "Plutonium Child".
Spiney starts with a very fast guitar solo. Bish joins in with

the guitar, singing in a staccato style at a very fast tempo set by Rep bashing away on the drums.

> *There's a nu-clear bomb in ma back garden.*

Bish breaks into a short dance between each line away from the mike.

> *A huv no shield against a can-cer threat.*

Bish is standing up front, sending the mic stand round and round, just missing the audience front row.

> *Whit cun A dae tae pro-tect ma child.*

The crowd pushs forward, Bish swings the mic stand round and round to push them back.

> *The law is made tae keep mae doon.*

I join in with the bass guitar with Spiney: dum, dum, dum... Bish is going mental on the floor.

> *Dis-ney child pick up a plu-ton-ium toy,*

Bish takes a gulp of beer and sends a fountain into the crowd.

> *Und catch a gen-etic mu-ta-ted moose.*

Another gulp sends a fountain of beer into the audience.

> *Each handful o earth a radio-active scare.*

Another fountain of beer goes through the air.

Con-tam-ination is the com-mun wurd.

Dum, dum, dum... Bish is back on the floor again doing his stuff.

The po-li-ti-cian and bigot and xe-no-phobe will fail.

A girl with closely shaved hair down the centre and big spikey bits to the side comes up on stage, dancing along side Bish.

Break the chains tae gither tae pull doon the walls.

She wraps herself around Bish's neck, making it difficult for him to move, but he still manages to sing into the mic.

Take heart let us dance tae gither.

The girl is still hanging around Bish's neck. Spiney moves over and unzips her dress in one movement almost down to her backside. She screams and runs back into the crowd holding onto her dress. There is a big cheer. Bish is back at the mic to sing.

A huv a dream where no one hus tae fight.

Dum, dum, dum... Bish throws the contents of his beer glass into the crowd, does a spin, lands on the floor, gets back on his feet, and starts singing into the microphone again.

This pla-net a com-mun trea-sure tae share,

Bish starts trying to imitate Rod Stewart.

But a dinnae owan a hand ful o earth.

This time he is ripping off some Bee Gees movement, swing his hips around, fingers pointing in the air.

Expected tae die fur cuntry o birth,

Bish does some effeminate Abba stuff, fingers running through his hair.

Not by sword, but a can-cer death.

Dum, dum,dum... Bish is back on the floor pogoing up and down.

On the Clyde the Po-laris sails.

Bish stares into the crowd with a lost look.

Frum an Ayr-shire field a plough man watches.

Bish walks casually away from the stage to the back behind Rep, then comes racing to the front to sing into the mic.

A tourist bus passes every-one looking but see nuthing.

Bish stares back into the crowd again.

Nu-clear bombs pointing nae-boady knows where.

Dubm, dum, dum... Spiney joins in with Bish, pogoing about.

Just about when Bish is to start the next verse, condoms full of white stuff come flying over the crowd. The condoms are aimed at Bish, but I get one in the face.

My Eastern friend A cannae see.

Bish does a quick dance and throws a condom back into the crowd.

But A dae know nu-clear bombs frum Hiven,

Another condom goes flying back into the crowd.

Will hurt ma heid.

And another one goes flying.

Dae they believe the same as me?

Dubm, dum,dum... Bish is back on the floor again – wriggling about.

Again if tanks run over Poland.

Bish spins around, arms spread out.

Di-vine inter-vention is the only way,

Bish spins again.

A look a-round in vain,

Bish spins again, looses his balance and goes into the crowd.

The crowd push him back onto the stage. He starts singing.

> Tae which God cun A trust and pray.

Dum, dum, dum... Bish stands still looking up at the ceiling as if he has just been switched off.

> The nu-clear bomb may solve yur pro-blem,

Bish drops to the floor with the mic and his whole body twitches on the ground in a dancing rhythm.

> But the po-lit-ician owes an ex-plan-ation.

He is still on the floor twitching away, then jumps up, spins round and sings.

> A black death dis-appears be-neath the-waves.

Bish stands in front of the audience, the mic half down his throat, and sings.

> Con-di-tion red is it practice or is it the end?!

The music abruptly ends.

Lucy starts playing a bit by herself. Bish takes a slug of beer before starting the next song.
A girl with short black hair and a flimsy blue dress tumbles onto the stage. In a rhythmic dance she starts to fondle her breasts, but trips over and in the process the dress falls around her shoulders, exposing her heavy chest. She gets up on her feet again and starts to pogo away alongside Bish, then

falls down to the floor with her legs apart, gyrating her hips and goes through the motions of rubbing herself off. Spiney puts his foot on her shoulder and heaves her back into the crowd in an undignified manner. Another couple of girls, each with a pint in hand, come on stage and dance alongside Spiney and myself. One has dyed blond hair, black eye make-up and is wearing a black bin bag and swastika armband. The other has a bright orange cut through the centre of her hair and bright red tufts sticking up at each side. She is wearing a dog collar with safety pins hanging off, a black and white stripy T-shirt, a tiny wee dress, stockings with big holes and a pair of bovver boots. We all dance away.

Somebody at the back of the crowd lets off a fire extinguisher and directs it towards the band. White foam goes everywhere. Soon, beer is flying through the air. Then, tomato ketchup is sprayed all over the place. Bog rolls fly around.

The audience are going wild, jumping up and down. The two girls still dance alongside Spiney and I.

Lucy stops playing. Bish caught his breath for a few moments then goes straight into "Capitalist Consumer Chaos", the last song before our break. Bish sings each line with a very fast tempo, Lucy playing a bit by herself after each line.

> *A huv every thing,*
> *but huv nothing... A want!*
> *It's a sad state o affairs,*
> *fur a de-ve-loped economy!*
> *So-Ciety expects tae con-form,*
> *spend und throw... Away!*
> *Con-sum-er-ism gone wiiild,*
> *Ma-ter-ial-ism the order o to-day!*
> *Chase the do-llar,*

> it's a drug tae Swallaaa!

Bish puts his fingers down his throat and makes a *Ehhh!!!* sound.

> *Ma-chines built no tae last,*
> *but buy new every other... Day!*
> *A dream o fast cars, designer clae-thes,*
> *und don't furget the bim-bo in the... Bi-kini.*

Lucy suddenly stops. Bish turns round with an anxious look on his face and loudly whispers over, 'Get that fuckin' thing goin'.'
I give Lucy a good slap on the back. The music blasts out again. Bish continues as if nothing has happened.

> *Only chance in life,*
> *is tae watch owan ma TV set!*
> *The rat race is fur rats,*
> *and no fur the an-i-mal in mae!*
> *It's the con-su-mer so-cie-ty,*
> *in the ca-pi-ta-list's... Pa-ra-dise.*
> *Huve we for-go-tten re-a-lity?*
> *chained tae ma TV.*
> *Soap opera und game shows,*
> *stare at a piece o fur-ni-ture.*
> *Ideal fur the ad-ver-t-i-ser,*
> *tae send the message... Hame!*

Suddenly everything went off. The music died instantly and the room went pitch black. A few seconds later, the lights in the room came back on again.
Everybody looked round to see what was happening. An old

grumpy bastard janitor in the corner shouted over, 'Fuck off! Noo! Y'yre Time's Up! Get the fuck oota here! Whit a fuckin' mess y've left. A've goat tae clean awe this shite up!'
Someone for the audience started to have an argument with the janitor.
'Uch! Away tae FUCK! We've paid oor money and we're dancing owan.'
A shouting match started.
'Get the fuck oot'a here or A'll phone the polis. It's the last time yis wu'll be back here!'
People reluctantly started to move out of the room. The janitor was in no mood to turn the power back on again.

The concert had finished. We had almost managed our complete repertoire.
It had been a good night. Bish was brilliant. He had a real presence on stage. His style was very particular: one moment a riotous rebel, the next an awkward insecure persona appeared, but he always performed with a certain humour.
The band played well. Much to our surprise, everything worked as planned. Lucy worked well. Everybody in the band was happy, even though the concert had been cut short. We felt like a real band for the first time.
After all the weeks of hard work putting everything together, there was a real sense of achievement felt that night. We congratulated ourselves. A sound was beginning to appear that could only be described as raw energy.

The crowd left grumbling, still wanting more. The rest of the team and half a dozen other punters went after the girl in the blue dress.
I was left to stash all the music stuff in a cupboard for collection later, but I took Lucy with me. Lucy was too precious to leave. I strapped her to my back.

≈ *Rock Rock* ≈

New Route

We all piled out of the union at some hour in the morning, still with dancing in our legs. The girl with the blue dress had disappeared. A big crowd were hanging about outside, wondering where the next party was going to be.
Bish spotted a building opposite, about five stories high. He took off, and started to climb up the outside of the building.
All I heard was, 'Fuck, just look at the jugs' here; new route, piece 'a pish. Rock! Rock! Rock! A'm goin' tae the top!'
Bish starts climbing the building. A few moments later, about seven or eight people were on the façade of the building, trying to get to the top. This was the challenge for the night.
Bish was out in front, Spiney and Rep behind, making good progress to get to the top of the building. I was near the bottom, making much slower progress with Lucy strapped to my back. Everybody else followed on.

≈

It was difficult to imagine what was going through their heads. Was it a mass suicide attempt? Was it a mass break-in by the K.G.B. into a top-secret vault? Was it a mass break out from a lunatic asylum?
It was too much for two cops to take in. On the beat, at night, in Glasgow, having to deal with pub fights, winos, drug addicts, muggings, wife beatings, murders, etc., something beyond their horizon – must be trouble: time to call in the reinforcements; everybody except the SAS.

≈

There was a shout from Spiney above, 'Shite, it's the polis.'

Somebody else shouted out, 'Let's get oot'a here.'
I looked around and saw two cops running towards us. Everybody was clambering down the façade of the building, then scampering in all directions. The two cops didn't have much of a chance holding onto anyone. I managed to disappear with Lucy on my back and watched from a distance. Everybody managed to bail out except Bish, Spiney and Rep. They were still high up on the building trying to reverse crux moves past a window ledge, the two cops underneath shouting at them to come down.

Soon the whole place was like a disaster zone. Police cars, ambulances and fire brigade all converged in front of the building. Sirens wailing, flashing lights everywhere. Spotlights picked out Bish, Spiney and Rep on the outside of the building. Ambulances with doors open waiting for bodies.

Bish, Spiney and Rep eventually managed to reverse back down without being rescued by the fire brigade.

There was no escape. They were dragged away by the cops.

That night, I drove up to Fort William by myself.

Hole in y'ure heid

I arrived in Fort William at first light and drove up to the end of Glen Nevis to pitch my tent. It was Saturday morning and I had nobody to climb with. After some breakfast, I went down to the campsite at the entrance to the Glen. I found an English punter who was wanting to climb Point Five Gully.

Why not try it again? Sneak up, climb Point Five Gully and get one over the rest of the team.

During the conversation, the English punter told me that he had fallen off a bit of rock in Derbyshire and had a compression fracture on his skull. The surgeon had removed a piece of his skull about the size of a 10p coin and had placed a temporary plate over the hole in his skull before the next operation. I was a bit concerned about getting stuck half way up the hill with somebody with a hole in his head.

'U're yae sure, pal, yae wanae climb wae a hole in y'ure heid?'

'No problem mate, I've just got to climb with a helmet at all times,' he replied in a funny northern English accent I had never heard before. He took off his cap to reveal a shaved head, criss-crossed with stitches.

'Nice bit o knittin' yae huv there, pal. Right, if yur game, let's get go'in up the hill.'

The two of us bombed up the hill as fast as we could and arrived at the bottom of Point Five by late morning. It was blowing a gale and the cloud was down – good ice climbing weather! We geared up and I set off up the first pitch of Point Five Gully.
I moved up on the left of the gully, over a bulge to the right, then up a small ice runnel to the belay on the left wall. I remembered the belay well. It was the place where I stood for hours waiting for Spiney at Christmas. I set up the belay and brought up the English punter with the hole in his head.
We changed places at the belay and I headed up the next pitch. The ice was steep, but each placement of axe or kick of crampon felt secure. The gully above became narrower and narrower. I moved up over an ice bulge, and then another. I hunted around for somewhere to put in a runner, but there was no place for protection on either side of the gully wall. I kept on moving up.
I came to a stop about 100 feet above the belay. I had run out most of the rope without any protection. There was a reasonable place to rest for a moment or two on the right side of

the gully. Above and slightly to the left the gully became very narrow, just about wide enough for one person. Snow poured down the vertical chimney in torrents, almost like a continuous waterfall of snow. All the loose snow higher up the mountain was getting blown down by the strong wind and focused tightly into the narrow chimney.

I waited for a few moments for the torrent of snow to stop, or at least subside a bit. It didn't. After waiting ten or fifteen minutes, I decided to try and climb the chimney. I moved into the full force of the falling snow. The weight of snow landing on my head was pushing me out, but I thought I could force on. I whacked in my ice axes, made a move higher and felt even more unstable. The further up I got, the more spindrift came down on my head and shoulders, pushing me outwards.

I was holding on for dear life, snow pounding down on my head. A fall from this position would be serious. I made another move higher, I could not see my ice axe placements, but just relied on the feel of the ice axe hitting good ice. There was so much snow pouring down on my head, it was difficult to keep balance. I tried to move higher, but the weight of the snow made me feel very unstable. It was a bit like climbing up a waterfall and I was the dam at the top blocking the flow.

I was stuck in a vertical chimney, with what seemed like all the snow on the Ben landing on my head. I reckoned that two or three moves would see me on easier ground. However, I was very aware that if I fell I would go a long way down the hill. I tried fumbling about to find some protection in case I fell off. I couldn't find anything.

Time passed.

The thought of trying to move up and being pushed off by the weight of falling snow was frightening. The thought of down-climbing what I had just climbed was also frightening. I did not know if I could get back to the belay without a fall.

I hung onto my ice axes hoping that the snow coming down the chimney would relent a bit to allow me to continue – it didn't.

I started thinking about Jacko and what he would do—jump off without a care?

May be that was the answer—can't turn left or right, can't go back down, can't go on any further in life—may be the only answer is to jump?

Fuck!!! My crampon slipped; the adrenaline hit the back of my head; a pulse bolted around my body. I took a few deep breaths to regain composure. There was a split second when I thought I was off. I kicked in my crampon again to find a better placement. I hung on.

Time passed.

I was jammed in the chimney for well over an hour, perhaps longer – too afraid to climb up, too afraid to climb down, and the longer I stayed there, the colder I was becoming. At any moment I felt I could be pushed off by the weight of snow coming down on my head.

I was starting to shake, but I didn't know if I was shaking with cold, fatigue or fear.

I could picture Jacko falling through the air. One second would be all it would take. I could see Jacko's head smashed, brains all over the place, buck teeth sticking out from the bloody mess. I could see myself flying through the air. One second to find out what was on the other side. May be I should smile and just let go.

Fuck!!! My ice axe slipped. Fear spun around my head like a tornado. The torrent of snow coming down overbalanced me. I took the ice axe out and whacked it back in again as fast as

I could. It was a good placement. I held on and waited for the adrenaline to settle down.
I started signing "Flying" to myself.

> A'm just hangin' owan tae a piece o rock
> A'm just holdin on tae reality
> A'm gripped oot'a ma fucking skull...

Time passed.

I was getting worried. I had only one small ice screw and with an almost superhuman effort I managed to get the thing two or three turns into solid ice, but no further. There was so much snow coming down, I couldn't see where the ice screw had been placed. I just stuck it in, turned it round a couple of times and hoped for the best. It went in only a couple of inches. I had to tie it off half way with a sling. I had little faith in the protection.

A decision had to be made: either climb up and risk a long fall on poor protection or climb down using the tied off ice screw for some security.

I decided to climb down. It seemed the better option. I made my way down, little by little, trying to down-climb what I had just climbed up. Every movement downward felt very insecure and I kept imagining I would be down the hill at any second.

After a great deal of effort and much to my relief, I arrived back at the belay.

We abseiled off the belay and into Observatory Gully. The light was starting to disappear. We climbed up Tower Gully, an easy grade I, onto the summit plateau and then descended down to Fort William.

Point Five gully had defeated me again.

I met the rest of the team in Fort William that evening and told them about the epic on Point Five. Bish still had the "C" on his forehead from the gig the previous night. It was glued solid to his head.

All the stories started to come out.

'A wis owan the Point again masel, way this English punter wae a hole in his heid; couldnae believe he wanted tae go ontae the hill. His heid wis like a hot cross bun. Awe stiched up like a ma's knittin'. Anyway got up tae the crux and goat jammed in a tight wee chimney wae awe this snaw cummin doon. A wis up there fur hoors A wis – really brickin meseal.

Totally spaced oota ma box; thought A wis doon the hill at a faster rate of knots. A wis just stuck there, way awe this snaw pourin' doon on ma heid, just shittin' ma keks—A wis. A cudnae move up. A wus up there fur hoors, A wus.'

'Told yae it wusnae a joke gettin' up the Point way awe that snaw cumin' doon.'

'Any way, A managed tae reverse doon the crux und abbed oaf the belay whit a nightmare it wus...'

'Anyway...where wis yae when the polis dragged us away?'

'A wis huven tae clean awe the place up when youis wur owan the Ran-Dan aifter that bird. A hud tae take Lucy away with mae; awe the rest o the stuff is stashed away. Anyway whit happened tae ursels and the polis?'

'Well, it started off as breakin' and entry, then it wus disturbin' the peace—couldnae believe it, it wus awe those fire engines and their sirens that wur disturbin' the peace. And then this polis pointed tae ma heid and asked whit wis the C fur. A sais, "CUNT!" Then this polis goat awefae stroppy – took it personal like. When yis try tae be honest wae the polis, awe yae get is a hard time. Anyway the polis just goat bored wae us and let us go in the morning.'

We had a few more drinks, and I decided to head back to the tent.

'Can yae gee me a run hame tae ma tent up the end o' Glen Nevis?'

'Nae bother, A've the old man's new motor.'

'A did'nae know yae cud drive.'

'Just passed ma test last week. Am noo legal.'

'Magic, let's get a fish supper first, then we'll be oaf.'

Off we went down Glen Nevis in Bish's 2-litre machine. It was a terrible night. Sheets of rain pouring out of the night. Bish was flying along Glen Nevis describing how good the machine was.

'It's a magic machine, cun dae the ton, drove up frum Glasga in an hoor 'n hof...fleein' up a wis.'

'Death owan the road yis ure... Ure yae sure yu've passed yur test? Ya must o geed the bloke a back honner or sumthin'?'

'Whit wis that?'

'Nuthin, just keep drivin'.'

We flew past the Youth Hostel doing some ridiculous speed and onto single-track road. The car was launched into the air at each rise in the road and came down with an almighty thud at the bottom, suspension bottoming out, and exhaust pipe crashing into the tarmac; sparks flying. This went on for some miles. I was surprised that the exhaust pipe had not been ripped off after the first few bumps on the road. At each bump on the road, I had to brace myself between the roof of the car and the dashboard to stop myself hitting the roof. Bish was enjoying playing at rally drivers.

The road along Glen Nevis is fairly straight, but coming towards the bridge over the river Nevis I started to wonder if Bish had remembered about the sharp turn to the left just before the bridge.

'Ah, Bish.'

'Whit's up?'

'Remember there's a...'

Bish interrupted my sentence with panic in his voice.

'Ahhh, where's the...' when Bish just realised the road had disappeared, followed by, 'fuckin' rooo...ad!!!' as we went flying through the air.

The car left the road and flew through the air, the ground disappeared beneath us. I braced for impact; neither of us was wearing seatbelts. The car hit a tree square on, about ten feet up and then dropped straight down on a peat bog. The car came to an abrupt halt.

The two of us started laughing. The tree had stopped the car going down a deep gorge and into the River Nevis. We were lucky that the car hit a young springy tree and not something solid otherwise the two of us would have been through the windscreen. There was a smell of petrol everywhere, the petrol tank had landed on a stone and cracked open. We got quickly out of the car in case it caught fire.

The two of us stood there in the pouring rain, completely soaked to the skin, looking at the mangled car. There was no way to get it back on the road that night. Bish decided to walk back to Fort William. I continued along the road to find my tent. It was raining like it can only rain in Fort William.

I got back to my tent. It was in the middle of a field, but now the field was a large pond of water. The tent had collapsed and most of it was underwater. I waded, knee deep across to the tent. I unpegged the tent, struggling to hold onto it in the gusting wind, and pitched it on higher ground. Everything was completely soaked. I wrung out my sleeping bag and crawled into it. It was going to be a long, cold, wet, miserable night.

Soon I was shivering and could not sleep. I lay awake, listening to the rain and the wind battering the tent. I started to think about getting stuck on Point Five and wondered what I would have done if I couldn't have climbed back down.

Maybe Jacko was stuck on the point of life, with too many problems? He couldn't turn left, he couldn't turn right, too afraid to continue and too afraid to go back—the only choice was to jump?

I scribbled down some words on a scrap of paper to pass the time.

> *Look out from my window,*
> *Don't like the world that I see.*
> *Blunt my ambition, bottle my spirit,*
> *To keep me in my place.*
> *Don't ask me why I'm a waste of space,*
> *I'm trying to escape the human shite.*
> *Born working class, die working class.*
> *Nowhere to go, no choice, no hope*
> *Go fighting, get pissed,*
> *Have baby, grow old, find a grave.*
> *Wreck this, destroy that,*
> *Only identity, is my writing on the wall.*

Looking down from a high cliff, there's a wicked temptation to step out, to tell your mind that it's an illusion, and trick your mind into believing that you can walk on cloud. Maybe a drug confused Jacko's reality. Maybe that's why he jumped?

I wrote some more.

> *Take a drug to fix my mind*
> *Chemical illusion clears my vision.*
> *Better than society-induced depressive plight.*
> *Only escape from the working class fate.*
> *Sniff glue to relax my state.*

≈ Rock Rock ≈

A nice glass of meths, after dinner taste.

At some small hour in the morning, I woke up. The storm was still blowing a gale. I was hungry and rummaged about in my rucksack for something to eat. I pulled out an empty Coke can. Somebody had crushed the Coke can and thrown it away on the hill. The red can stuck out against the white snow. I had picked it up and stuffed it into my rucksack to bring down the hill.

I lay in my wet sleeping bag, looking at the crushed Coke can with my head torch. There was something about the coke can that made me annoyed. The way it as casually thrown away on the mountain. If it was lying on a street somewhere, beside a bus stop or in a back lane, it wouldn't have bothered me, but it was thrown away on the mountain.

I started to write a song about it.

> Cellophane wrapped,
> pre-packaged sterilised world,
> there's nowhere to escape.
> It's a Coke can culture,
> buy one and throw away.
> You need to buy, don't question why,
> I'm in a moronic state,
> There's no escape,
> It's a Coke can culture.

I called it "Coke Can Culture".
That was the song-writing finished for the night. I was getting tired. I stuffed the scrap of paper in my pocket to work on later. I felt asleep.

≈

Next morning the rain had stopped. I packed up the wet tent and went back down the road to find the car. Bish, Rep and Spiney were there with a minivan trying to pull the car out of the ditch. The car was eventually dragged out. Bish and Rep disappeared back down to Fort William to get it repaired.

Spiney and I went up the Ben again. This time we avoided Point Five Gully and went for Orion Face Direct on the north face instead.

We climbed it.

At the top we congratulated ourselves. It was the first grade V ice climb we had managed to complete. We got off the hill late at night. The only doss we could find was an abandoned factory in Fort William.

The Buachaille

I awoke with a fright. A rat had just crawled over my head. I quickly sat up from my sleeping bag and looked round to survey were we were. The place was completely derelict. It looked as if it had been set on fire some time ago and then the winos had moved in. There was a large collection of empty cans and bottles lying about everywhere. There was a strong, stale, alcohol, rotten food, urine smell about the place. Somehow the doss didn't seem as bad last night.

We got organised and headed into town for some breakfast and to get dried out. Today's plan was to head down to Glencoe and meet the rest of the gang from Glasgow. We set off late from the Fort. Spiney and I were in front on the bikes. Bish and Rep were behind in the car. Bish managed to get his car repaired and was driving very sensibly. He had also been to hospital to get his "C" removed. There was now a big plaster across his forehead.

≈ *Rock Rock* ≈

The four of us drove through Glencoe heading towards the Rannoch moor.
Spiney stopped his bike at the side of the road beneath Buachaille Etive Mor, at the eastern entrance to Glencoe. The light was starting to fade, it was cold, the wind was picking up snow and sending it round in spirals. Bish and Rep pulled up behind us.
The four of us at the side of the road were discussing our plans for the evening and trying to find out where everybody else had camped.
Spiney interrupted the whole proceedings, 'Whit the fuck is that!?' pointing down the road towards the Kings House hotel. Everyone turned round and saw a punter wearing a kilt on a motorbike coming towards us. The bike was all over the road, the kilt was flapping up around his face, due to the speed of the bike and the gusting wind, exposing himself to the elements. The punter was trying to steer the bike with his left hand and struggling to keep his kilt down with his right hand. He was not wearing a helmet. His red hair and beard were all over the place.
The bike crossed the main road in front of us and went straight into the ditch. The punter went over the handle bars: head planted into a large snowdrift, feet in the air, his kilt lying around his neck.
The four of us rolled about in laughter and clapped and cheered.
    'Fuckin' brilliant! Let's see that again!'
    'Ha! Ha! Ha!'
The punter didn't move. A couple of us ran over to get the punter out of the snowdrift. He was totally pissed and reeked of booze.
    'Ure yea all right pal?'
We got him on his feet.

'Ya fuck...in'. Ya fuck...in'...bassstards...take yis awe on.'
The punter started to try and kick and punch Spiney, but was nowhere near him.

'Y'ure pished, ya drunken bum.'

'Fuck yis awe, y'ure awe a bunch o fuckin' wankers! Cum owan take yis awe owan, cum owan square fuckin' go! Cum owan! Square fuckin' go!'

The punter took another swing at Spiney, but completely missed, overbalanced and fell back to the snow. There was some movement on the ground as if the punter was trying to get to his feet, but couldn't. Instead he crawled away into the snow.

At this point the punter throws up over himself.

'Whit a fuckin' state yae ure.'

There were a few more grunts and groans from the punter. He realised that he could not get on his feet without our help.

'Gee'us a fuckin' hon pal...'

'Y'ure'is ma best pals, yis ure, ma best fuckin' pals yis ure, ma best pals yis ure...'

The punter starts a singsong.

'Hallleoo darlin', a luv yae darlin...greeen uuus'the heather bonnnie blummin' heather... Marrry uuus'the heather... isss'ma bonnie heather.'

'Stick sum snaw in his mooth fur christ sake.'

The punter is swaying about, just about managing to stand by himself, singing to himself, then he throws up over his costume.

'Awe shite... Get this wino oot'a here.'

Spiney got the punter's bike out of the ditch and back on the road. He started it after a few attempts. Bish found a piece of string in his rucksack that I cut in two and tied his kilt around his legs as best I could.

'That'll keep y'ure balls warm, till y'ae get hame.'

The punter is still on his two feet singing away and trying to carefully wipe the vomit off his shirt with his hand but, in fact, was doing a good job of evenly spreading it about.
He was still singing away.

> *A'll tak the high roaaad,*
> *und yu'll take the low roaaad annnd*
> *A'll be in Scotland before yae...*
> *Cumowan sing away will yis...*
> *nd A'll be in Scotland be fore yis...*
> *before yis...*
> *A'll be in bonnie Scotland before yis.*

'Cumowan, pal, shut yur face und get back owan yur machine.'
We put him back on his bike, still singing his head off and sent him on his way down the Glen.
'A'll tak the low road nd A'll be in Scotland...before yis!
The four of us stood watching the bike weaving its way down the road and into the distance. You could hear the sound of his drunken song getting fainter, then there would be crunching gear changes and over revved engine.
We speculated if he could navigate the next corner.
'Yes... He off...'
'No, not quite...'
'Oh shit, yes...'
'Oh no... Oh! that was close.'

The bikes and car were parked just off the main road. The four of us made our way across to a group of tents camped on a flat spot of land underneath the Buachaille. Bish was out in front, ploughing his way through a snow drift.
Suddenly, the snow gave way underneath Bish and he disap-

peared up to his armpits down a hole.

'Ah shit! A'm fuckin' soaked.'

The snow had blown over and covered a river.

'It wus time yae hud a bath anyway. Yae wur startin' tae ming.'

'Very funny, geeus a hon tae get oota here.'

Bish gets pulled out. The lower half of his body was soaked.

'Looks like yae huv pished yursel here Bish, ha, ha, ha!'

'Yes, very funny... A'll pish owan yae if yae dinnae shut yur cake hole.'

We moved over to the tents. It was the rest of the squad from Glasgow. Darkness was setting in, we started to get unpacked and the camping gear out.

Somebody had brought along a couple of roadside traffic hazard lights. They were turned on. Beacons of orange light flashed around. Bish got his cassette recorder out and started blasting out punk rock. We all danced away, rolling about in the snow, jumping up and down. Sometime into the dancing Spiney noticed a police car had stopped on the main road and two figures with torches were making their way towards us.

'Shite, it's the polis, hide these bollards fur goad's sake.'

The bollards were stashed under a snowdrift.

'Cumon... Quick...move along a bit...dance a bit oor there so the polis dusnae see that hole in the snow.'

We danced along a bit to where the spin drift had covered a deeper part of the river and carried on dancing.

The two cops headed in our direction. The cops waded through the snow, then, suddenly both of them disappeared from view as the snow collapsed into the river.

We rolled about in laughter on the snow.

'Ha! Ha! Ha! Oh Jesis!'

A couple of us ran over, looked down and asked.

'Got a problem doon there officer?'
'Very funny.'
'Dae yae want a hand tae get oot?'

The cop tried to get by himself, but was having difficulty. Reluctantly, he took Spiney's hand and was pulled out of the snow. The cop then pulled his friend out. Both of them were soaked.

Two wet cops arrived at the campsite. We were dancing away.

'What are you up to?'

Bish replied.

'We wus just having a wee swim aboot in the snaw. A cun see yae huv been doin' that already.'

Spiney joined in.

'We're daein' sum gardenin'... Plantin' tatties we ure.'

The cops weren't impressed.

'Smart bastards aren't yis.'

'Just trying to keep warm officer.'

'Yae look a wee bit cauld there.'

'Why don't yae join in if yae want?'

There was a suspicious eye cast, trying to figure out what we were really up to.

'Turn that thing off.'

'We're no disturbing the peace ure wae?'

No reply.

'What are you lads up to?'

'Uch, we're no up tae anythin', just here tae get a bit o climbin' done.'

'What were the flashing lights?'

'Headtorches.'

The cops gave up and walked away. Leaving a trail of water in the snow behind them. The flashing bollards came out again once the cops were some distance away. We carried on dancing.

≈

The next morning we went up and climbed Raven's Gully on Buachaille Etive Mor. I reached the summit as the last few beams of sunlight disappeared over the horizon. It was the end of a great day. I stood on the summit, looking over Rannoch Moor far below, wondering how people could have survived over the centuries in such a hostile climate and through such social unrest. I stayed on the summit until the last of the light, bracing myself into a freezing northerly wind. Clouds were racing over the sky, almost touching the top of the mountain. I was starting to feel cold and eventually descended Great Gully by myself in the darkness.

I wrote a song about The Buachaille. It took weeks to finish.

≈

I gave the song to the band some time later in the garage.
Rep came out with, 'Is that wan no a bit heavy? A bit deep, like? A bit like Andy Stewart or Sidney Devine?'
　'Naw it's a ballad yae tosser.'
　'Whit dae yae mean? Like the Bay City Rollers?'
　'Naw ya daft bugger. It's a bit like folk punk. Punk fur the common man... Prols punk, yae know... Workers punk. Punk fur the people.'
I hadn't really thought much about it but that's what came out.
　'Wur takin' punk tae the man owan the street no the commercial shite owan Top o the Pops.'
　'Anyway, it'll gee Bish a break between awe the fast stuff he sings.'

I had a discussion with Bish about how best to do the song. In the end we decided it would be best done as a rip-off, a bit like "My Way" by Sid Vicious. It would give him a breather between the fast songs.

Bish had a shot at the song. He started off in a sensible slow monotone droll then started to speed up in more aggressive tones towards the end spitting out the words. Bish made the song work.

≈

The final exams were coming up, so that curtailed our climbing for a period. We did one other concert to an audience of six. The snow was disappearing from the hills and soon the rock would be bare.

Between swotting for the final exams, we met in the garage to work on the new songs, fixing bikes and scheming about trying to go to France in the summer to climb some big mountains.

≈ *Stephen Najda* ≈

The Old Man

Hitching

I awoke in a panic. There was a shock of cold water on my legs and a feeling of not knowing where I was. My feet were under water.
Last night I had dossed on a steep slope underneath a bridge. I kept rolling down the slope in my sleeping bag, so I built a small stone wall to stop me rolling over, but it wasn't big enough. Twice in the night, I had rolled down the slope in my sleeping bag before getting out and crawling back up under the bridge. On the third occasion I was too tired to get out of my sleeping bag and simply stayed where I was and hoped it would not rain, but I must have rolled further down the slope and stopped with my feet in a burn.

The morning cold made me get organised quickly. I wrung out my sleeping bag and put it on the top of my sack with the wet end hanging out to get dry. I headed back into town to find some breakfast.
I had to hitch-hike from Glasgow since my machine was out of action. I crashed the bike into a tree the previous weekend coming home from a wild party. The bike got a bit mangled, but I was all right to climb.
Yesterday, the hitching was not very good and I only managed to get as far as Ullapool.
The plan was to meet the rest of the gang at Achmelvich campsite at midday and climb the Old Man of Stoer the following day. The Old Man of Stoer is a 250 feet sea stack that stands out from the sea cliffs about 20 miles north of Achmelvich. Spiney was already at Achmelvich and Bish and Rep probably

passed over the bridge I was dossing under at some time in the night on their way to Achmelvich.
I had a plastic cup of tea and a fried egg sandwich for breakfast at a small stand near the harbour. Then I walked across town to hitch north to Achmelvich. I was still hopeful of getting to Achmelvich by lunchtime. There were only 50 miles or so to go.
Several hours on the road and I could still see the Fáilte gu Ullapúl road sign. There were not many cars on the road and the ones that were, were pulling caravans. Cars pulling caravans never stop for hitch-hikers. Despair was setting in. I tried to look enthusiastic and walk and hitch at the same time, but had given up and ended up sitting on my rucksack with my chin in my hands. I was trying to think up some more songs for the band, but nothing was coming into my head.

Randy and the Radiohead

A VW dormobile drove past, stopped turned round and drove back down the road towards me. Magic, a lift at last!
They drove straight past and back into town. Shite!
Ten minutes later the van reappeared, drove passed, stopped, turned round and drove back down the road towards me.
They drove straight past. Tossers.
The van turned around, came back up and stopped beside me. Magic.
The window wound down.

    'Where yaa go'in, bud?' a loud American accent asked.
    'Achmelvich.'
The driver looked at me in a curious way.
    'Is that a sign from Epona?'
I looked at the punter and wondered what on earth he was talking about. Did I miss something?

'Naw, its just doon the road here,' I replied.
'Geee, love your accent man. Are you Scotch?'
Shite, here we go.
'Jump in bud, I'll take you where you wanna go,' the American said.
I slid open the side door of the Volkswagen and threw my rucksack in. I was greeted with a resonating, 'Hiii,' from three girls in the back of the caravanette.
'Hiii there,' I said, trying to sound like John Wayne.
The girl closest introduced herself as, 'Anna-Ma-Rieee,' the other said, 'Su-Sannn,' and the girl in the corner, 'Meee-Cheaaal.'
Then Anna-Marie said, 'Geee, you speak with an accent.'
I was a bit confused about this. It took me a few seconds to work out a reply, hoping not to offend.
'Yae speak wae an accent as well.'
Anna-Marie replied in a brisk determined voice, 'No, I don't, I'm an American.'
Again, I was a bit confused about the reply and wondered what to say next. Should I mention that she's talking with an American accent or just keep quiet?
'But, yur talkin' wae an American accent.'
Anna-Marie looked confused.
'Yae know, Scots talk wae a Scottish accent... Americans talk wae an American accent.'
Anna-Marie looked more confused.
I gave up.

There was an awkward period of silence.

The passenger in the front seat leaned over and said in a very bold and loud American voice, 'Hiii, I'm Randy,' shaking my hand vigorously.
Shite! What was I supposed to say? That's interesting? Is it not

a bit early? Do you want a cold shower?
There was a long pause, before I replied in a quite confused way, 'A'm not.'
A few seconds later a confused Susan asked, 'You're not what?'
I was starting to feel embarrassed and I thought for a few seconds before replying, 'A'm not randy.'

There was another pause in the conversation when everyone looked at each other.
The driver said, 'Hay man, is that your name? Not Randy?' and sort of laughed.
I didn't reply.

There was another uncomfortable period of silence.

I tried to start the conversation again.
  'Where ure yis goin'?' I asked nobody in particular.
  'We're going to meet our destiny,' replied Randy.
Oh shite, what have I teamed up with?
Without much prompting Randy starts off, 'I'm the reincarnation of an ancient Highland Chieftain. I was born half-human, half-alien. My father was taken by aliens for experimentation and it's my destiny to return where my father was taken, so I can be projected into the future. I have to inseminate an alien to further my spirit in the universe.'
Randy was keen to tell me more, but had to keep reminding the driver to drive on the left hand side of the road.

There was a period of silence again.

  'Where are you going?' Susan asked
  'A'm go'in tae climb the Old Man o Stoer,' I replied.
  'How old is he?' One of the other girls asked.

I was confused by her question and wasn't sure what to say.

'Old enough.'

The reply seemed to satisfy her.

Everybody seemed interested in the old man in a curious, but not really understanding way. One of the girls muttered something to another that I could just about make out, 'I think he's talking about having a date with an old man.'

I just left it.

The inside of the caravanette was full of some kind of writing script. I was curious to know what it all meant.

'Whit dus this bit say? Dus that bit mean anythin'?' pointing to some scribbles on the wall.

Randy looked over from the front seat and said, 'My pop wrote me instructions how to find him in his afterlife.'

'Oh, so it's like a map?'

'Sure thing boy! The future and past are out there – its not under your control. We are merely passengers in our bodies.'

'Awe that writin' stuff tells yae awe that?'

'Sure does bud.That's what we're here for!'

At that point Randy broke the conversation and indicated to the driver that there was a turn-off coming up. He started giving him instructions on how to drive the caravanette on a dirt road. The driver pulled off the main road and started driving down a small dirt track. Everybody in the back was bouncing about and things were falling off the inside of the van. Randy was giving directions. He seemed to know where he was going. He looked like the boss.

I was starting to get a bit concerned, and asked, 'Where ure wis goin'?'

'Home base,' Randy replied.

'We've been shopping in town for groceries.' One of the girls said. 'We're having something to eat soon. Why don't you join us?'

I was starving and the thought of some food really did appeal.
'Is home base far?' I asked inquisitively.
'Just round the next hill, boy,' Randy replied.

We turned round the next bend and there was another VW dormobile. I counted four people, two men and two women. There appeared to be a big telescope, radio equipment and electronic stuff lying around all over the place.
'Ure yae bird watching or plane spotting or something?' I asked.
'Tonight is the night they're comin',' said Randy.
'Who's cumin'?' I felt obliged to ask.
'My father,' Randy looked at me in almost a state of disbelief
'Oh, but A thought yur faither wus deid,' I replied.
'Dead! He's not dead!' he didn't seem to like the word dead.
'He's comin' tonight to project me into the future,' he replied in a very forceful voice.
'Where's he cumin' frum?' I had to ask.
'From the third planet in Cassiopeia.'
'How does he know where tae come?,' I asked.
'Because this is the place he was taken from,' he could have ended the sentence with stupid.
I was getting more intrigued, but the conversation was getting a bit heated so I left Randy to play with his radio bits and went over to talk to some of the girls preparing food.

'Hi there, that looks tasty,' I said to Susan in my John Wayne voice.
We ended up talking about music and how she liked the Bee Gees and the Beach Boys. I mentioned that I was into punk rock and how crap everything else was.
Susan suggested to, 'Go and have a word with Anna-Maa-Reee,

she's really spunky.'

I was a bit confused by the word spunky. Did she mean to say punky? Or maybe she was trying to tell me she's pregnant? Or maybe there was some connection with the food that I had missed?

I felt obliged to go over to speak to Anna-Marie.

'When is y'ure wain expected?' I asked.

'I'm a lifelong abductee', was the reply.

I was trying to look and sound interested, but couldn't follow her track of thought and assumed that she must have misunderstood something. I had no idea what she was going on about, but thought it best to keep the conversation going.

'Really, that's amazing.'

'I didn't want to tell anyone until I met Randy. He has helped me so much. Nobody would listen to me – except Randy. He has been a great help. I didn't understand the purpose. I had to ask them. I had to ask them several times. I need to understand why you are here and why you are doing this.'

'Very important tae ask,' I reassured her.

'The ship came and hovered over my house. It was a huge round flying object with bright lights everywhere. It just sat there. I couldn't move... I just couldn't move an inch. The bright lights went off and I could see it was a bright silvery colour. There was no noise, but some wind. Then, three lights came on in a triangular formation. Then a light in the centre of the triangle came on; it was a sort of blue colour. I was really, really, really scared, but I couldn't run away. There was something inside pulling me forward, a voice telling me to go closer. A ramp came down from the centre of the space ship. There was a dazzling light coming from inside, too bright for me to see. I felt my feet weren't on the ground. I could hear a voice inside my head inviting me in. I felt I had no choice, it was my destiny, I had to go aboard. It was really, really spooky, but I had to go inside.'

She paused.

I felt I had to ask something.

'Did yae need a ticket tae get owan board?'

Then, she carried on, as if I had said nothing.

'They have come back many times since that first encounter. Most times, I'm taken on board the craft and the room is round and brightly lit. The aliens ask me to lie on a couch, a bit like an operating theatre. It's a bright room with lots of aliens. I was really, really scared the first time, but there was a calming voice saying, 'we are here to help you'. They do not speak to me, but there's a voice inside my head. There are aliens moving all around with funny looking instruments with beams of light coming out and lights flashing. They are not very tall and are a greyish, whitish, greenish colour. Some look a bit more greyish others look a bit more greenish; with sort of blotches here and there. Funny looking things. They have feet with four toes and three long fingers. They have huge, staring, almond shaped black eyes that never blink and two little holes for a nose, a tiny little mouth and no ears. Their skin looks like leather. All communication takes place mind to mind, through those big black eyes. I can feel those eyes going straight into my head and extracting my thoughts—everything. I have no control, but its not frightening.'

'Incredible,' I was starting to look round to see if there were any aliens hanging around the campsite.

'They stuck an instrument into my womb to extract an ovary. One time they actually removed my skull to look at my brain and then replaced it. I can see everything happening. There is no pain; there's never any pain. You cannot see any scars after they finish. They told me telepathically that they were doing these things to ensure our species continued. They didn't want to colonise us or occupy us. They said they were here to help.'

She paused again.

'They've implanted something in my stomach. See, look.' Anna-Marie lifted up her T-shirt.

'If you feel there, that lump is an electronic receiver. They can contact me at any time and I have to go.'

I felt Anna-Marie's electronic receiver. It felt like rib to me.

Anna-Marie then explained to me, 'My doctor doesn't know what it is.'

I could see that Anna-Marie wanted confirmation that her electronic receiver was still there.

'Aye, A see whit yae mean. It does look a wee bit strange.'

There was another pause.

I tried to keep the conversation going.

'Dae yae no need tae plug in a battery sumwhere tae get it goin or sumthin?'

Anna-Marie wanted to do more talking.

'I'm helping a new life form to be created. I've seen the children of the new species inside the spaceship. I was taken there to help me understand. I had to understand. They were lying motionless inside these large plastic tubes filled with some sort of gooey, greeny liquid. Hundreds of them all in line – as far as you could see. I was told that they are being kept in storage to repopulate the planet after the next mass extinction. It's coming, you know. The world is going to change as we know it and we'll have to be prepared. So, you see, I'm helping the world create a new life after we all destroy ourselves. I feel as if I'm creating a new world.'

Anna-Marie stopped talking and looked at me as if expecting I should agree with her or say something.

I was lost for words. There was an uncomfortable period of silence when I was thinking what to say. The only thing I could think about was mentioning the ghost at Ben Alder cottage.

'Ah... A've seen a ghost, mibby one of yur alien pals has got a base there too? A've been there a few times. A've seen the ghost and goat a bit o' a fright but A huv'nae seen any space ships nearby. Mibby the space ship came doon owan the other side o Ben Alder.'

It was the first time we appeared to understand each other. Anna-Marie was wanting more information.

'Geee...you've seen a ghost?'

'Aye, that's right.'

'It's a connection to your inner space.'

Anna-Marie had lost me again.

'If y'ure interested. A'll draw yae a map, how tae get there like, it's a wee bit difficult tae get there, yae huv tae walk a wee bit, unless yae cun get y'ure pals in the space ship tae take yae there. D'yae huv a pencil and sum paper?'

Anna-Marie disappeared and came back with a pencil and paper. I drew a rough sketch of how to get to Ben Alder, but made a few mistakes.

'D'yae huv a rubber?,' I asked Anna-Marie.

'It's all right, I'm on the pill,' she replied.

It was another conversation stopper. I looked at her in a confused way.

She looked at me honestly. I looked away not sure what to say and continued with the map as best I could and gave it to her.

'Here yae ure. A'm sure yur spaceship captain will find it awright.'

I went over to talk to the other girls preparing food.

'We try to be as self-sufficient as we can,' Susannn said.

She showed me boxes full of herbs and other green stuff.

'This one' alfalfa, and that one's bean sprouts for tofu,' she said.

I was thinking to myself, alfawhat? Was it toffee she said?

I thought I had better not ask any questions, in case she said it was farmed on Mars or bought in some market in the nearest star system.

After a bit of time, a cloth was put down on the ground and the food appeared. My imagination of food quickly disappeared. I was hoping for pie and chips. Instead I was given carrot juice and a plate of leaves and grass, with some white cheesy stuff. I thought it was disgusting but put on a brave face and ate it. I was looking forward to the toffee and a cup of tea to end. Instead I was given some tea that looked and tasted revolting.
  'D'yae huv any milk and sugar fur ma tee?'
Everybody seemed horrified.
  'That comes from a cow,' replied Randy in a very forceful manner.
Good point. Was I supposed to agree or disagree?
  'Ah, yes...of course.'
I reckoned that I wasn't going to get any milk and just carried on taking small sips of the disgusting tea.

After the meal, Randy leaned over and asked,
  'Hai, dude, wan some grass?'
I replied, 'No Ta, A've hud plenty already,' not wanting any more alfawhat stuff.
Randy looked a bit confused.
  'Hai, man, what planet are you from?'
I could have asked him the same question.
  'Do ya not wanna smoke?' Randy tried again.
  'Naw, a dinnae touch fags,' I politely refused.
Randy backed off with a very confused look on his face. It was the first time Randy was short of words. I could see his face going through several contortions of insult, anger and laughter.
I wasn't sure what was going to come out. I just sat there won-

dering what his problem was.
After a few moments Randy came back with.

'I'm talkin' about drugs, man, you wan some?'
'Yae need a clear heid owan the rock, otherwise yur fuckin' pâté.'
'Was that pataaay you mean, man?'
'That's right it's a French wurd fur getting minced, deid like mangled.'

I gave up with Randy and tried to keep the conversation going with the rest of the group,
'Ta very much fur ma dinner, that was pure dead brilliant,' trying to sound grateful, but really glad that the dinner was over.
'There ain't nothin' dead in it, boy,' Randy interrupted and looked at me very seriously.
Randy then goes on about seeing relatives and friends who have died on earth and have been brought back to life inside a spaceship.
'You don't die, it's more like going to sleep for a short time. Why don't you come along and see for yourself?'
My imagination was running riot, what was he going on about? But, I thought it better not to accept, otherwise I would never get to Achmelvic on time.
'Thanks, but A'm meeting ma pals later. Cun yae beam me over, like they do in Star Trek?'
Randy didn't like the word Star Trek.

Everybody started smoking rolled up cigarettes. I was offered one, but politely refused.
'Smokin' dus nuthin fur ma climbing,' I said.
Everybody ended up rolling about on the ground and laughing their heads off. I couldn't figure out what the joke was.

'The dude says smokin' dos nuthing for ma climbing,' Randy kept saying, trying to put on a Scottish accent.
Everybody burst into laughter.
'You're ace, man—far out!'
Everyone bursts into laughter again.
'The dude says smokin' dos nuthing for ma climbing.'
Randy starts rolling about in laughter on the ground.
'Dos nuthing for ma climbing. The dude says...dos nuthing for ma climbing.'
Everyone is rolling about laughing I just sat here.

After their smoke everyone started getting ready for something. Some sort of radio headset with an aerial pointing up from behind each ear was being put on everyone. Randy started playing around with the big radio-looking thing. The radio thing started making all these strange sounds.
Everybody started to take off their clothes.
'Come on join in... We're having a practice for tonight.'
'Naw, naw, it's a wee bit too cauld fur mae. Anyway A'll huv tae head oaf soon und team up wae ma pals.'
It was getting too far out for me. It was time to head back to the main road and get hitching again.
'A hope it disnae rain fur yis, und yae find yur spaceship. Byeee!' I shouted over.
I picked up my rucksack from the open caravanette, waved goodbye and headed back down the track.

Eh!*??*?!

Back on the main road the hitching was still not going too well. Randy had only managed to take me a few miles down the road. Only an occasional big flashy car whizzed past. I sat on my rucksack beside the road with pen and paper and start-

ed to write a song called "Randy and the Radioheads".
I scribbled down a few lines but didn't get very far. Occasionally, I looked down the road, but there were very few cars today. I thought that I should have told Randy that there would be an alien spaceship landing at Achmelvich this evening and I could introduce him to the captain if he could get me there on time.

It must have been well over an hour later, when an old beaten-up Citröen Dyane stopped. It was left hand drive. The machine looked a complete mess: the bumper half off dragging along the road, and rust everywhere. The licence plates were foreign, but I couldn't recognise from what country. The driver opened the window flap on the door, even though it would have been easier to converse over the rolled back sunroof. I had to lean down to speak to the driver. He was wearing a big floppy hat, but I could see he had a long, miserable looking face.
The driver asked in broken English, 'Whare go-in?'
I could not work out the accent.
 'Ach-mel-vich,' I pronounced each syllable carefully and pointed in the direction they were going in.
There was a girl in the passenger seat. I couldn't help notice that she was wearing a very revealing short dress. I couldn't stop looking at her legs while talking to the driver.
 'Ach-mel-vich. Doon-the-road-here. Straight-on.'
There was some discussion between the two, I could not make out what language they were speaking. The two kept arguing. I could feel a certain tension in the air as if they had been arguing all day.
 '¿Cómo es él?'
 'Cállate y sujétate los cojones un rato!'
 'Me gustan sus ojos azules.'
I interrupted their conversation and shouted out each sylla-

ble, 'Ach-mel-vich Loch-in-var No-rth,' and pointed almost frantically down the road.

The two in the car kept on talking, as if I was not there.

'¿De que hostias va este tío, quiere que se la casquemos?'
'¿Le doy un susto?'
'Siempre andas asustando a jovencitos.'

I didn't seem to be getting anywhere. There was a lot hand waving and gesticulation from the driver, then there appeared to be some sort of an agreement, so I opened the back door and tried to get inside the car. The back was full of rubbish, clothes, bits of food, books and the like. There was also a smell of stale beer.

I went in, rucksack first, and tried to clear a space by pushing some of the junk to one side. In the process, I almost tripped headfirst through the opposite door when I stepped into the car expecting to stand on the floor, but suddenly realised there was no floor. I stood inside the car, feet on the road, head and shoulders above the sunroof. I closed the door with some effort and tried to clear a space to sit down.

I realised that most of the rubbish I had just cleared from the back seat was now lying on the road. I put my rucksack down on the space I had just cleared and began picking up all the rubbish from the road.

There appeared to be no alternative, but to sit on my rucksack, head sticking out above the roof, one foot jammed against the door and the other between the two front seats. The two in the front appeared completely unconcerned about my difficulty or about losing their stuff from the back of the car.

I settled down for the journey. The driver was wrapped up like Toulouse Lautrec with a big floppy hat and scarf.

I leaned forward to try and start a conversation, but I could not stop looking down at the girl's cleavage. She had a large chest.

There was a lot of chit-chat up front.

'*Me parece que le gusto.* I think he fancies me.'

'*Cállate, puede que hable castellano.* Shut up, he might speak Spanish.'

'*Tiene ojos bonitos.* He has nice eyes.'

'*No me avergüences, ¿vale? Siempre andas haciendo lo mismo.* Don't embarrass me, you're always doing this.'

'*No te preocupes, no entiende nada...¿verdad que no, monada?* Don't worry he doesn't understand, don't you dear?'

The girl turned around. I got a big, long, sexy smile from the girl. She out-stared me.

I felt I had to say something and try and get a conversation going.

'A-um-frum-Scot-land', speaking in a very deliberate manner and pointing to myself, and then asked, 'Where-dae-yae-cum-frum?'

The girl replied, '*Quiero joderte!* I want to fuck you!'

She gave me another long, sexy look and then started arguing with her boyfriend again.

'*Te lo dije, no entiende lo que estamos hablando.* Told you, he doesn't understand what we're talking about.'

'*No me pones celoso, tu pequeño amante se va a llevar un buen susto cuando se de cuenta que es lo que escondes bajo tus bragas, tesoro!* You can't make me jealous, your lover boy is in for a shock when he realises what you've got under your knickers, dear!'

'*¡Que te jodan!* Fuck you!'

I thought I had better get my map out and clear the confusion. I leaned over and pointed to Achmelvich on the map. This seemed to cause even more confusion. The girl took the map, then gave it back a few seconds later without looking at it, smiled at me and said something.

'*Ahora no, cariño, la tengo dura.* Not just now, love, I've got a hard-on.'

I smiled back, thinking what a cute girl and what a horrible boyfriend.
We set off cruising down the road at not much more than 30mph, the driver struggling to keep the car in a straight line with each gust of wind. The conversation between the two went up and down between periods of arguing and silence. At the height of each argument, Toulouse Lautrec would inadvertently pull the steering wheel to the left, the car would hit the verge and then the conversation would stop for a moment until the driver regained control of the car. On each occasion we hit the verge some junk fell off the back seat and onto the road. I thought about mentioning that they were losing stuff out of the car, but reckoned that it would take me several miles to explain and I didn't want to spend the next couple of hours going back and looking for some old, dirty clothing. I was more concerned that Toulouse Lautrec would completely lose control of the car, and was preparing to launch myself through the sunroof.
The girl started to peel a banana in a very slow, deliberate manner.

'¡*No te comes tu plátano!* Stop eating that banana like that!'

'*Lo como como quiero.* I can eat it any way I like.'

She didn't say anything to me but broke off the top part and gave it to me. I smiled and ate it. She smiled back.
We had not travelled much more than ten miles down the road, when another shouting match started.

'¡*Para el coche, me muero por echar una meadita!* Stop the car, I'm dying for a piss!'

'*Es culpa tuya, por beber tanta cerveza.* It's your fault for drinking too much beer.'

'¡*Para el coche o salto!* Stop the car or I'll jump!'

The car pulled up abruptly at the side of the road. I was not sure if it was a planned stop or mechanical failure. The girl

in front made a fuss about getting out of the car. She dashed out and went round to the side of the car and started going through the motions of doing the toilet.
I was trying to look straight down the road as if nothing was happening, but the girl was making no attempt to hide. There was something not quite right. She started peeing like a man! There was a confusing few seconds when my reality had been shattered. I took a quick second glance to make sure I hadn't made a mistake. My mind was going round in circles trying to figure out what was going on. It was too much for me to take in. I decided it was best to head off.
I pointed out Suliven in the distance to the driver.
    'Mountain over there. A go and climb. Bye!'
I stood up inside the car, picked up my rucksack, threw it out the sunroof, jumped out through the sunroof and took off at a brisk pace directly away from the car.
The girl was laughing her head off and shouted something in my direction.
    '¡Vuelve, cariñito! Come back darling!'
    '¡Te quiero! I love you!'
I hid behind a small hill and watched the girl rolling about in laughter. The laughter seemed to go on for some time. Toulouse Lautrec just sat patiently in the car as if nothing had happened. Eventually, they disappeared.

I came back down to the road, sat on my rucksack and hoped not to get picked up by any more nutters. There were still few cars on the road.
Time passed. I was getting bored and started to write a song about the two in the Citröen, but I was a very confused youth and didn't get very far.
It started to rain. Achmelvich was still some distance away. I gave up trying to write and started to walk a bit further down

the road. There was still some distance to go. I walked as far as a telephone box at the side of the road. It was the only shelter for miles around. It was early evening and the rain was now pouring down. I looked down the road as far as I could see, patiently waiting for car headlights to appear in the distance. When a car was close, I would jump out of the telephone box, get rained on, stick out my thumb, the car would fly past covering me in spray, then I would jump back into the telephone box and wait for the next. Nobody would stop. I thought I was going to have to spend the night in the telephone box. I remembered Randy and the Radiohead and started to get spooked. Randy had been so adamant, so convincing, that I half expected to get beamed up at any moment into an alien spaceship. Then, I started thinking, maybe it is better to be abducted by aliens than spend the night in a telephone box.

I spotted a car in the distance. I jumped out and stuck my thumb out. I couldn't believe my luck; the car pulled up and stopped beside the telephone box. It was a police Landrover, very nice of them to stop.

Just at the moment I opened the back door of the Landrover, the two police got out of the front and went over to the telephone box to make a call. I sat in the back of the Landrover for some minutes, thinking to myself that they did not see me hitching and will kick me out into the rain again once they see me in the back.

The two police got back into the Landrover and drove off without acknowledging my presence. I was sitting in the back keeping quiet.

'Where are you goin' son?' Eventually, one of the cops asked.

'A'm tryin' tae get tae Achmelvich and climb the Old Man o' Stoer ra morra, but the hitchin' husnae been very good. Ta, very much fur pickin' mae up, otherwise it wid o been awe

night in that telephone box.'
The police were climbers too and soon we chatted about the hills. The police dropped me off at the road to Achmelvich. The police Landrover disappeared down the road to Lochinvar. I was by myself again.

It was late at night and still raining heavily. I thought about finding a doss for the night, but couldn't find a decent one, so I decided to walk the last six or seven miles to Achmelvich.

I walked along the road for some time. The rain had stopped and there was just enough moonlight to walk without a torch. Everywhere was darkness and black shadows.

Suddenly, there was a sound in the distance that made me stop. I was not sure what it was, but it made me hesitate to go further. The night started to make my imagination run riot. Maybe an alien spaceship had landed on the other side of the hill and Randy and all his pals were about to beam me aboard. I told myself it must have been an animal, and started walking. I stopped again, then something instinctively told me to run. I turned off the road, down an embankment and into thick bracken and gorse.

I heard a voice, 'Get him,' from somewhere in the distance.

I could hear someone after me. I jettisoned my rucksack to move faster, but was tackled to the ground and ended head-first into a bramble bush. There was a struggle. I got hold of a bramble branch and slashed it across the face of the punter that was holding on to me. There was a sound of pain. He lost his grip. I struggled free and managed a few more steps before another tackled me to the ground. My right arm was twisted up my back. There was a click and I could feel a handcuff going on. My left arm was twisted up my back to meet my right and the second handcuff went on.

I tried to get to my feet with my arms connected behind my back, but was met with a violent kick to the left of my stomach just below the rib cage.

'Y'a fuckin' bastard!!!'

I fell on the ground gasping in pain.

'Whit the fuck's goin on… Y'ure yis the polis?'

A torch was shown in my face.

'Shut the fuck up!'

There was a shout from above that they had found my fishing rod. I was dragged back up to the road. There were a couple of other men there.

'Caught you red-handed ya wee bastard.'

'Whit dae yae mean? A wis just walkin' doon the road here, when awe yur animals jumped owan mae. Look owan o them booted mae in the side.'

'What's the fishing rod for?'

'Its fur sea fishin'…catching haddie's.'

I was taken over to a Landrover and put in the back. There was another character there.

'Nice evening fur fishin'?' I asked the punter.

I got a wry smile back.

Somebody came over and started asking questions.

'A'm tellin' yae, A wis just walkin' doon the road here, tryin' tae get tae Achmelvich when A goat set upon by those big bastards oor there. A'm goin' climbin' the Old Man of Stoer ra morrow and A'm meetin' ma pals at Achmelvich. If yae dinnae believe mae just ask yur polis friends; they dropped mae oaf at the bottom o' the road just an hoor ago.'

There was some discussion in the distance. I was released a few moments later and left to walk the last few miles to Achmelvich.

I arrived at Achmelvich campsite almost at dawn and found the rest of the team. I squeezed into the tent and woke everyone up in the process.

I was met with a chorus of, 'Awe fuck off...' from half dazed bodies lying in slumber.

'Where the fuck huv yae been? We've been waitin' awe day fur yae.'

'It's a long story.'

Spiney got up and started cooking some breakfast. A smell of bacon soon wafted around the tent. I started recalling my hitchhiking tales about meeting up with Americans from outer space.

'Yae cannae be serious.'

'D'y'ae mean tae say, they hud ariels sticking oota their hieds?'

'That's right...started dancin' aboot in the scud, waitin' fur a fuckin' spaceship tae land. Bunch o' fuckin' bampots, totally oaf their hieds.'

'Well did yae wait fur the spaceship?'

'Naw, hud tae bail oot. It wus gettin' a bit too wild fur mae. Then the next thing wis, A goat picked up by this punter wae a big floopy hat and a bird wae big tits. Yae widnae believe it, but the motor stopped and the bird goot oot and started pissin' like a man. A jist cudnae believe it—pissin' like a man she wis. A cundae handle it. A just hud tae bail oot.'

Everybody was looking at me as if I was taking the piss. The American story was just about believable, but nobody believed me about the girl.

'Fuck off! Yur talkin' shite.'

'A'm tellin' yae, she started pissin' like a bloke.'

'Yur mooth is awe broon.'

'A'm tellin' yae...'

'Huv you been on sumthin'?'

'A'm tellin' yae, she started pissin'.'

'Bet yae wis fuckin' steam boats, blottoed oota yur mind.'

'A'm tellin' yis, this wuman started pissin' like a bloke, serious!'

'A bet yis, it wus sum fuckin' punter in a kilt. Did she huv a beard? This is the hiellands, remember, this is Teuchterland.'

I was too tired to argue, so I finished my breakfast and went to bed.

The Old Man

I awoke about midday, had a bite to eat and got organised as quickly as possible. My left side had swollen up where I had got kicked the night before and my hands were cut from the bramble bushes.

We set off on two bikes to find The Old Man of Stoer. Spiney in front, with eyeballs between the speedo and knees up to his ears. Rep riding pillion, holding a brolly in one hand and a bottle of wine in the other. Rep had found a tin of paint and had hand-written on the back of his mountain jacket in big, bold, white letters "Copulation Station", "Plutonium Child", "Glue sniffin' tosser", "The Clash", "White Riot" and other lyrics from the band. On the second bike, Bish was going through his Mod look, wearing a thin black tie, and smiling at everyone, while trying desperately to catch Spiney, who was doing ridiculous speeds on single track roads. And I was on the back of Bish's machine, trying to stop two sets of climbing gear and a tent falling on the road.

We went as far as the road would take us, parked the bikes, pitched the tent beside a nearby lochan, and then set off on foot to find The Old Man.

We walked to the Point of Stoer, then along the edge of the cliff, occasionally looking, down to the sea several hundred feet below, trying to figure out where The Old Man was, and wondering if somehow we managed to walk past a 250 feet high pinnacle of rock without realising it.

A lonesome figure was walking his dog along the cliff edge coming towards us. I was just about to ask him if he had seen a sea stack. However, his dog came bounding over towards Rep and jumped on him in a sort of friendly way. But Rep turned, and in trying to avoid the dog, pushed it aside. The dog went a bit further in its leap than it expected and continued over the edge of the cliff and into oblivion. There was a surreal moment of silence. We all looked at the space where the dog had been, then over the edge. There was no sign of the dog, only the sea crashing onto rocks several hundred feet below.

One second the dog was there, the next gone. We looked at the dog owner in a sorry, tough shit, not our fault, sort of way. The dog owner looked perplexed, confused, angry, sad.

I thought it better not to ask if he had seen The Old Man; the dog owner obviously thought it better not to hassle four punks. Rep muttered, 'A don't like fuckin' dugs,' and the four of us continued along the cliff edge.

A little distance further round the coast, The Old Man suddenly appeared—it looked very impressive, an impossibly steep pinnacle of rock 250 feet high, overhanging around the middle, and coming to a point at the summit. We stopped at the top of the cliff and looked at it in awe for a while.

A gale force wind was blowing into our faces. The sea was grey and ugly; big Atlantic rollers came crashing in over the base of The Old Man. It was difficult to imagine that The Old Man had stood for centuries facing the might of the sea.

The four of us scrambled down the cliff face opposite The Old Man and down to a rock plinth at the bottom. There was a narrow channel of water separating The Old Man from the mainland. The plan was to set up a rope traverse or Tyrolean traverse in the evening to save time, and come back in the morning to climb The Old Man. That meant that somebody would have to swim the channel. It wasn't an evening for swimming.

The channel separating The Old Man from the mainland was only about 20 or 30 feet wide, but it looked deeper than it was wide. It was low tide. The rock on either side went in sheer and was covered in barnacles. The choice was to climb down and get slashed to bits by the barnacles or jump straight in, swim across, and get slashed to bits by the barnacles climbing out the other side.

Lots were drawn to decide who was going to swim across the channel and set up the Tyrolean traverse. Rep drew the short piece of seaweed; he would be swimming.

Spiney hammered in a peg to set up the Tyrolean traverse on the mainland side. Bish and I were getting the rope organised. Rep was getting ready for his swim. He went into his rucksack and brought out all his heavy mountain gear. A large selection of elastic bands of all sizes and shapes also appeared. He put on his mountain gear, then started to tie elastic bands around his neck, arms and legs of his mountain jacket and overtrousers. He was standing fully clothed, wrapped up for the high mountains with his big climbing boots on, strapped up with elastic bands.

'Whit the fuck ure yae daeing, Rep?'

'A wanna keep dry.'

'Ure yae fuckin' stupid, y'ure goin' tay sink like a fuckin' stane.'

'Fuck off! No worries.'

'Ure yae goin'tae walk along the bottom tae get tae the other side?'

'D'yae want a plastic bag fur y'ure heid as well. Stop y'ure hair gettin' wet!'

'Fuck off!'

'Ure a fuckin' bampot!'

Rep dug himself into a corner and was adamant that he would swim across the channel fully clothed in this mountain gear with his elastic bands to keep him dry. Rep tied a rope onto his climbing harness and started psyching himself up for the swim. Spiney whispered to the two of us to be ready to pull Rep out. Rep went over to the edge, paused for a few seconds, then jumped into the water with brolly in hand for effect. He went straight down and there was no sign of him coming back up. His brolly surfaced, and then a few bubbles appeared.

'Get him oot,' Spiney said.

All three of us hauled on the rope as hard as we could to get Rep back to the surface.

Rep appeared, like a half drowned rat, coughing and spluttering, gasping for breath, and happy to have been dragged back to the surface.

'Y'ure a fuckin' tosser, told yae, yae wid sink like a fuckin' stane.'

Rep seemed to accept this and didn't want to go back in, his pride dented.

Spiney drew the next short piece of seaweed. He stripped off, tied a piece of string to his waist and jumped into the channel that separates the Old Man from the mainland. You could feel the shock of cold water making him swim vigorously, and in a few seconds he was at the other side. A hammer and a couple of pitons were set over on the string to set up the other side of the Tyrolean traverse at the base of the Old Man. The old hawser rope was then pulled over. The rope was fixed at both ends and made as taught as possible. Spiney came back along the hawser rope, hand over hand. We went back to our tents for the evening, satisfied with our day's work.

Next morning we were back at the bottom of the cliff opposite the Old Man. The wind had dropped, the sea was calm and the tide was out ideal conditions for the climb. I was first across the Tyrolean traverse. The rucksacks came across, then Bish, Rep and Spiney last. Bish and Rep got organised quickly and took off up the first pitch of the Old Man. Spiney and I followed. There was seaweed lying about all over the place from the storm last night, making the first pitch quite slippery. I led up to the first belay ledge on a rock platform about 80 feet above the sea.

I brought Spiney up to the belay ledge. We were exchanging equipment at the belay when there were shouts from Bish and Rep up above in a tone of voice that sounded like they had just experienced an unexpected bowel discharge.

'Ah, fuck!!! Fuckin' hell!!!'

'Ah, fur fuck sake!!!'

Spiney and I shouted up trying to find out what the problem was.

'Ure yis alright?'

Spiney and I looked at each other, wondering what all the fuss was about.

'A dinnae know whit there problem is. Sound's like as if they've hud a dose o skits in the bath!'

The next pitch looked steep over bulging rock. Spiney took off up the pitch over layered strata of Torridon sandstone. The rope moved quickly through my hand. Soon Spiney was belayed. I followed up to the belay.

The next pitch was a traverse along a horizontal fissure in the Torridon sandstone that ran across the landward face of the Old Man. It was my lead. I started to shuffle along a small ledge that became smaller and smaller the further I moved round. The handholds were not very good, nor was the protection and it was exposed, which made me feel very aware that if I came off I would swing in a huge pendulum across the face. I shuffled along the ledge.

Then, I met my first seabird. It was standing above me on a small ledge. I looked at it; it looked at me; then it projected a bundle of rancid vomit onto my head. I couldn't remove the dollop of vomit for fear of falling, but tried to shuffle along the ledge more before I got another in the face. I traversed further round the narrowing ledge and straight into another seabird. It watched me for a moment, deposited a pile of vomit in my ear, then it flew off to my shouting and cursing.

I continued to move round until the ledge came to an end at the base of a system of chimneys. I put in a couple of good chocks and set up a spectacular hanging belay at the bottom of the chimney. Looking down, it looked a good 150 feet straight into the sea. I tried to remove the bits of vomit from my hair.

Spiney came round to the belay a bit later covered in vomit, and cursing and swearing at the seabirds. Spiney continued up the chimney to reach the summit. I followed.

We had reached the top. The summit was spectacular: a small pinnacle 250 feet above the sea. The four of us sat on top of the stack, proud that we had climbed the Old Man.

It was a fantastic day. The sun was out. The sea calm. We had a long leisurely lunch on top of the stack. It had been a great climb and we were in no rush to leave.

After eating, Bish's tape recorder came out of his rucksack. The Undertones were the first track, blasted out of Bish's cassette recorder. We started jumping up and down to the sound, having a disco on top of the stack.

Suddenly, I slipped off the side of the stack during a dance

movement and went headfirst over the edge. Fuck!!! My heart jumped out of my chest. Just as suddenly, I came to an abrupt halt a few feet down when the rope held me to the belay. I was looking at the sea 250 feet below.
The rest of the team hauled me back up, a little shaken. The Jam was next on the cassette recorder. The four of us were soon back dancing again.

After the dancing an abseil was rigged up. We abseiled off the summit and down to the first belay edge. It was a spectacular abseil off the south east corner of the stack. A second abseil took us to the base of the Old Man.

I had drawn the short piece of seaweed for the return trip and would have to dismantle the Tyrolean traverse and swim back. It was now high tide and the water level was only a few feet below the Tyrolean traverse rope. It was obvious that we were all going to get wet. Spiney and Rep stripped off, jumped in and swam back across to the mainland. On the other side they threw over a couple of polythene bags weighted with stones. Bish and I put all the climbing gear and clothes into the bags and sent them over in rucksacks on the Tyrolean traverse. The rucksacks went underwater as the rope sagged half way across the traverse.
  'Looks like yae'll huv tae swim back too Bish.'
There was a long pause from Bish.
  'A cunnae,' Bish was looking very nervous.
  'Whit dae yae mean cunnae, can't yae swim?'
  'A'm afraid o' water.'
  'This is a fine time to tell us noo. Why the fuck didn't yae tell us before?'
  'A didnae realise A wid huv tae get wet.'
Not only could Bish not swim, but he had a paranoid fear of

water. He almost drowned as a child. In fact even taking a bath was a major traumatic experience for him – at least that was his excuse for not washing.

There was some discussion about Bish's water phobia, whether he should stay overnight on the stack and we would collect him in the morning at low tide or try an underwater Tyrolean traverse. Bish decided to try the "underwater Tyrolean traverse". He was looking terrified, more terrified than when gripped on any piece of rock.

'Bish, yae might as well strip off and A'll send yur stuff oor in a poly bag.'

I gave Bish a few words of comfort.

'Just remember, when yae hit the water start pulling yursel along the rope as quickly as yae cun, Spiney and Rep will be pulling yae frum the other side.'

Bish moved to the edge of the water and summoned all his nervous energy to jump in.

'Remember tae hold y'ure breath and no playin' at submarines.'

He was as white as a sheet.

Bish jumped in and went straight underwater. You could see the panic underwater as Bish was moving hand over hand, Spiney and Rep at the other end pulling as hard as they could. It was all over in a few seconds, but it must have seemed an eternity for Bish.

Bish appeared at the other end looking very relieved to be on hard rock. I dismantled the Tyrolean traverse, took out the piton, threw all the gear over, jumped in and swam across.

We got back to the campsite, packed up and headed back to Achmelvich for the evening. This time, I was on the back of Spiney's machine. Bish and Rep were in front. Spiney was trying to catch up with Bish.

We flew down a steep hill on a single-track road. At the bottom, I could feel a panic in the braking. For some reason, Spiney only realised at the last moment that there was a very sharp bend coming up. There was no way we were going round the corner. A split-second decision had to be made.

The choice was to go straight on and off the end of a small harbour and into the sea or alternatively to try motorcycling through somebody's front garden. Spiney chose the latter.

A group of kids playing football jumped aside, as we came sliding through their game and ploughed right into a front garden, flowers and vegetables flying in the air. The bike hit something solid and came to an abrupt stop. I was thrown off the back and landed in a heap in a vegetable patch. The tent, which was strapped to the petrol tank, parted from the bike, flew through the air and went straight through the front door of the house!

Everything came to rest, Spiney was lying trapped under his bike, intermingled with the front lawn and some vegetables. I ran over to get the bike off Spiney. He was lying at some strange angle with his head planted into the ground. I pulled the bike off him and got him to his feet.

A woman appeared from the house with the tent under one arm and a cup of tea her hand. She gave me the tent and the cup of tea to Spiney.

'Ahh...thanks missus. A took the corner a wee bit too fast. A hope a dinae gee yae a fright.'

He finished the tea in almost one gulp.

'Ta very much.'

The woman said she was a nurse and kept going on about neck injuries. Neither of us paid much attention to her, Spiney and I got the bike up, quickly strapped the tent to the petrol tank and removed some soil from the engine.

'Cumowan let's get goin', we're miles behind Bish noo.'

Spiney kick started the bike. It started first time. I jumped on the back and Spiney blasted off down the road again to catch up with Bish and Rep.

Underwater

We were back at the campsite in Achmelvich. It was the morning and it was raining. The four of us lay in our sleeping bags making brews and watching the rain come down. Spiney was getting bored and had a great idea about snorkelling for flounders or crabs. Bish wouldn't go near water and Rep was happy to go along with that.

Spiney disappeared from the tent. He reappeared some time later with two wets suits borrowed from a nearby caravan park. Spiney fitted into his wet suit like a glove, but I was having a real squeeze putting mine on, eyes almost popping out of their sockets.

Off we went down to the coast in our wet suits. We jumped in at a rocky point and finned along the coast. The wetsuits made the water just about bearable. We worked our way around small bays and rocks, through the kelp and the swell. We didn't catch any fish, but we finned underneath a sea cliff that looked interesting for climbing. There was a deep chasm at one side of the cliff. We finned in for an explore. It was deep water and the rock went in shear on both sides. We started snorkelling about.

Spiney announced that there was a huge chock-stone jammed in the chasm some 40 feet down.

    'Look oor there... There's a big boulder doon there. A reckon A cun swim underneath. Looks a piece o piss.'

I wasn't so sure and tried to convince him it was a bad idea.

    'It might be blocked underneath.'

Spiney was unconvinced.

'Nae bother, A cun swim under that nae problem.'

Off he went underwater. I could see his yellow fins disappearing down into the depths. Some 30 seconds or so later, he appeared back on the surface gasping for breath.

'Almost got there!'

'Y'ure daft, y'ull dae yursel in and A'm no cumin' in after yae'.'

'No worries, piece o pish.'

'Well, A'm headin' oaf, 'cos A'm fuckin' freezin.'

Spiney disappeared under the water again. It seemed more like a minute this time before he surfaced again gasping for breath.

'A goat tae the chock-stane. A reckon A cun get under next time.'

'Y'ure a fuckin' heidcase! A'm gontae climb oot here and run hame, 'cos A'm brassers.'

I was starting to climb out of the water and up an easy part of the sea cliff. I was 40-50 feet up the cliff when Spiney announced he was going under again. I stood and watched. His yellow fins disappeared into the dark depths. I stood there expecting to see Spiney surface after about the same time period as before. He didn't.

Seconds passed. He's not coming back up.

Seconds passed. The thought passed through my mind "Do I jump into the water? But there's nothing I can do."

Seconds passed. At last a figure appeared from underwater, broke the surface with a huge gasp for breath.

'A did it! A did it! A did it!' was all he could manage to say between large gulps of breath.

'Yae dead good noo let's get goin'. Let's cum back wae Rep and Bish and climb sum o these cliffs.'

I was just happy that Spiney came back to the surface.

Spiney and I jogged back to camp in the wet suits to warm up. Bish and Rep were in the tent, making a brew. There was still a distinct odour of seagull vomit that I thought had disappeared the day before.

'Whit the hell's that smell, ya bunch o mockit bastards.'
'Whit smells that?'
'Huv yae no hud a wash yet? Y'ure just a bunch o clatty-cunts.'
'Oh, fuck off!'

We had something to eat, got organised, then the four of us set off back to the sea cliffs with climbing gear.

We got to the top of the cliff, abseiled down to the bottom and climbed back out. The four of us spent the rest of that day, and the following day, putting up some new climbs. At the end of each day punk rock was blasting out over the sea cliffs and we danced away.

Devil's Delight (part2)

The weather was still not very good. We were lying in our sleeping bags chatting away, cooking some breakfast, watching the rain come down and wondering what to do. Bish and Rep were talking about going back home. Spiney wanted them to stay on a bit longer and was trying to think up something to keep them from going.

'Its kind o funny that story wae those Yanks yae wur talkin' aboot. Last year aboot this time it wis wan o those balmy nights and a just cudnae sleep, so a went oot fur a walk. It wus a smashing night...full moon...you cud walk fur miles in the moon light. Any way A hud been paddin' aboot fur a good time when A heard this drummin' sound cummin frum sumwhere in the distance. Whit the fuck is that? A sais tae masel. Who the fuck wid be oot drummin' in the middle o the night? Anyway, A follow the sound fur whit seemed like hoors, then A came oor this wee hill and a just cudnae belive whit a saw...'

'Well don't keep us waiting, whit the fuck did yis see?'

'There wis awe these folk dancin' aboot in the scud. Fuckin' freezing it wus as well...dancin' aboot in the scud they wus. Anyway, they wur daein' this devil worship stuff or sumthin', prancin' aboot in awe this fancy gear. Then in cums this big bastard wae a sheep's skull owan his heid dancin' aboot...and ends up shaggin' this bird lying doon owan the rock... A cudnae believe it.'

'Fuck oaf! Yur talkin' shite'

'A'm tellin' yis, there wis aboot twelve o them dancin aboot in the scud. There wis this punter beatin' away owan the drum and awe the others were dancin' aboot this big fire. A wis owan the top o this wee hill lookin' doon owan everythin...this bird appears wae a robe...she walks oor tae this rock...drops the robe...lies doon owan the rock...und the punter wae the sheep's skull owan his heid starts shaggin her.'

'A fuck oaf, that's shite, naebudy wae dae that.'

'A'm tellin' yis a saw it wae ma ain eyes... This punter wae a sheep's heid starts shaggin' this bird. And whits mare... A saw the big bastard that hud the skull owan his heid in the campsite today. A reckon they'll be at it again tae night. It's a full moon tae night and A'm goan tae check it oot.'

Bish wasn't so convinced.

'Full moon, we'll be lucky tae see anythin' wae this weather. Well A'm no goan if it's pissin' doon.'

That was the end of the conversation about the devil worshipers for the time being.

The rest of the day was spent back at the sea cliffs getting wet and putting up new climbs.

In the evening, the weather was looking better and the discussion was back on about going to see the devil worshipers.

'This hud better be worth it... A'm no lyin' aboot fur hoors in the middle o the night waitin' fur sum nutters tae prance aboot in the scud.'

'Dinnae worry, A've brought along some entertainment. We cun gee them a wee surprise the night.'

Spiney had a mischievous look in his eye, but we all knew him well enough not to ask, otherwise some long tale would be spun.

After dinner, the four of us headed off to the place where Spiney reckoned it all happened the previous year. We hiked for a couple of miles around the coast, through bogs and over hillocks, until Spiney announced, 'This is it.'

There was a deep hollow between three hillocks that made a natural arena. At the centre there was a large flat rock and nearby was a ring of stones for a fire. We went down into the arena. Spiney pointed out.

'That's where the bird got shagged...that's where their fire wus...and A wus up here owan top o that wee crag oor there...and this is where the punter wae the sheep skull owan his head came frum...doon frum that wee gap oor there...and the other came doon frum there.'

The story seemed consistent so far.

It was starting to get dark.

'Hurry up geeus a hon tae get set up...start digging a hole under the fire place oor there.'

We started digging away. Nobody asked any questions.

'Right that's deep enough noo.'

Spiney pulled out a couple of containers from his rucksack.

'Sorry A hud tae borrow sum sugar frum yae.'

'Is that ma sugar yae huv? Ya bastard...that's awe a huv left.'

'Dinnae worry, its gauin tae a good cause.'

'Yae must o raided the whole campsite fur awe that sugar yae huv there.'

Spiney starts measuring out the sugar and mixes in some other stuff into bottles.

'Right stick these in the hole like this...and cover them up with sand.'

'Is that ma gas cylinder yae huv there, ya bastard?'

'Aye, stick it in there at the centre wae awe the rest.'

'Huald owan a minute, that's the last o the gas...we cunnae huv a brew in the morning if that goes up.'

'Its awe fur the cause... Right cover it awe up wae awe that loose soil.'

'Ure yae sure this is gontae work?'

'It'll work...it's tried and tested.'

Spiney makes the final touches to the fireplace, leaving it looking undisturbed.

The four of us retreat back to the top of the wee crag overlooking the arena. We settled down in the thick heather.

It was now dark. We waited quietly for a few minutes.

'What time is it?'

'Shhh.'

'It cun only be ten minutes since we wur doon there.'

'Shhh.'

All was silent for sometime.

'A cud dae wae a brew.'

'Shhh.'

'Ma arse is getting' wet.'

'Shhh... Shhh the fuck up will yae!'

We lay on our backs listening to the wind and looking up at the full moon moving between dark clouds.

'Nice full moon fur ware wolfs the night.'

'Ahooo... Ahooo...Ahooo...'

'Shut the fuck up!'

All was quite again.

Sometime later.

'A bet yis they don't cum.'

'A bet yae they do.'

'A bet yae they don't.'

'A bet yae they do.'

'Shhh...keep quite.'

'A bet yis it wus just a bunch o boy scouts roastin' tatties yae saw.'

'Fuck off!'

'A bet yae were pissed watchin' Dr Who or sumthin'. It wus the fuckin' daleks wae sheep's heids buzzin' aboot... Exterminate! Exterminate! Exterminate!'

'Shhh... A think a cun hear sum wan cummin'.'

'A wish it wus mae cummin'.'
'Shhh...sum wan is cummin!'
Spiney was right, you could just about make out voices.
'Whit happens if they cum up behind us?'
'Shhh... Shut the fuck up!'

The four of us looked down. Three people appeared in the arena. You could make out dark shadows moving around organising stuff from their rucksacks. Not much later a second crowd arrived; then another bunch of people arrived some minutes later. It was difficult to work out how many were there altogether. Maybe as many as twenty. There were two or three people around the fire trying to light it, but they appeared to be having difficulty getting it going. Other people were arranging things. Torch light shone back and forth across the arena. You could hear the clinking of bottles and cans and a bit of conversation that was difficult to make out.
Eventually a small fire was underway. Drums appeared and two people started drumming. It looked as if a ceremony was about to begin. The four of us lay at the top of the crag overlooking the whole scene unfolding below, heads peering out from between the thick heather. The fire was now bigger and lit up most of the arena. Many of the people had disappeared. I whispered across to Spiney,
'Where huv they awe gone?'
'Shhh.'
A few minutes later the two drummers start drumming a slow beat in unison.
'These punters wid look great in the band.'
'Shhh.'
'A cud dae wae sum o those drums... A wonder if they ure intae punk?'
'Shut the fuck up and watch!'

The drumming stopped. A chime sounded, then a slow monotone drumbeat started.
Two columns of people appeared either side of the crag walking in beat to the sound of the drums. Everybody was wearing long black robes and carrying long black sticks. The two columns moved into the arena and formed a circle around the fire. Four people with bigger sticks formed in a square around the rock in the centre.
The drumming stopped. A chime sounded out. Another character appeared. He was wearing a fancy robe and had a deer antler headset.
 'Fuckin' hell look at him...whit a prick.'
 'That wid be great head gear fur the band.'
 'He looks like fuckin' Davros. Next it'll be the Daleks cumin' in!'
 'Shhh...keep yur voice doon.'
The punter with the deer antlers moved slowly to the centre of the arena, his hands were in the air and he was chanting something that was difficult to work out. Everybody else started chanting out some rhythmic sound.
The drums started going faster and faster, people moved round the fire in a sort of dance and chanting at the same time. The drumming stopped. A chime sounded. Everyone stopped. The robes fell to the ground.
The drumming started again. People were running about naked, dancing and laughing away. Drink was being passed around. The fire was by now blazing strong. The flames illuminated the bodies as they danced.
 'Whit the hell ure they sayin'?'
 'Dinnae know, cunnae work it oot...must be sum devil stuff.'
 'Its sumthin' like Tra Embra Dram, Tra Embra Dram.'
 'Shut up and watch!'

'When is yur thing gonae go oaf?'

'Shhh...be patient.'

A dead deer was dragged into the arena and placed on the rock.

'Jesis... Whit the fuck ure they gointae dae wae that?'

'Shuut, just watch will yae.'

The punter with the deer antlers was presented a large dagger by one of the people standing in the square around the fire. He took the dagger with both hands and moved over to the carcass. The music started going faster and faster again. Everybody was dancing and chanting faster and faster.

The music suddenly stopped. All went quite.

A chime sounds out. The punter with the deer antlers plunges the dagger deep into the animal. There's a loud cheer from all the characters in the arena. The man with the deer antlers buries his hands deep inside the dead animal cutting away. He pulls out the heart and holds it above his head. The animal's blood was dribbling down his arms and body.

The four of us looked on. It was all starting to get really spooky. The punter with the deer antlers was looking very serious.

The drums started again and everyone, except the punter with the deer antlers, started drinking and dancing. Another gowned figure appeared in the arena and moved slowly to the centre. The robed figure stood facing the man with the antlers on his head.

The drum music stopped. The arena went quite. A chime sounded.

The robe dropped. There was a big cheer from the rest of the crowd.

The drums and dancing started again. A naked woman stood in front of the man with the deer antlers. The man placed the heart on the flat stone then raised both bloodied hands and wiped the blood on the woman's breasts.

There was another chime. The woman lay down on the stone with her legs apart. The drum beat started slow, but got faster and faster. Everyone danced away.

The music stopped and there was another chime. The punter with the antlers dropped his gown to reveal his naked body. The drum beat started again slow at first then went faster and faster as everyone danced around the fire.

A funny gurgling sound started to get louder. A few faces turned round looking towards the fire wondering what the sound was. Then, it became more of a rumbling sound that got louder and louder. The drummers started to slow down trying to figure out where the sound was coming from.

Suddenly, a huge Roman Candle flame burst out into the night sky. The whole ceremony stopped in an instant. Everyone turned round and stood back to witness this bizarre occult phenomenon. You could hear gasps of amazement and cries of fear from the performers as the flame reached 40 feet into the night. The whole arena was lit, bright as day, for a few seconds. The punter with the antlers dropped to the ground and started prostrating himself as if expecting Satin to walk out from the flame.

The four of us looked at this huge flame.

'Holey shite...whit the hell did yae put in there?'

The flame started to die down a bit. The punter with the antlers got on his knees and shuffled forward to the fire, hands outstretched as if giving an offering.

Suddenly there was an almighty explosion that blew the punter back to the ground, antlers whisked straight off his head by the shock wave. The noise echoed around the arena and disappeared into the night. A cascade of fire ash fell from the sky, covering the whole arena. It was a chaotic scene. People ran about in all directions trying to escape red-hot embers falling from the sky on naked skin.

The four of us rolled about in uncontrolled laughter.
'Ha! Ha! Ha!'
'O Jesis!'
'Ha! Ha! Ha!'
'Oh ma goad!'
'Ha! Ha! Ha!
'Look at them go!'
The next thing, Rep stands up on top of the cliff with a torch under his face and shouts out at the top of his voice.
'A am the devil! A am yur master! Yur ma slaves!'
A few angry faces turned round and look up at Rep.
'Cummon lets get the fuck oota here!'
Rep is still standing there shouting his head off, arms outstretched, giving out commands to his flock.
'A um yur lord! Obey me! Or yu'll die'
'Cummoan tae fuck... There's goina be sum upset folk aifter us soon. Cummoan time tae disappear.'
The four of us turned tail and ran into the night as fast as our laughter would allow. Looking back you could see torch light and hear a lot of shouting and swearing from a group of people out after us, but they had no hope of catching us.

Back at the tent, and in our sleeping bags, we were trying to get to sleep for the night, but Spiney's surprise kept us going well into the night.
'Awe Jesis a huvnae laughted as much as that fur years. Did yae see that big bastard's face when yae stood up there and shouted oot... A um the devil! Absolutely priceless. Awe... shit... A nearly shat maesel.'
'Did yae see that bird wae the blood owan her tit's. Whit the fuck wur they up tae daein' that stuff? Did yae see how she took oaf intae the night as if she'd seen a ghost. A huvnae seen anywan move as fast as that.'

'Awe shit, mae side is still splitin'...fuckin' hell that wis sum night.'

'Did yae see that flame go up...whit a fuckin' sight.'

'How the fuck did yae get that flame goin' up like that.'

'Takes years o practise.'

'...and when the gas cylinder when oaf...did yae see the face owan that bloke.'

'Did yae see those birds jumpin' up and doon when awe those red hot embers came fawin' oota the sky like rain. Daein' an Indian war dance they wur. Ah shit! Whit a sight! A nearly shat maesel!'

'Right calm doon, let's get sum sleep.'

The four of us went quiet, then a minute or two later Bish would erupt in a burst of laughter.

'Did yae see that big bastard starts prayin' tae that flame… Awe fuck… A've a pain in ma side.'

'Calm doon fur Christ sake.'

It went quiet again, then a minute or two later, you could hear the tears of laughter coming from Rep.

'Shut the fuck up and let's get sum sleep.'

'A'm sorry, A cunnae stop.'

There were more sniggers from Rep.

It was a late night trying to calm down after all the laughing exertions.

Gone Fishin'

The next day, it was raining again. Bish and Rep took off back to Glasgow. Spiney and I planned to stay a few more days. The weather was still unsettled, so a bit of fishing was in order to get something to eat and pass the time.

That afternoon, Spiney and I went off to do some sea fishing in a 12 feet mirror dinghy. The plan was to go out to a large hole, which Spiney had spied on the maritime charts and fish for haddock. The fishing spot was about a mile and a half offshore, in a line between Sgeir na Tràghad and Soyea Island.

By the end of the day, we had caught no haddock, but a boat full of dogfish. We gave up fishing for the evening. There was a heavy swell, and I was feeling seasick. As the boat reached the top of a wave you could see the coast as a thin black line against a grey horizon.

Spiney started up the engine. There was only a feeble, "phut, phut" out of the engine. Spiney tried again and again to start it. There were another couple of 'phuts' out of the engine, but the thing wouldn't start. The last few minutes of light were spent fiddling about with the engine, but we couldn't get it to start, and we had no torches.

It was now dark. The oars were out. I started to row back as Spiney bailed. By this time he too was feeling seasick.

We were out at night in a heavy swell with no lights, not really knowing if we were heading towards Achmelvich or Greenland. There was no time to worry, we took turns at rowing the boat or bailing it out. Sometimes, it was difficult to judge the wave direction in the dark. There was anxious feelings of "Oh! No! We're going over!" when the boat met a wave side-on. The thought passed through my mind on several occasions—what are we going to do if we end up in the water? I was beginning to wonder if it was such a smart idea, coming out so far to do some fishing.

At the top of each wave, the wind would catch the bow and push us side-on into the next wave. It took a lot of energy to reposition the boat to face head-on for the next one. I looked up occasionally from the top of a wave to try and identify anything against the night sky.

We had been rowing and bailing for a couple of hours and had no idea if we had rowed miles out into the Minch or miles round in circles. Spiney reckoned the current was taking us south, but then changed his mind and thought it could be north.

At some point in the night, a faint light appeared in the distance.

'We're go'in the wrong way ya plonker, there's a light oor that way. It must be the coast. We cood o drifted as far south as Lochinver.'

I was pointing in almost the opposite direction to where we were going. Spiney didn't believe me.

'Dinnae talk shite, there's no way land's oor there.'

'A tell yae, look oor there, there's a light and it's no a boat.'

We changed places, taking care not to capsize the boat.

Spiney was up front and looking over my shoulder.

'Fuck! Y'ure right, there's a light oor there and it's no far away.'

I turned the boat around and started to row in the direction of the light. The boat felt very unstable as I turned it onto a wave, trying to follow a course to the light.

'Quick more tae port! More tae port! Left! Left! Quick fur fuck sake before the next wave cumes in!'

After a few minutes' rowing it became obvious that the light was coming from a boat after all, probably a trawler.

'Let's go over and get directions.'

It took another good 10 minutes to get within shouting distance. There was a dim light from a cabin, otherwise the boat was dark. I could hear a chug-chug-chug sound from the engines.

'Haaallooo there!' Spiney shouted over several times at

the top of his voice.
Somebody on deck appeared with a powerful searchlight and shone it in our direction. You could just about make out a figure holding the torch.
Spiney shouted in slow deliberate words to make himself heard over the wind.

'Hallooo! Which-way-ss-Achmelvich?'
'What the fuck are you doing here?' There was a distant reply.
'We're going tae Achmelvich. Ure we going in the right direction?' Spiney replied.
'Turn round, you're go'in the wrong way.' A reply came.
'How far tae the coast?' Spiney shouted over.
'Two miles,' a reply came.
There was a pause, then another question.
'Where have you come from?'
'Stor-na-way,' Spiney quickly replied.
'Why did you tell him that?' I asked.
'Ouch! It'll gee him sumthin tae talk aboot in the pub.'
'Ask him if he cun geeus a tow.'
'Cun yae geeus us a tow?'
'Fuck off!' Came a distant reply.
'Thanks! A think he's fishin' illegally,' Spiney said.

I turned the boat around and started rowing away from the trawler. The sound of the boat disappeared into the darkness. We were alone again in a heavy sea.

We rowed all night. Eventually a greyish haze appeared on the eastern horizon. A thin black line of a coast started to appear. A few features on the coastline could be identified. We were not far from where we were fishing last night. The wind and the swell had dropped. Both of us took an oar and started rowing as hard as we could to Achmelvich Bay.

An hour or two later, we rowed onto the beach to an anxious reception party.

Darkness

The weather turned bad again and after a few days watching the rain come down we were getting bored. We started talking about heading back home and getting our trip to France organised.
However, there was one more thing on Spiney's mind.
There was a cave Spiney discovered near Inchnadamph the previous year that he was really keen to explore. I was not so keen since I was worried about feeling claustrophobic and about bumping into Randy and the Radioheads again. Also, neither of us had been down a cave before and didn't really know what to expect.
The weather forecast was not good for the next few days. Climbing was out, so we decided to explore the cave instead.

≈

The next morning we were off to Inchnadamph to try and find the cave. We had brought about 100 meters of nylon fishing line (to mark our passage into the cave in case we got lost), a bunch of climbing gear, and a rope ladder that we had made up. Neither of us had any idea how big the cave was nor how difficult it would be.
We left the motorbike at the end of a dirt track and walked for a couple of miles along a shallow valley, then turned north and went up to a boulder field on the side of a nondescript hill. After a bit of time wandering through the boulder field, Spiney found the entrance of the cave on the side of a wee rocky crag. It was not much of an entrance. Spiney went first, I followed.

It was a tight squeeze between two large boulders and then a belly crawl under a large boulder. This was as far as he had come the previous year. In front, I could see Spiney was struggling to get through a tight constriction, then suddenly he disappeared down into a dark hole. I stuck my head into the hole and asked.

'Y'ure yae OK?'

'Aye, just be careful when yae cum through. There's a wee bit o' a drop here.'

I passed the rucksack through and started to squeeze into the hole. It was like going into a room through a tiny hole in the ceiling. It was pitch black inside. My eyes weren't used to the darkness. My hands were flapping around trying to find something to hold onto and at the same time trying to squeeze through the tiny hole.

Suddenly, I popped out of the hole and landed on top of Spiney. The two of us got to our feet and fumbled about inside the rucksack to find our headtorches. We fiddled about in the dark with the wires to get the batteries connected.

A light came on and illuminated the inside of a large chamber. It was the first time that either of us had been inside a cave. It was dry and the atmosphere was warm with stale air.

The plan was to explore as much of the cave system as we could. At either end of the chamber there was a tunnel that ran for as far as we could see. I fixed the nylon fishing line around a large rock. We chose to explore the right hand tunnel first.

We made our way some distance along the tunnel, half-crawling, half-crouching, feeding out the fishing line. At the end of the long passage we came across another large chamber with a collapsed floor, exposing another tunnel system beneath the level we were on. A small burn was flowing at the bottom of the chamber. The sound of rushing water was amplified in the confinement of the chamber. We decided to use the rope ladder to get down. I hammered a piton into the rock, fixed the rope ladder, and threw it down into the hole. It was too short to reach the bottom. So we set up an abseil with our climbing rope, but it would mean that we would have to climb back up the rope hand-over-hand to reach the rope ladder. I tied the end of the fishing line to the piton. Almost all the fishing line had been used.

Spiney went down the rope ladder, then abseiled down to the bottom of the chamber. I followed. The abseil rope and rope ladder were left to get us back out.

The two of us followed the stream down through another tunnel system. The water had cut channels into the rock and had polished it into weird shapes. After some distance down the tunnel the stream ended in a large pool. The roof of the cave came down to meet the water: our passage was blocked. However, it looked possible that there could be another chamber on the far side of the pool, but it would mean crossing the pool and going underwater to investigate.

I drew the small stone and was elected to get into the water first. Justice was done since Spiney was first in the water at the Old Man.

I stripped off and went into the water. My legs were numb within seconds. The water was ice cold. I came back out and put on my clothes to keep in some warmth and went back in again. I waded across the pool holding my helmet and head torch, going around stalagmites, to where the rock face met the water. The water was now up to my waist. I felt the rock face underwater as best I could with my feet, to try and find an opening or undercut that could possibly reveal another chamber. All I found was a rock face that went down to the bottom of the pool.

There was no possibility of further progress. I waded back

across the pool, got out of the water and jumped up and down to get the blood circulating again.

We backtracked down the passage to the abseil point, had something to eat, then went up stream to explore another passage.

We made our way up through a narrow tunnel into a bigger chamber. In the big chamber, were smaller passages running in all directions. We decided to explore one of the narrow passages, it was not much more than a foot in height. The headtorch beams shone into the dark passage of unknown length. The passage looked very tight and narrow. Spiney was keen to explore and quickly disappeared down the hole. I followed. All I could see was the soles of Spiney's boots shuffling about in front of me. We crawled some distance into the passage, head, shoulders, bum, feet hitting against the ceiling. Sometimes it was a really tight squeeze to get past a particular constriction, or we had to work our way around a narrowing.

We wriggled further into the passage. Suddenly, 'CRASH! THUMP!' Rocks from the ceiling fell and whacked my head and back. Everything went black, like turning off a light. My sense of vision had gone. It flashed through my mind that I was dead.

One second before I could see where I was going, my hands in front, Spiney's boot's; now nothing...absolutely nothing... just black. I lay stationary for some seconds trying to work out what had happened—perhaps I was in some unconscious state? The only thing I could feel was the adrenaline pumping around my body. I wriggled my toes and fingers, and pinched myself several times for reassurance that my body was still working.

I started coughing. Dust and sand in the air made breathing difficult, I was too afraid to move in case more stuff came down, but I couldn't stay where I was for very long.

I slowly and very carefully crawled backwards, feeling each movement in the darkness, until I found better air. I fiddled with my head torch to try and get it working again, but couldn't get it to work. My elbows, arms, head, shoulders, backside, legs kept hitting the ceiling, restricting my movement. I was concerned Spiney was buried in front. I was concerned that the roof would collapse again. I was concerned that the roof had collapsed behind me and blocked our exit. There was total darkness. Breathing was difficult. There was no room to move. The only sense was adrenaline going into overdrive, thumping around my body.

I started to panic; the panic turned to terror; the terror turned into blind fear. Eyes open, eyes closed, it was just black—nothing.

The fear started to run out of control. I closed my eyes and tried for a few moments to calm down by taking a few deep breaths.

I fiddled about in the dark with the wires and bulb of my headtorch to try and get the thing to work. The thought that the headtorch had been smashed and I wouldn't be able to get back out passed through my mind. I continued fiddling about for sometime, trying to get some light.

At last, a beam of light came on and I could work out what had happened. I could see the soles of Spiney's feet about 10 feet in front of me. I pushed some of the debris in front of me to the side and moved slowly forward to where Spiney was. There was still some loose stuff coming down from the ceiling. I knocked on the sole of Spiney's right foot as if I was knocking on someone's door. Spiney's right leg moved. I moved some of the debris beside Spiney's feet to the side. The ceiling above him was very loose and more came down. I could make out a few words Spiney was saying.

'There's a boulder pinnin' ma right shouder doon.'

I gave Spiney a few reassuring words.

'A cun see it. A'm afraid the whole roof will cum doon if yae move.'

'A wus afraid o that.'

'Can yae breathe OK?'

'Yeah, nae probs, so far.'

I checked the ceiling, removed a few loose blocks and set them aside. There appeared to be a fissure of very loose rubble above Spiney. He must have disturbed one of the boulders and the whole lot came down. I removed a few other larger rocks that looked as if they could come down at any moment and scooped away handfuls of sandy soil to give Spiney more room. Spiney was lying still.

Once I had cleared as much as I could. Spiney started to move back, inch by inch, trying to work as much of his body away from the stone that was holding him down. When he could move no more, I held Spiney's ankles and when he shouted, I pulled as hard as I could. The ceiling collapsed on top of Spiney. I kept pulling his ankles and managed to get him away from the rock fall.

The air was full of dust. It was difficult to breathe. Both of us were coughing. Even with the headtorch light, the visibility was almost nil with so much dust in the air. Spiney and I crawled backwards as quickly as we dared to get out of the narrow passage and get back into a larger tunnel.

I popped out into the large chamber and clean air, grabbed Spiney's ankles and dragged him out from the narrow passage. The two of us sat there coughing and spluttering, clearing our lungs of dust. Shaking the sand out of hair and clothes, picking sand out of our ears, nose, eyes and mouth.

Both of us were very relieved to get out of the narrow passage and into more space. That was enough for today. We followed the stream back to the rope, climbed back up hand-over-hand to the higher cave system. Then backtracked along the fishing nylon and made our way to the entrance. I appeared back on the surface. It was early evening. We had been in the cave most of the day without realising how much time had passed.

≈

It was the end of the Spring break. I had to hitch back to Glasgow the following day. Spiney gave me a run on the back of his machine to Inverness, to give me a head start. We were flying down the road doing some ridiculous speed, trees at the side of the road zapping past, when the engine seized. The bike came to a slow stop with smoke pouring out of the engine. There was nothing to be done but push the bike to a nearby farm and dump it there.
I hitched on one side of the road to go south to Glasgow, Spiney on the other side to go north back to Achmelvich.

≈

It was finals back at school, but our thoughts were more about going climbing in France. France has some of the biggest mountains in Europe. We had read the Chris Bonnington, Dougal Haston, Joe Brown books from cover to cover, digesting every piece of information. The photographs and stories of climbing on the Chamonix Aiguilles, Mont Blanc and the Grandes Jorasses were imprinted in my mind. Chamonix was our target; the centre of alpine climbing in Europe. There were real mountains there, one's that tower into the sky, unlike the small rounded bumps you get in Scotland. Going to climb in the French Alps was like going on a pilgrimage. If Chris Bonnington can go to Everest, then the BCT can go to Chamonix. Maybe the following year the BCT will be off to Everest.

≈ *Stephen Najda* ≈

But how to get out to Chamonix in the French Alps with all the climbing gear, stay a few weeks to get as much climbing done as possible, and to get back home was a major headache.

≈ *Rock Rock* ≈

The Van

The exams were over, school had finished, and we were looking forward to a long summer holiday, climbing in France. Each of us scrimped and scraped enough money doing odd jobs here and there for our biggest adventure. After all the hard work, planning and organising, our dream was starting to take shape, but nobody had thought about the logistics of getting out to France, and back again.
None of us had travelled much outside Scotland and the thought of having to cope in a foreign land, with people not speaking English, was really daunting, but the thought of climbing in the French Alps was just too attractive to miss.

≈

Bish and Steevie are in the garage working on a new song. Rep is tapping away on the drums.

'Whit wus that A hurd yis sayin' tae that punter at the last gig?'

'Eh?'

'Yis wur givin' awe that bullshit tae sum punter, remember.'

'Ouch, it wus nuthin.'

'Wus that punter sayin' he wus wanting tae make a recording o us?'

'A told yis, the record companies will be lining up… We're better than the Sex Pistols, the Clash…'

'Yeh, yeh, sure thing Bish…next thing yu'll be tellin' us is the Pope will be cumin' tae watch us.'

'As a matter o fact, A goat a phone call the other day from the Vatican.'

'Yeh, yeh. Fuck oaf, Bish.'

Bish was up to his usual antics.

'Cumoawn, where were wae? Whit wus A singin' again? Oh right...'

Bish clears his throat and starts to sing, 'Chem-i-kal does ma heid in!'

'Naw, naw, Bish, it's awe wrong...yis need tae sing... GoTa chemical in ma heid.' Steevie interrupts.

'That's shite...it hus tae be more like... Chem-i-kal does ma heid in!'

'That's no what A wrote.'

'Well it's pish. Yis will just huv tae rewrite it then.'

Rep stopped playing with the drums and looked up.

'Whit the fuck is that?'

An old clapped out mini-van, smoke pouring out the back, drove up to the garage. The window winds down and Spiney sticks his head out, proud as punch.

'Look whit A've got...and it wus only 25 quid!'

'25 quid!' Rep bursts out, '25 quid for a rust bucket! That's a fuckin' fortune!'

'It's a bargain! And it's oor ticket tae France!'

'It's a rust box, clapped oota heap o shite!'

'It will never make tae the end o de street, never mind France!'

'Aye it will...nae fuckin' bother...and get us back!'

'So A need some dosh tae pay fur the van.'

'No fuckin' way, hosey!'

'Cumowan Rep, don't be such a prick.'

'25 quid... That's almost awe the dosh we huv tae get tae France.'

'So, whit's the plan? Ure awe four o us gontae squeeze in d'ere?'

'Nae fuckin' bother.'

'Oh aye...think we're sardines? A'm gonae end up owan the roof.'

'That cun be arranged...so geeus the dosh.'

'A'm no spendin' 25 quid owan that heap! No fuckin' way, Hooosseyyy!

'Cummoawn don't be such a prick...just give us the 25 quid.'

'Fuck oaf! Yis huv been done.'

'Cummoawn, it's no your dosh, it's oor dosh...remember. We awe made it playing the gig's remember...it's oor dosh. The plan is tae save up some dosh tae gotae France...remember. We buy the van und awe go tae France. If we don't buy the van, we'll end up watchin' Coronation Street on the telly. Simple eh?'

Rep was having none of it and started bashing away loudly on the drums.

'Fuck sake! A know where yis huv stashed the dosh. A know where yis have stashed the dosh. A know where yis have stashed the dosh...eh, eh, eh.'

Spiney squeaked out like a child, then made a sudden dash behind the drums. Rep jumped on him, and tried to wrestle him to the ground, but Spiney managed to get to an old can with the dosh in it.

'A know yis yur a mean fucker – that's why we gave yis the dosh tae look aifter.'

The two are on the ground wrestling; Spiney turns Rep over in an arm lock and sits on him. Spiney stuffs his hand into the tin and starts peeling manky notes apart.

'Whit the fuck huv yis been deanin' way oor dosh, it's minging?'

Rep is moaning under Spiney's weight.

'But...we need tae buy food, a ticket for the boat, petrol money.'

'Thanks very much fur oor 25 quid... Fuck sake Rep, why huv yis suddenly awe become sensible awe o a sudden? If we don't get goin' soon tae France, then the summer will be over soon, und well be goin' nowhere, proto.'

'Good, we awe agreed, the van is a good idea. Everyone happy?'

Bish looked at Steevie unconvinced. Rep is really pissed off, grumbling and moaning.

'Whit's wae awe the looks? Any better ideas?'

Spiney opened the door of the van.

'Look yur buying luxury...look.'

Bish put his head inside the van.

'O fur fuck sake! It's fuckin' boufin' Cun yis no ask for a discount 'cos o the smell?'

'Beggers can't be choosers. Look whit maer dis yis want? It's got a steering wheel, a couple o seats, yis cun see oota the windae's...luxury! Eh?!'

Nobody was convinced by Spiney's blather.

After a lot more squabbling at last the van was bought, £25—a bargain at twice the price—no questions asked. It was one of those mini vans, dark brow-blue in colour, just big enough to carry two people in the front and a whole load of luggage in the back.

A few problems had to be sorted out. First, with the engine running, the exhaust fumes did not quite manage to reach the exhaust pipe and instead the whole interior of the van would quickly fill up with a blue noxious haze. The solution was ingenious. A large piece of flexible industrial ducting was found and installed to run from inside the front grill, over the engine, through a hole cut in the dash board, up the front of the wind screen to the mirror and then turned down – providing fresh air for the driver and passenger – but only when the van was moving. Second, hours had to be spent on the engine, fixing the timing, changing the electrical cabling, cleaning out the carburettor, etc. The van burned a lot of oil. A bit of fine sawdust in the oil helped, but a long, blue trail lingered in the air long after the van had passed. Third, the brakes did not work that well. In fact, the hand brake did not work at all. New brakes were fitted, but that did not make much difference. However, with a bit of imaginative use of the gears the van could be stopped in a reasonable distance. Fourth, the previous owner had been a farmer (so we were told) and the van had a distinct pig/chicken/cow smell about it. Congealed blood and other solidified body juices could be found in every nook and cranny. Hours were spent with a steam hose trying to clean the inside, getting covered in all the shite of the day. Fifth, the petrol cap got pushed through rusty bodywork on our first attempt to put petrol in the tank. A bit of wire wrapped around the petrol cap, attached to a couple of rivets on the outside of the van, took care of that problem, but there always remained a faint petrol smell. Anyway, the good news was that we had a M.O.T. for the van that was valid for the next couple of weeks – enough time to get out to France.

After days spent working on the van, a few more modifications were made and a quick dab of paint on the burnt bits restored it to almost good as new. "BCT on Tour" was written across the back doors, "Copulation Station" was on one side and "Suicide Express" on the other side of the van.

Test drive

A test drive seemed a good idea since the plan was to drive over 1000 miles from Glasgow to Chamonix and go climbing, then back again to Glasgow, but we did not know if the van would make it to the end of the road...and we still needed more money to survive out there.

'Right who's up for a test drive?'

'We cun go up tae the dams?'

'Naw A mean, we cun go tae the Fort, A've been in discussion about a gig in the Fort, at the weekend.'

'Where did this cum from, A thought we wus gontae France?'

'Look, we need some more dosh tae get tae France, ya plonker!'

'The Fort is miles away, we don't know if the van will get round the next corner?'

'We need the dosh, und we cun goes up und climb the Old Man o Hoy...the last time we climbed the Old Man o Stoer, this time we cun go and climb the Old Man o Hoy, simple.'

'That's miles away...we're goin'in the wrong direction... und we cunnae awe go in the van.'

'We cun travel light, awe four o us will get in the van, nae fuckin' bother... Leave Lucy here, no drums...und we cun solo somethin'?'

'Eh? How are we supposed tae play a gig without Lucy and drums?'

'We cun improvise.'

'Improvise?'

'Whit dae yis mean, improvise?'

'Yae cunnae improvise a shag in a whore house.'

'Dae yis mean, we huv tae mime? B.C. fuckin' T...the best band in the world that mimes... A punk rock band that mines that will pull in the crowds etc...that's a brilliant idea! A wish A thought o that. B.C funckin' T, the best silent band in the world.'

'No climbing gear und solo the Old Man o Hoy?'

'Well, maybe not solo the Old Man o Hoy... Right... OK... Me and Rep cun go owan ma machine, und youis two cun go in the

van way Lucy and sum music gear, sorted eh?!'
After a lot of arsing around, we managed to get Lucy in the van with legs hanging out the back, a guitar and a drum and some climbing gear.

'Were ooaf now, see yis in the Fort.'
'We'll pass yis owan the road, und we'll blow some smoke in yur faces.'

≈

The van is creeping along as we made our way up north.
'Cun yis gee it sum more laldy? A cun walk faster.'
A "you must be joking" look from Spiney.
'Is this as fast as we cun go? It will take us weeks tae get tae France.'
Another look from Spiney.

There was a hitcher at the side of the road. We stopped.
'We're oafta the Fort. We cun take yis up the road pal?'
'No worries, jump in the back here and hold owan, it's a bit o a squeeze...and the suspension is a bit rough.'
'Ta, very much.'
The hitchhiker squeezed in the back. He laid stomach down in the back of the van, holding on to the top of the seats, bouncing about like a pea in a tin can and trying not to breathe too much. Occasionally a white face would appear between the two seats from the blue haze in the back.
'Ure yae all right pal?' I would ask every few minutes.
He did not say very much, but appeared happy enough.
We were driving down a long straight, when Spiney announced.
'OK A'll geeit more laldy.'
Then... Woosh!

An almighty flame appeared from the back of the van. The van instantaneously filled up with smoke and a pungent burning plastic smell. The poor bastard in the back must have thought his time was up. What with being knocked about, gassed and now being flamed, we did not have a happy passenger: he wanted out. Our passenger went into panic mode and took a lunge over me for the door.

'Fuck! Let me oot!!! Let me oot!!!'
I had to beat him back.

'Get the fuck back in! Wait a second! Will yis. Wait till the van stops, ya eejit!'
Spiney turned off the engine and brought the van to a stop as quickly as possible. Both of us jumped out and threw dirt and some wet grass over the back of the van to extinguish the flames. The back of the van was scorched; most of the paint work had been flamed. The hitcher was struggling to get his rucksack out over the driver's seat. He was in no mood to hang around. Cursing and swearing and coughing he took off down the road.

'Fuckin' cunts! Mental bastards! Whit the fuck ure yis tryin' tae dae tae mae...'
There was some smoke coming off his clothes as he stormed down the road. Spiney shouted out a farewell.

'Next time we'll run yae oor—ya bastard!'

It was back to square one. The two of us went under the bonnet to figure out what had gone wrong. It looked like a gasket had gone, not a quick job to fix and it was starting to get dark. Bish and Rep pulled up, revving the engine of his machine. Bish shook his head.

'Tut, tut, oh dear! Oh dear, oh fuckin' dear! The boys ure stuck. Oh dear, oh fuckin' dear!'

'Told yis that fuckin' shite heap wus a waste o money!'

Rep pipes out.

Spiney and Steeve look up from under the bonnet not amused. Bish keeps revving the engine.

'Told yis the van was a waste o money. That's 25 quid doon the drain. Fuckin wankers!'

'Fuck oaf Rep!'

Rep gives a V in return. Bish keeps revving his machine.

'We're oaftae the Fort, und leave these losers here.'

Bish revs up his machine higher, let's in the clutch and wheelies down the road. Rep is hanging on the back giving multiple V's.

'Bish und Rep will be back. They can't do anythin' without us...we've awe the gear. Cumowan, we cunnae do much, it will get dark soon, we need tae push the van oaf the road fur the night.'

Sometime later the sound of Bish and Rep re-appear at the van where Steevie and Spiney are having a brew.

'Thought yis were gontae the Fort, ya fuckers?'

'Cumowan we need tae get tae de gig. You should o fixed the van by noo.'

'Fuck oaf! A told yis it's fucked. Well yis cun help push the van tae the Fort if yis want?'

'Told yis the van wis a waste o fuckin' money.'

'Yeah, yeah, Rep yis sound like a broken record.'

'There's no way we can fix the van tonight. We'll doss oot here and get it fixed in the morning.'

'But the gig?'

'Whit fuckin' gig? Sum dodgy punter has offered yis a gig, weeks ago, but yis hunvae managed to contact him since. It's no gontae happen, so just dream owan, und huv a brew.'

'Fuckin told yis the van is a waste o fuckin' money.'

Spiney gives the evil eye to Rep.

'A told yae the van was a waste o money.'
'If you say that again, A'll take your fucking head off!'
'Fuck off wanker!'
Spiney is getting upset.
'Fuck oaf! Und don't come fucking back next time! That's the end o France und the end o the band so fuck off!'
'Naw it's no. The two o us will get tae France und we'll set up another band.'
'Like fuck! Yis will.'
'Aye A'll will.'
And Bish joined in.
'You should o fixed the van proper!'
'Just fuck off will yae! You wanted the test drive up here. You and yur fucking imaginary gig. Get it into ure heid—there's no fucking gig!'
'Fuck off! A'm gointae the Fort.'
'Told yae the van was a waste o money.'
Spiney is getting more upset.
'Well fuck off will yis!'
Bish storms back to his machine, tries to kick start it, but the machine and Bish topple over head over tit into a drainage ditch. Rep runs over and helps Bish pull the machine out of the ditch. Steevie and Spiney roll about in laughter at the slapstick antics. Bish is furious and tries to kick over his machine again and again but cannot get it to start.
'Ha ha ha... Away yis go und hitch up tae the Fort, ya wankers!!!'
Rep gives a "V" and both storm away into the darkness.
'Fuck oaf! Und don't come back! Und fuck oaf with yur band!'
'They'll be back... They can't go far without the bike.'
'Fuck the midges are oot big time, let's get a fire goin'.'

≈ *Rock Rock* ≈

Steevie and Spiney are sitting round a small fire having a brew and something to eat.

'Rep really gets on my tits sometime. He's a real pain in the arse. Goin' on and on'. A could kill him sometimes, A could. A could wring his neck, sometimes. And Bish just keeps going on and on and on aboot gig's everywhere but we're no making any money. Bish and his fucking band. It's oor band. I bet, he hus hud this gig thing in the Fort in his heid fur weeks und husnae told us… It wus just Bish fucking scheming away. Bish keeps going on and on until he gets his way. He just keeps fucking scheming away awe the time. Bish and his fuckin' scheming will be the end o the band. Und we'll never get tae France at this rate…the van is fucked! That's the end o France.'

'Hopefully it's naw as bad as it looks. We cun check it oot in the morning.'

The conversation was getting quite depressing as everything appeared to be falling to bits. Steevie swipes the back of his head.

'Shit! These midges are out in force this evening.'

The two are sitting looking into the fire. Steevie's imagination runs riot as Jacko appears out of the darkness. Jacko is stoned, laughing and taking the piss.

'Born workin' class, die fuckin' workin' class, there's nae where tae go, nae fuckin' choice, nae fuckin' hope. A say, why ure we livin' in such a fucked up state? The whole world is against mae because they don't like what a say—it's the only escape. A'm stuck owan the fuckin' point o life. Yae know whit A mean. Whit is the fuckin' point o life, if there nae fuckin' choice, nae fuckin' hope. You're just the same, yis cannae escape, you're trapped, your fate is mapped oot. You'll go fucking nowhere. Do nothing. You're just spineless like everyone else. Yur just A waste o fucking space. Ha ha ha! You're just a waste o space!'

Steevie starts writing down a song on a scrap piece of paper.

'A don't know why yae ure still writing yur songs. That's the end o the band. A cunnae see us getting' together again.'

'Funny, A just remembered the time up the Jerries when we wus roasting tatties at a camp fire, just like this, und Jacko appeared oota the darkness, totally spaced oota his box und started goin' owan aboot the point o life.'

'The point o life is that the van is fucked, the band is funcked, un we're no goin' tae France. It's awe Bish and Rep's fault aboot this gig in the Fort'. A'm off for a kip. Shit! The midges are bad the night. Make sure you put that fire oot in case the van goes up and close awe the van windows otherwise we'll be eaten alive.'

'No worries. A wonder where Bish and Rep are now?

'Who cares? Shit, these midges are bad!'

≈

The night is as black as coal, Spiney and Steevie are snoring away in sleeping bags, squeezed in the back of the van with Lucy and the rest of the junk. Suddenly, there is loud banging on the roof of the van.

'Aargh Come on let us in! The fucking midges are killing us!' it was Bish.

'Let us in!, fuckin', let us in!'

Bang! Bang! Bang! On the van roof.

'Come on let us in! The fucking midges are killing us!' Bish pleaded.

'Fuck oaf!'

'Come owan let us in!'

'Fuck oaf, ya wasters.'

Bang! Bang! Bang! On the van roof.

'Aargh, cum owan, let us in fur fuck sake!'
'Fuck yis oaf tae the Fort.'
'Aargh let us in! Aargh!!'
'Youis deserve to have a long slow death.'
'Cumontae fuck, let us in!'
Bang! Bang! Bang! On the van roof.
'Let us in! Let us in! Let us in!'
'A thought yis didn't like the van, Rep, eh?'
'Let us in! Fur fuck sake. Aargh!!!'
Bang! Bang! Bang! On the van roof.
'Hoi! Careful o the paint work.'
'Let us in! Fur fuck sake! Aargh!'
'Aargh!!!'
'Cumowan, Let us in! Let us in!'
Bang! Bang! Bang!
'Whit wur yis saying Rep, the van is a waste o money, eh?'
Bang! Bang! Bang!
'How about saying, the van was a brilliant idea.'
'Fuck oaf!'
Bang! Bang! Bang!
'Well that's no a very nice thing to say.'
'How about saying, the van was a brilliant idea, and we'll think about lettin' yis in?'
'Come on let us in! The fucking midges are killing us!'
Bang! Bang! Bang!
'Fuck oaf!'
'Cunt let us in!'
'Fuck oaf!'
'Fuckin' cunt, let us in!'
'Fuck oaf!'
Bang! Bang! Bang!

The angry shouting match between Spiney and Rep was

brought to an end when Steevie blasted on the car's horn until both of them shut up.

'Nobudy says anything, right.'

Rep was about to start again, when Steevie pressed the car's horn again.

'Nobudy says anything. Right, get in quick and don't let any o those wee bastards in. Yis will huv tae doss the night sittin' up in the front seats. And now will everyone shut the fuck up and let's get some doss.'

Steevie opens the door of the van. Bish and Rep get in with a lot of attitude and angry silence.

'Now everyone, shut de fuck up und let's get some doss.'

≈

It's first thing in the morning and pouring down with rain. The four are in the van, still with depressed rage from last night, not saying very much. Steevie trying to lighten the atmosphere handed the words for the new song to Bish.

'A've got a new song fur yae Bish, A scribbled down last night. It goes something like. "Born working class, die working class. The loop of life goes on...".'

'There's no point writing any more. The van is knackered. We cunnae get tae France now. And the band is fucked,' Spiney interrupts.

Everyone is in a huff, listening to heavy rain bounce off the van roof.

The rain poured down and down for hours. The only thought was how to get the van fixed and get home.

'Well that's the rain oaf a bit.'

'Well fuck this for a laugh, let's try und get the van fixed und oota here.'

≈ *Rock Rock* ≈

≈

The van comes alive.

'That wus a lot easier tae fix than A wus expectin'.'

Bish and Rep are still fiddling about with Bish's machine, trying to get it to start.

'That's us headin' back doon the road.'

Spiney continues to rev up the van engine.

'See yis back hame! Bye!'

'Hold owan A minute will yis, cun yis no geeus a bump start eh?'

'Fuck oaf will yis! Who wus slagin' oaf the van, eh? Und noo it's awe pally wally.'

'Yis cun fuck oaf back hame, but A've goat awe the dosh, remember,' Rep blasted out, 'und yis ure no gotae France, 'cos yis don't huv any dosh, yis ure fucked! Youse ure skint!'

'What's this dosh your talkin' aboot? Enough tae buy a lollipop? And remember Rep, it's oor dosh, no your dosh, und youis urnae gotae France either,' Spiney blasted back.

'We huv enough dosh tae go tae France.'

'Naw yis huvnae. And it's no yur dosh, it's oor dosh.'

'Aye A huv.'

'Naw yis huvnae.'

'Aye A huv.'

Rep and Spiney are starting to eyeball each other. Bish jumps up abruptly from his effort at trying to start his machine and rummages about for his cassette player. Music blasts out. Bish is pogoing up and down as if there's no tomorrow, shouting out.

'We're gontae France! We're gontae France! We're gontae France!'

'Eh Bish, whit the fuck ure yis goin'owan aboot?'

'We're gontae France! We're gontae France! We're gontae France!'

'We've got nae fuckin' dosh. We're ure no goin' anywhere.'

'A've got a idea. We huv enough dosh tae drive oot tae France. So we'll organise a gig or two over there tae pay fur tae get us back hame. We're gontae France! It's the BCT owan a world tour.'

Everyone looked at each other—was Bish serious?
Bish is jumping up and down, shouting and singing out.

'The BCT owan a world tour. We're oftae France! We're oftae France! We're oftae France!'

Soon all four of us were pogoing to the music and shouting out.

'The BCT owan a world tour'. We're oftae France! We're oftae France! We're oftae France!'

The BCT World Tour

The next test run in the van was not to be so rigorous, a couple of times round the block and that was it.

To cut costs to the bone, the van was loaded up with as much food as we could plunder from home: porridge oats, sugar, dried milk, flour, raisins etc. All the food was unboxed and transferred into plastic bags to save weight and space. A couple of shelves were installed on the inside to take all the bags of food. The van was loaded with a spare tyre, extra oil, and the minimum of tools to get us to France and hopefully back. The climbing gear was next, and then finally the musical stuff. By the end of the day, the van was crammed, jam packed, full to the roof. Everything was packed except Lucy. She was still lying on the ground waiting to be loaded. There was no room for her in the van. A few things were unloaded and we tried to squeeze her in, but she was such an awkward shape, that there was no way she would fit. We sat beside Lucy and figured out how we could get her out to France.

An old frame was spotted at the back of the garage, which was quickly adapted as a roof rack. I dismantled Lucy into two sections. Spiney found some old fishing net at the back of the garage. The top half of Lucy was sat vertically with her head sticking through a big hole in the net and her lower half rested horizontally along the roof rack with her two feet sticking out of the front. A drum was at her back. I put an Écosse sticker on the back for good luck.

It had been a long day, the van was packed full, but we were now ready to roll.

We're oaf tae France

Next morning we were off on our great adventure to France. The plan was to get to London by nightfall, to avoid the traffic,

then get to the south coast by the morning and worry about France when we got there. The van happily cruised along at about 40-45mph on the motorway, Lucy sitting on top with her tinsel hair blowing in the wind, everything else on the road was flying past, giving us strange looks.
After a very long day and night we finally reached the English south coast. It was almost dawn and we were both knackered. Spiney had driven all day and night since I couldn't drive. We parked in a lay-by somewhere in Kent and crashed out for a couple of hours.

≈

A few hours later a brew was on, then we were back on the road to find a cross-channel ferry. However, we soon got lost in the Kent countryside and were driving around all these small country lanes arguing about who got us lost, where we got lost, and which way to go.
 'Fuck, it's the polis.' Spiney interrupted the argument.
I turned round. All I could see was a headlight in the side mirror. They drove with us for a mile or so, before the blue flashing light came on.
 'Awe shit, this is awe we need noo.'
Spiney pulled over. Two cops came over. One of them asked Spiney for his driving licence and M.O.T. The other one went around inspecting the van, checking tyres, the good set was on.
 'What is the tube for?' The cop, pointing at the industrial ducting running up the windscreen, asked Spiney
 'It's an engine performance enhancer.'
The cop looked very unconvinced.
 'And what's the doll for?'
 'Lucy is no a doll. She's oor lead singer. We're the BCT owan a world tour.'
The cop looked even less convinced.

'Where are you off to?'

'First stop owan the world tour is tae Cham, climbing.'

They seemed not to believe our story, that we had driven from Glasgow and were on our way to climb in the Alps. They wanted to see if all the lights & indicators were working—they were. We had done a good job on the wiring after the fire. They wanted to hear the horn. Spiney pressed the horn. It did not work.

'It wis working an hoor ago,' Spiney tried to reassure the cop, 'when this cat run oot in frontae us...honest.'

'Get out of the car,' one of the cops said.

Both cops put their shoulders to the van and heaved.

'Good hand brake,' Spiney said, knowing full well that there was no hand brake. But he had casually put the van into gear when getting out. The two cops gave up trying to push the van.

The cops were starting to get bored. I asked for the direction of the nearest ferry but got a frosty reply.

'We want to hear your horn before you go,' said one of the cops.

They went back to their car to do some paperwork and we went under the bonnet to try and get the horn working. One of the wires had broken. Spiney shorted a screwdriver across it and got a sound out of the horn.

The cops drove away. We waved goodbye to them. The horn was left disconnected.

We continued on our journey through the small country lanes, getting lost and arguing which way to go. Eventually, we found a ship that was about to cross the channel.

Culture Shock

On the French side, when we came to disembark from the

ship, the van wouldn't start. Both of us got out and under the bonnet to figure out what the problem was. All the cars had disembarked from the hold. The van would still not start. A few of the crew came over and pushed the van out of the ship's hold. We rolled down the ramp and came to a halt a few yards on French soil. The next few hours were spent trying to figure out what the problem was. By this time it was dark. The engine was completely dead and nothing we could think of would make it start. In the meantime, our ferry had taken on a new cargo and disappeared over the horizon, and another ferry had come and gone. Eventually, at some small hour in the morning, the engine started. Neither of us could work out why the engine started all of a sudden and put it down to some dodgy electrical wiring or a bad earth.

At long last we were off on our adventure into France. Hands and faces covered with oil and dirt, we looked more like a commando raiding party than a couple of plukey kids just escaped from school. The docks were deserted, there were few lights and the whole place had a run down, abandoned feel about it. It was not obvious to figure out which way to go. There were dark corners everywhere with no signs for direction. Each time we took a turning, we ended up facing a fence or looking out over water. There were containers and a few parked trucks in the distance. Spiney drove over and stopped beside a large truck. It looked as if there was somebody inside. I jumped out and banged on the window to ask for some assistance.

'Hay, mister cun yae tell us how tae get oot'a this place.'
A curtain was pulled back in the driver's cabin and an ugly brute with a hammer was shouting his head off in some foreign language. He was one disgruntled punter. Time to make a quick exit back to the van.

'Well whit did he say?'

'A'm no sure...but he wusnae very happy.'

We drove off again into the night trying to find a way out of the docks. Eventually we found what looked like an exit and drove through. Not much later, Spiney noticed two cars in the distance, driving fast in our direction with full beam on.

'A wonder whit their problem is?'

'Dunno, but they're movin' fast.'

Wanting to stay out of trouble and keep a low profile, Spiney nipped in between two parked trucks, turned the lights off and crawled away slowly into the darkness, navigating on instinct and good luck. Two cars went flying past, their headlights disappearing into the distance.

We sneaked away, back the way we came, still without headlights. A few moments later there was a distant screeching of brakes. I leaned out of the window trying to work out what was going on. I could hear the car engines getting louder and again coming in our direction.

'They've turned roond. Get back roond and hide behind that auld building oor there. A'm no wantin' tae deal wae any cops at this time in the mornin'.'

Spiney stopped the van behind the building and turned the engine off. We sat for a couple of minutes until there was nothing to be heard.

'Right, the coast is clear. Let's get oota here.'

Spiney started the engine, turned on the lights and we set off again. Not much later, progress was stopped by another fence.

'Jesis, when will we get oota this place, thur's fences everywhere.'

Within seconds of us stopping, a car drove at us at speed on the other side of the fence. It braked violently, coming to a screeching halt only a few feet from the fence. The full beam of the car blinded us. Spiney put the van in reverse, did a quick manoeuvre to turn around, and drove away in the opposite direction.

'Whit the fuck's goin' on?'

'A don't huv a fuckin' scoobie.'

'These boys ure just arsin' aroond.'

A minute or two later saw us driving alongside another fence. The second car caught up with us, driving on the other side of the fence.

'It's just like the fuckin' Keystone Cops here. Head oor there,' I pointed to a group of trucks parked in the distance.
We drove away from the car on the other side of the fence. It drove away at speed into the distance following the line of the fence. I was hanging out the window trying to work out where the two cars had gone.
We crept in between two parked trucks and then Spiney turned off the engine. Just as the engine was turned off, a car came to a screeching halt straight in front of us. Spiney started the engine and put the car in reverse. A second car pulled up abruptly behind, blocking our retreat.
Large trucks blocked our escape to the left and right. We were trapped. I counted at least three getting out of the front car. Something in French was screamed at us, *'Sortez de la voiture! Vos mains en l'air!* Get out of the car! Get your hands in the air!' There was a second shout.

'Sortez de la voiture! Get out of the car!'

Spiney and I had no idea what was going on. We looked at each other contemplating the next move.
There was another shout in French, *'Allez! Sortez immédiatement! Les mains en l'air.'*

Spiney was getting ready for a fight.

'A'll try and ram the car behind then make a run for it.'

'Get the ice axe oot' in case there's trouble.'

There was an argument about what to do.

'Hold on, they may be cops?'

'There's no cop signs or flashin' lights owan their motors. They're no wearin' any cop uniforms.'

'Let's make a run fur it.'

The French was getting more agitated.

'*Sortez tout de suite de la voiture, bande d'énfoirés!* Get out of the car, arseholes!'

Spiney and I looked at each other.

'Whit the fuck's goin' on?'

I could see what looked like a gun coming out. I had only seen a gun on the telly before.

'*Mais sortez, bordel de merde, sortez!*'

'*Les mains en l'air et plus vite que ça!* Get the fuck out of the car and put your hands in the air!'

The French seemed to be getting more agitated. The three characters in the front car, dressed in black overalls, came running towards us, guns pointing. As soon as we saw the guns, our hands went into the air.

'Fuck, it must be the polis,' said Spiney.

A cop stopped in front of the windscreen and pointed a gun at us. We just looked at him not knowing what to do.

Spiney wound down his window with his right hand; the other was still in the air.

'Aaa... excuse me, A'm tryin' tae find mae way oota here...'

A cop grabbed Spiney by the hair and arm through the open window, another cop opened the door, dragging Spiney out. The door on my side was opened and I was dragged out onto the ground, then up and spread-eagled against the outside of the van. I turned round to see Spiney getting pressed down on the bonnet of the van. As I tried to look round a hand lifted my head back and whacked it against the side of the van and held it there. A second person searched me.

There were some French words shouted at us.

'*Tu joues à quoi!? connard, hein?* What the fuck are you playing at?'

A few seconds later one of the cops took my right hand and twisted it up my back. I could feel the cold steel of a handcuff going on. Then my left hand was taken and snapped into the other handcuff. I was then picked up by the handcuffs and dropped face down at the front of the van together with Spiney. A cop was kneeling on my shoulders making it difficult for me to breathe, pushing my face into a puddle of water. There was a diesel taste in the water.

'*Allez, voir dans la bagnole si ces branleurs nous cachent quelque chose!* Search the van, see if these arseholes have anything!'

Two of the cops got into the van and started poking about inside. A few moments later there was a shout:

'*Hein! Les gars devine ce que j'ai trouvé.* Bingo! We've got some thing here. Take a look at this.'

'*Bon, embarquez-les.* OK Take them away.'

I was picked up by the handcuffs and tossed into the back of one of the cars. Spiney was dragged away to the other.

A cop got into the back of the car either side of me. We drove off. The cop sitting on my left had his arm resting on my shoulder with his elbow against my head, every time the car went over a bump his elbow would hit the side of my face. I looked at him. There was a smirk on his face, as if he was enjoying it. He didn't look much older than me.

The car stopped outside a building. I was dragged out of the car by the handcuffs, and into the building. Spiney was already there, standing handcuffed in front of a desk. Some old grumpy official looking bastard was sitting behind the desk.

'*Qui sont ces connards?* Who are these arseholes?'

'*Ils sont détenus pour passé la douane sans s'arrêter. Et pis ils ont resisté à l'arrestetion. On a trouvé de la drogue dans la bagnole!* Detained for driving through customs without stopping, resisting arrest, dangerous driving and suspected drug smuggling.'

A big black plastic bag was put on the counter.

'*Tenez!* Here's the stuff!'

The grumpy old bastard official behind the counter looked at the plastic bag, then looked up at us and asked for something.

'*Papiers?* Papers.'

Spiney and I looked at each other, shrugged our shoulders not understanding what was going on and not knowing what to say.

'We wur tryin' tae find a way oota this place but we wis gooin' roond and roond und were gettin' nowhere when we wus set upoan.'

The grumpy old bastard official was becoming more grumpy.

'*Vos passeports, bordel!* Your passports fucker's!'

Spiney sussed out what he was going on about.

'A did'nae huv it, it's in the motor, y'ure cloons dragged us oot'a oor motor and kicked oor fuckin' heids in. Look polis brutality,' he pointed to a small bleeding cut on his arm.

The grumpy old bastard official interrupted.

'*Eng-lishe?*'

'Naw, Scottish,' I replied this time.

'*Quoi?*' Came a confused reply from the grumpy old bastard official.

'Bagpipes, kilts, haggis yae know.'

The grumpy old bastard official still looked perplexed.

I thought I had better clear up any confusion.

'Remember we beat Holland 3-2 in the last World Cup. Argentina? The Tartan Army? Cun y'ae no remember the Archie Gemmil goal? Its wus pur dead brilliant—a real stoater. He went roon three Dutch defenders and ploncked the ball in the back.'

The grumpy old bastard official interrupted and spoke to one of the young cops.

'*Mais qu'est-ce qu'ils me racontent, ces cons?!* What the fuck are these nutters going on about?!'
The young cop shrugged his shoulders. The grumpy old bastard official started giving him a hard time.

'*T'es censé parler l'anglais, hien?* You're the smart arse that can speak English?'

'*Mais chef, je comprends rien.* I haven't a clue what there going on about.'

'*On en a fait que six mois au lycée—vous savez.* I only had a six month course at school.'

'*Je crois, qu'il parlait de l'Argentine.* I think he's going on about Argentina.'

'Euh, you are freum Argentine?' One of the young cops asked in broken English.

'Naw ya daft bugger, A'm talkin' aboot fitba' in Argentina! A'm no frum Argentina.'
I then remember about the Écosse sticker on the back of the van.

'A'm frum akoss.'
The cop shrugged his shoulders again.

'A-um-frum-A-koss,' I tried again.
There was a look of desperation on the official's face.

'*Fouillez-les!* Search them and lock them up!'
We were briskly searched. A few coins were taken from our pockets and put on the table. A piece of paper and a pen were put in front of our faces.

'*Signez.* Sign this.'

'A'm no signin'nuthin,' Spiney replied.
This caused a bit of a debate.

'*Allez, emmenez-les. Et qu'on trouve quelqu'un demain qui parle l'anglais. Analysez-moi ça au labo!* Just put them in the cell, get someone that can speak English here by tomorrow, and get this stuff tested!'

Spiney and I were lead down a corridor with reinforced doors on either side. I was trying to explain to the cop.
    'A um frum Akoss. A um frum Akoss. A um...'
A cell door was opened. Spiney and I were led inside, uncuffed, the door slammed shut and locked behind us. The two of us sat there wondering what was going on. We dossed the night in a wire-framed bed. It was the best doss we had had for days.

Freedom in France

We were released in the morning when the French police realised that their massive haul of cocaine was in fact a few pounds of flour. I was given a big black plastic bag containing a selection of ripped plastic bags mixed up with flour, porridge oats and dried milk powder the police had taken from the van. The two of us were escorted to the door. The van was outside. It must have been towed from where we were stopped last night. Lucy was fine on top. In the daylight it was a bit more obvious what we had done – we had driven straight through the French customs without stopping and they weren't very happy about it.
A student interpreter, working for the cops was standing looking at the van and asked in pretty good English, 'Where do yoz go now?'
    'We're the BCT owan tour.'
    'What iz ze doll?'
    'It's no a doll. It's Lucy; she's oor lead singer.'
He did not understand me and shrugged his shoulders. I shrugged my shoulders and said, 'Bye...see yae when we get arrested owan oor way hame.'

We set off, a bit bruised, but otherwise none the worse for our ordeal. I had a feeling that we had not seen the last of the French police. The drive through Calais was traumatic. It was a busy morning and Spiney was looking nervous driving on the wrong side of the road. All was going well until we came to the first roundabout. Spiney went round the roundabout the wrong way. He realised that something had gone wrong when three lanes of cars were all heading towards us and they didn't look like they were going to stop. He pulled sharp on the hand brake to do a hand brake turn, but then there was a look of anxiety in Spiney's face when he remembered that the van didn't have a hand brake. In panic mode he put the steering wheel into full lock and tried to get the van round. The van turned round onto the pavement and hit a table and a couple of chairs in some roadside café. A couple of the café's clientele got a bit of a fright drinking their morning café when they saw a van heading straight towards them and had to jump out of the way.

'Ah sorry there. Shite! Let's get oota here before the polis get ontae us again.'

'Yur dam right.'

We drove off, heading back down to where we had just come from.

'How the hell dae wae get oota this town?'

We seemed to drive round the town in circles looking for signs for the N43 to St. Omer or any road that headed south or east. Eventually, we found a way out of town and managed to put some miles on the clock, driving along small French roads. The plan was to drive on small roads (avoiding paying for the motorways), across northern France (avoiding Paris to the north) then south east towards Geneva and the Alps. We had enough snack food to keep us going for a couple of days. Both of us were nervous of stopping to ask anybody anything and having to cope with dealing with the locals in French.

Pierre

We tried to be as inconspicuous as possible driving across France, but the mini van always seemed to attract attention everywhere we went. For example, driving through a small town, the local punters would drive up on their Mobilette-lawnmower, moped-bike things, tooting horns and trying to hold on to the van for a free ride. Sometimes old, beaten up Citröens would follow, tooting their horns and waving at us. We could never understand what the attraction was. I thought it might be Lucy on top and put a plastic bag over her head with two holes for her eyes, but that made no difference. I thought it might be the "BCT on Tour" writing on the back and tried to rub in some mud, but that made no difference either.

On one occasion we got a bit more attention than we bargained for. We were driving at night, along a quiet country road, somewhere north of Dijon, heading towards Geneva. There were few cars on the road.
 'Sum punter's drivin' up ma arse and turned his headlights oaf.' Spiney commented.
I looked over the back to see what Spiney was talking about. There was too much rubbish in the back of the van to see, so I wound the window down and stuck my head out. I could make out a silvery white Peugeot. The Peugeot was very close to our tail.
 'Whit the fuck's his game?'
 'Ouch, its just a blind frog that cunnae drive.'
The Peugeot drove with us for some time only inches from our tail. By this time Spiney was getting more and more aggravat-

ed. He touched his brakes a couple of times to try and get him to back off a bit further. A few seconds later, the punter in the Peugeot turned on his headlights full beam, illuminating the whole inside of the van.

'Shite! It must be the polis again…better slow down in case we get dun oor again.'

Spiney indicated to pull in and slowed down almost to a halt. The Peugeot drew parallel to us and the French punter made some sort of gesture that I had never seen before but presumed was some kind of French obscenity. I felt an obscene reply was in order and gave two fingers back.

'Ah, A don't think it's the polis this time,' I mentioned to Spiney.

'It's just a local frog arsin' around.'

Spiney pulled away from the edge, cursing and swearing, and started to drive off. The Peugeot slowed down in front of us. The driver kept stamping on his brakes to slow us down, bringing us almost to a halt.

Spiney tried to overtake, but as soon as the van started to accelerate the Peugeot would match the van inch for inch. The two cars moved very close to each other almost touching. Soon we were racing down the road, side by side, at maximum speed towards a bridge and a narrowing of the road. There was a grinding metallic sound as the two cars hit. The back of the Peugeot scraped along the front wing of the mini.

Spiney braked as hard as he could. The van skidded and went side on, then Spiney just managed to regain control; otherwise we would have hit the bridge. The van came to a shuddering halt in the middle of the road, in the opposite direction to the one we were travelling. There was a strong smell of burning rubber.

'Fuckin' bastard!' Spiney shouted out at the top of his voice.

'He's trying tae kill us!'
The Peugeot's tail lights disappeared into the night. Both of us hoped that was the last of the Peugeot.

Not much further down the road we caught up with a car moving very slowly. It was the Peugeot again!

'Shite! It's that fuckin' frog Pierre again, he's back fur mare! Get the ice axe oot'a the back, don't let fuckin' frog Pierre get close again.'

I leaned over the back and rummaged about to find an iceaxe. Spiney drew up behind the Peugeot and put his full beam on. The punter started to brake hard, forcing Spiney to break hard. Then the punter pulled away and braked hard again, forcing Spiney to break hard again. This happened several times. Each time a collision was just avoided. Spiney tried to overtake, but the Peugeot moved over to stop us. Spiney moved to the inside and again the Peugeot moved over to block our progress.

'If that bastard tries tae force us oaf the road again, get that ice axe oota the windae und re-arrange sum o his paint work.'

There was a tree standing by itself at the side of the road some distance away. The Peugeot started to move over and push us off the road.

'Fuckin' hell! This frog is deadly serious!'

I wound down the window and stuck the end of the iceaxe out. The Peugeot came close and hit the iceaxe spike. There was a horrible, grinding, metal-to-metal sound for a second or two. Sparks were flying off the end of the iceaxe. A large gash appeared in the Peugeot's side panelling.

Instead of getting him to back off, this seemed to raise the stakes. The punter pulled in behind the back of the van, turned on his full beam, then rammed the back of the van. The force of the impact pushed both of us forward onto the seatbelts. A few bits and pieces fell off the inside of the van. He rammed the back of the van again.

'Ure yae finished wae y'ure Iron Bru?' Spiney asked.

'Next time that frog comes along side, chuck that ginger boatle oot at his tyre'.

The Peugeot started to overtake again.

'Right he's cumin' along side again; get that fuckin' ginger boatle ready.'

I looked in the wing mirror. The Peugeot came alongside and started to drive close to the van. When the front grill of the Peugeot filled the mirror, I threw the bottle onto the road under the driver's wheel. The punter lost control of the Peugeot, hit the backside panelling of the van, then swerved away off the road. I stuck my head out of the window and could see he was having a bumpy ride over a ploughed field. The Peugeot came to a stop some distance from the road.

'Thank fuck for that! Jesis, A hope wae dinnae met any mare frogs like that... A dinnae know whit his game wus, but he wus trying tae take us oota the game.'

'A think that Pierre, hus been watchin' too many cowboy films.'

We turned off at the next junction and drove on for a few more miles, then stopped to inspect the damage.

Lucy was fine. There were a few bashes to the side of the van, the exhaust pipe was lying at a strange angle and the back door was difficult to open and close. One of the tail lights was all cracked and the other was knackered, but it looked repairable.

We drove on for another few miles, far enough to feel safe in case Pierre got back on the road again and was looking for us. We pulled up in a little wood and decided to doss the night in the van.

The fence and telegraph pole

We had a brew-up in the morning and started driving again. Progress was slow, driving along small country roads, occasionally getting lost and trying to figure out the best way to go. Spiney had been driving for almost two and a half days and wanted a break, so we changed places and I had my first driving lesson in the van. Everything was going fine and I started to feel reasonably confident behind the wheel.

I was driving along a small country road, straight as far as the eye could see. Suddenly, there was a bang and smoke started pouring out of the bonnet. The van lost power and slowly came to a halt. It looked serious.
The bonnet was opened, steam rising everywhere. We waited a few minutes for the steam to clear to have a closer inspection. The engine had sheared one of its four supporting bolts and had fallen forwards onto the radiator, cutting one of the radiator hose pipes. It looked bad. We tried to figure out how to repair the damage. The sheared bolt looked difficult to repair since the thread had been stripped on the chassis. Drastic action was necessary, an improvised solution had to be found. We had a brew at the side of the road and tried to come up with some ideas. There was nothing in the toolbox that could do the job. The nearest town was some distance away. The two of us sat in the morning sun wondering what we could do. The first thoughts of failure started to creep into my head. It looked like the end of the trip.
Out of the blue, Spiney suddenly sat up.
'A know. A piece o wood. We need a piece o wood.'
'A piece o wood...whit the fuck ure yae goin owan aboot? A piece o wood?'
'A piece o wood und we cun suspend the engine.'

Supporting the engine from a piece of wood seemed totally impractical, but it was the only thing we had to go on. The problem was how to make it work.

We had a wander through a nearby woods to look for a suitable piece of wood to use as a support for the engine. We came across a small fenced field in a clearing. There were a couple of horses in the field.

'Magic!' said Spiney, looking at the fence.

'Just whit we want.'

I just looked at Spiney wondering what he was going on about.

'Yeah? OK?'

One of the fence posts was removed and we cut about 10 yards of wire from the fence.

Back at the car, the fence post was cut into shape to fit under the bonnet. I bashed a couple of support grooves in the front inside wing with a hammer to take the fence post and deformed the bonnet so it would shut with the fence post underneath. This gave the van a designer-styled mean look to the bonnet. I punctured a hole through the front of the bonnet and tied it down to the front grill to keep the bonnet from flying open when driving.

I was bashing away at the bodywork with the hammer.

'Right A'm oaf tae get sum mare stuff tae set up the block und tackle,' Spiney announced.

He had a saw underneath his arm and I presumed he was off to saw down some trees. He reappeared sometime later with a long length of pole.

'Geeus a hon tae get the other bits A left. It took mae hoors tae saw up the bits.'

The two of us set off to collect the other bits. We walked through the woods. As the woods cleared into open farmland, I couldn't believe what I saw. In the distance, there was a line of telegraph poles going into the horizon, but one was missing. The telephone cable in the missing section almost sagged to ground level, weighed down by the top section of the pole. Spiney had climbed up the telegraph pole, sawn through the pole about one foot below the cable and then sawn the pole at its base. He then sawed the pole into three bits. We came back to the van, set up a tripod with the lengths of telegraph pole and attached a small block-and-tackle to lift the engine. The fence wire was then wound around the engine and supported by the fence post. A dozen or so lengths of wire were wrapped around the engine until it was as solid as a rock. The radiator hose was then repaired.

The breakdown took almost a full day to fix. The van was running fine again. The only difference was the slightly raised bonnet.

That night we camped by the van, pleased at the repair. The dream of getting to Chamonix was alive again.

Chamonix at last

It was another full day's drive to get to the Chamonix valley. We drove into the valley in late afternoon. It had been raining and there were still storm clouds in the air. It felt much colder compared to the stifling heat of the plains of northern France. Occasionally a rock pinnacle or glacier would appear through the clouds. I looked out of the window in awe, straining my neck skywards, wondering what else was hidden behind the clouds. The mountains looked formidable, imposing and frighteningly high; much bigger than anything we had seen before. It was now evening, as we drove into the centre of town and headed for the Bar National, commonly known as the Bar Nash, the famous climbing café. Glasses of cheap wine were downed in quick succession in celebration of reaching our goal. We had made it.

The wine went straight to our heads. We staggered out of the Bar Nash and back to the van and fell asleep on the seats at once. Sometime during the night, the two of us woke up almost in unison, threw up the wine we had just drunk, and then fell asleep again.

≈

This was our first day in Chamonix. The morning was beautiful: a clear sky, and a very fresh feel to the air. The white summits of the Aiguilles towered above the town. We spent the day getting our bearings, finding the campsite and buying some food. We camped at the Bioley, a bit of rough land just north of the train station. This would be our base for the coming weeks, and it was free.

It rained almost all the next day and there wasn't much to do except wander around the climbing shops and read climbing books. That night there was an almighty storm: thunder rolling down the valley, lighting flashes zapping across the night, torrential rain poured out of the dark sky. The thunder kept me awake. I lay in my sleeping bag watching the night sky light up, listening to the rain hammering down on the tent, and thinking that I didn't want to be stuck on a mountain in this weather.

The storm had passed by morning, but it was still raining. We were impatient to get into the mountains and so decided to head into the hills for a walk regardless of the weather.

We hiked up through steep woods to Montenvers, and along a flat strip of moraine at the foot of the Chamonix Aiguilles. The clouds were down and it was cold and wet. There was nothing to be seen. I tried to imagine where the mountains should be. The night was spent under a boulder near the Plan du Aiguille

télépherique station.
In the morning all was clear and we looked out in amazement at the mountains. It was the first time we had been so close to such large mountains. We sat in the morning sun, watching avalanches coming down the huge face of Aiguille du Midi, thousands of feet high. Aiguille du Peigne was straight in front, its summit looked impossibly narrow. The sheer scale of the mountains was overwhelming.
The clear sky held only for a few hours and by afternoon the mountains had disappeared behind a shroud of mist and rain. We gave up for the day and decided to head back down to the valley.

Communication

The weather remained unstable for some time and our frustration was growing day by day. We spent long days in the tent, watching the rain come down and eating too much food for our budget. Out of boredom and the realisation that the money was running low, I plucked up enough courage and decided to try and organise a gig for the band.

I had been practising my French with the help of a little pocket phrase book and had memorised a few sentences. I went into a music shop in town to try and communicate with a local behind the desk.

'*Ah, bonjour* pal, es-s-k voo parly an-dg-laz?' I started off confidently.
There was a look of incredulity on the punter's face.
I thought I should try some more of my French.
'*Je suisis* a punk band frum Scotland, sorry A mean A-koss. Avey voo gig fur band?'
The punter just stood there wondering what to say.

I tried something different.

'Play music fur punk band?' and went through the motions of playing a guitar.

The punter just looked at me as if I was a complete idiot, and said a few words.

'*Je n'ai aucune idée de quoi vous parlez!* I've got no idea what you are going on about!'

I had no idea what he was talking about.

The punter shrugged his shoulders and waved his hands around a bit. I realised I was getting nowhere, turned around and walked straight out of the shop.

I tried another couple of music shops in town and got a similar blank response. They had no idea what I was going on about and they couldn't care less. Communicating with the locals was going to be a lot more difficult than I imagined.

It had been a long frustrating day and I was getting nowhere. I found a cheap café, sat down, and tried my French again to order a cup of coffee. It was the only thing I was confident that I could order since there was a sentence written in my phrase book.

'Hay Jim. Avez-voos un tass dae caffay?'

The waiter just looked at me.

'Gee-us un tass dae caffay, see voos playet.' I tried again.

The waiter just looked at me.

'A... *Bonjor*. Caffay. Pronto?' I tried again.

I gave up after a few feeble attempts and instead just pointed to the phrase book. My coffee arrived.

I got my French phrase book out again and set about writing a few sentences to try and explain that I wanted to set up a gig for the band. However, my attempts at written French were probably totally incomprehensible to the average French person. After several cups of coffee and much deep thought about France and the French language, nature called, and I headed into the back of the café to look for a toilet.

I spied the toilets in the bottom right hand corner of the café. On the way, I caught the eye of a girl sitting by herself. She was reading a book, but glanced up as I walked towards her. I walked briskly past trying to look cool and casual.

Suddenly, 'Thud!' as I walked straight into a mirrored wall; the café was half the size I had imagined. I bounced back off the mirror with a bloody nose and into the path of a waiter coming out from behind the bar with a full tray of coffee and beer. He stumbled trying to avoid me; just about regained control, then lost it completely as his tray of beer and coffee went flying over a couple of nearby customers. They got soaked. The waiter went right through their table, chairs flying in all directions. Glasses and cups crashed to the ground. All the conversation in the café suddenly stopped and everybody in the café turned to look at what happened. A group of student types started to cheer. I was sitting on the ground with my hand over my nose trying to stop the blood.

The waiter apologised profusely to the people he had just drenched, then came over and started shouting at me.

'*Mais, qu'est-ce que vous faîtes???!!! Vous allez me payez les dégats?!* What the hell do you think you were doing? You're going to pay for the damage?'

I tried the little French 'puut', shrugged my shoulders and replied.

'Sorry pal, no ma fault. It's a daft place tae put a mirror.'

The waiter didn't seem to like this and started to manhandle me out of the café. The girl came over to help and started to take my side in the argument.

'*Mais, ce n'est pas de sa faute! C'est votre stupide mirroir.*

J'ai presque fait la même chose! It's not his fault, it's your stupid mirror. I almost did the same.'
The girl and waiter started to argue with each other. I stood there holding my nose, blood dribbling through my fingers and onto my T-shirt.

'*Taisez-vous donc, petite sotte! Mêlez-vous de vos stupides affaires?* Shut up you stupid cow! It's got nothing to do with you.'

'*Comment ôsez-vous me parler ainsi!* Don't call me stupid!'
I understood the word stupid from their conversation or at least I thought I understood the word stupid. The argument was getting more heated. There was lots of gesticulation and hand waving. Eventually we both got thrown out, much to the amusement of the crowd of students.

The girl and I ended up outside on the pavement. I said thanks for helping. She could speak reasonably good English and we ended up talking. She was in Chamonix on a walking holiday with her parents, but couldn't do anything because of the rain. I mentioned that I was in Chamonix to climb the mountains, but couldn't do anything either because of the weather and was trying to organise a gig for the band. I asked her to help. She agreed to help, but had to go soon, and arranged to meet at a café opposite, at the same time the following day.

≈

Tomorrow couldn't come quick enough. I hadn't washed for some time so an ice cold dip in a nearby stream that ran off the glacier was in order. I put on my best T-shirt and headed into town.

I met Sophie at the café as planned. I was a bit surprised that she had turned up. She was sitting reading a book as she did the previous day in the café opposite.

Soon we were chatting about the weather, what she did, etc. We had something to drink, but neither of us had enough money for something to eat. Sophie suggested that she could cook something in her holiday chalet.

We went back to the chalet. The place was locked up. She explained that her parents were out for a special meal and weren't expected back for some time. Sophie cooked something to eat. I watched.

The evening went on. One thing led to another and the next thing we were in bed.

'Ure yae sure yur parents will no cum hame?' I kept asking

'*Oui, oui*, no problem, no problem.'

She kept reassuring me that they would not be back for some time since it was their last day in Chamonix. However, just in case they made an early appearance I put a chair across the front door.

Not much later, there was at lot of banging and shouting at the door. Of course, with my luck her parents did come back home early.

Shite, it could only happen to me—time to make a quick exit.

The only obvious option was out through the window and onto the balcony. Out I went. Sophie drew the curtains behind me. I stood naked on a tiny balcony, three floors up, wondering what to do next.

Seconds later, a bundle of clothes was thrown out of the window, quickly followed by my shoes, then the window shutters closed abruptly. Very thoughtful, but Sophie had thrown my clothes over the balcony and they had landed on the outermost branches of a tree. I could hear my shoes landing on the

ground. A heated argument was starting inside.
The only way to the ground was down a plastic drainpipe. Plastic drainpipes are bad news, never as solid as the old ones. Not only that, but I would have to traverse across an adjacent apartment to get to the drainpipe. I moved across in a bridging move to get to the next balcony. Lights were on in the apartment. I looked in through the window. A couple was watching TV. Another bridging move took me to the end of the building and the plastic drainpipe. My imagination was running wild as I remembered the climbing escapade on the building after Bish's birthday party. I was half expecting the police and fire brigade to arrive at any minute and could see my picture on the front page of the local newspaper with headlines reading something like 'Scottish jewel thief caught exposed without kilt.'
I climbed over to the drainpipe. It was wobbly. I took a chance that it would hold my weight. It did. I climbed down.
On the ground, I searched around for my shoes, but could only find one. The tree was difficult to climb and I tried to throw stones up to get my clothes. Nothing came down.
Eventually I gave up and decided to head back home with nothing but one shoe. I found a cardboard box left outside a nearby shop. I wrapped it around my waist and headed back to the tent.

I got back to the tent and woke Spiney up in the process of trying to get in. I was greeted with tears of laughter.
    'Oh ma Goad! Whit the fuck huv yae been up tae? Ha! Ha! Ha! Did that bird nick yur clathes?! Ha! Ha! Ha! Oh Jesis A huvnae laught as much as this in ages. Ha! Ha! Ha! At least yu'll dae us Scots proud no wearin' anythin' under yur cardboard box! 'Ha! Ha! Ha!'
    'Yeh, yeh very funny.'

'Ha! Ha! Ha!'

'Noo shut yur goab and let mae in, A'm freezin' oot here.'

'Well A hope yae hu've goat yur translation dun,' he calmed down and asked.

'Naw.'

'That wusnae very smart wus it?'

'But A huv her number.'

'She's goat yur clathes und yae huv her number. That's no bad fur a nights work.'

≈

The next day I went back to find my clothes and also to find Sophie. I found neither. Somebody had removed my clothes from the tree and nobody answered the door of her apartment. She must have left very early in the morning.

It was back to square one, sitting in a café with the phrase book, trying to work out what to say on the telephone in case Sophie didn't answer the phone.

Evening came, I had Sophie's telephone number so I thought I would call her up. I had memorised one French phrase and I had it ready in case somebody else answered the phone.

I dialled the number, somebody answered, it wasn't Sophie.

'Ah, *peu ju paerlez avek Sophie?*'

I got a reply I didn't understand.

'*Désolé. Vous avez le mauvais numéro.* Sorry you have the wrong number.'

I thought I would try again.

'*Peu ju paelez avek Sophie?*'

I got a similar reply.

'*Mais, je vous ai dit que vous avez le mauvais numéro!*'

Again I had no idea what the person was saying. Maybe I dialled the wrong number? I put the receiver down and tried again.

'*Peu ju paelez avek Sophie?*'
The lady was starting to get more aggressive.
'*Désolé vous avez le mauvais numero!*'
I put the phone down and went away.

The next day I was back at the telephone box and went through the same routine again. I tried again at night, still no Sophie. And again the following day.
'*Peu ju parlez avec Sophie?*'
This time it was a man's voice.
'*Elle n'est pas ici. Foutez-moi la paix!* She's not here, so fuck off!'
He had a hostile voice. Sophie had said she didn't like her father. I put the phone down and tried about an hour later.
'*Peu ju parlez avec Sophie?*'
It was the same voice again.
'*Allez vous faire foutre!* Fuck off!'
I put the phone down and tried again a bit later. This time, I only managed three words of my phrase.
'*Peu ju parlez av...?*' before he started shouting down the phone.
'*Allez vous faire foutre! Allez vous faire foutre! Allez vous faire foutre!!!* Fuck off! Fuck off! Fuck off!!!'
I put the phone down and went away confused.

There was a *beau temps* forecast for the following day, so we decided to head into the hills.
I tried Sophie once more. I could only manage two words this time.
'*Peu ju...*' before I was interrupted.
'*Allez vous faire foutre!!!* Fuck off!!!' He yelled at me down

the phone.
I put the phone down wondering what the problem was. I thought her father was being a bastard, not letting her answer the telephone after the incident the other day.

≈ *Stephen Najda* ≈

Aiguille du Plan - Up the North face and down the West face

The next day the forecast looked good and we set off on our first Alpine climb. It was raining as we left the van at the campsite. The rain became heavier and heavier as we walked up the steep wooded valley to the Plan de l'Aiguille. We arrived at the boulder doss where we had stayed a few days before and settled down as best we could for the night.

≈

It was a fantastic morning, clear blue sky without a breath of wind. The Aiguille du Midi rose a thousand metres straight in front of us. The Aiguille du Piegne to the left looked as impossibly steep as a church spire. All morning was spent looking at the mountains, the arêtes, couloirs and spurs, trying to figure out where all the routes go. The mountains were plastered with a lot of fresh snow. Occasionally our conversation was interrupted by the thunderous sound of an avalanche coming down the Aiguille du Midi. The size and power of the avalanches were overwhelming.

There was a tent nearby our boulder with a couple of English climbers in it. We spent the rest of the day drinking tea and chatting with them finding out, what they had done and what they were planning. The mountain was left for the day to let the snow settle.

Spiney and I had two routes in mind: either the Frendo spur on the north face of Aiguille du Midi or the north face of the Aiguille du Plan. After watching avalanches coming down the north face of the Midi all day, we reckoned that the north face of the Plan would be a safer option, even though we had never had seen the north face.

The guide book described the route as consisting of a rock arête for about 400 metres, then followed by a 400 metres icefield to the summit at just under 3700 metres. The plan was to climb the rock spur the following day, bivouac underneath the ice field, get up at first light and climb the ice to the top of the Aiguille. We would then descend south down the Envers du Plan Glacier, return to Montenvers by the Mer du Glace and back to our boulder doss for the evening.

≈

Next morning, we had something to eat and started to get organised for the climb. Our rucksacks were heavy and too full to climb with, so we decided to sacrifice a lot of stuff, including our sleeping bags, to save weight and bulk. Only one bivouac was planned and we reckoned we could put up with a couple of cold hours. The sleeping bags weren't very warm anyway.

We set off, late as usual, from our boulder with all the time in the world. The two of us wandered up towards the towering Aiguille du Peigne, traversed over a small glacier and scrambled over moraine rubble. The closer we got to the Aiguille du Plan, the bigger the mountains became. As we moved around the base of Aiguille du Peigne, the arête on the north face of the Plan came into view. The arête was to be our first objective. As we traversed further an enormous hanging serac came into view. The huge serac was squeezed in between the top of the rock spur on the left and the Aiguille du Pèlerins on the right.

'Fuckin'hell, just look at that serac; it's huge!'

'Let's get a move on pronto in case that thing cums doon.' Just looking at the serac made me feel nervous. We had several discussions about whether the serac could take us out from where we were standing.

We quickly traversed further around into the Blaitière Glacier and to the base of the rock spur. Aiguille du Blaitière was at our back; strong sunshine warmed the enormous granite slabs of the west face. It looked more appealing than the cold, dark spur that was our objective. The route started up a system of broken chimneys rising steeply to the top of the rock spur.

We jumped over the *bergschrund* from the glacier and onto rock. I set-up a belay and Spiney started off up the chimney system. This was our first rock climbing on Chamonix granite. The climbing was relatively straightforward. A single rope was used for climbing easier rock, but we had a second rope for the more technical sections and for abseiling. We moved up the chimney, interchanging leads. However, progress was slow, so we decided to lead several pitches at a time before changing.

The rock was becoming steeper the higher up we got. We were making good progress and the crest of the ridge was getting nearer. I stopped and set up a belay beneath a steep chimney. It only looked like one or two pitches to the top of the ridge. Spiney came quickly up to the belay ledge, took my climbing gear, and then took off up the chimney above. I stood on a small belay ledge looking out at the last of the sun on the West face of the Blaitière, trying to figure out the line of the Brown-Patey route.

I noticed that the rope had stopped moving through my hands for sometime. There had been no shout of "climb" from above. May be Spiney had come across a difficult section? I strained to look up, trying to see if there was a problem above. To my horror I could see the rope had snagged around a large loose flake of rock at the top of the chimney about 50 to 60 feet directly above my head. The large flake of rock was moving at each tug of the rope from above.

A shiver of fear went down my spine. The piece of rock looked big and its flight path was straight down the chimney and onto the belay ledge I was standing on.

'Stop pulling the rope!!!' I shouted at the top of my voice.

'Stop pulling the rope!!!' I strained my voice louder.

Before I could manage a third shout I could see the large flake detach itself. Suddenly the rope started to move through my hands. Fuck! I'm dead.

There was nowhere to hide. It was one of these occasions, when you can see the end coming and there is nothing you can do about it. I was standing fixed to the rock on a small ledge barely big enough for two people, a couple of hundred feet up the mountain. I could only move a fraction to my right and there's a rock the size of a television set coming down on my head. It's a sense of helplessness. There is nothing you can do except feel as small as possible. I pushed my face as close to the rock as I could. I braced to feel pain. The adrenaline raced. There was a sensation of something big passing very close to my left shoulder. Followed by an almighty bang, which left ringing in my ears. There was a kind of a cordite smell of rock against rock in the air. Some light debris hit my helmet. A second or two later, there was a sound of bouncing rock on the cliff below. I moved only when the sound had stopped. There was no sensation of pain. I quickly checked myself over, to convince myself that the rock had missed me. There was an exhilarating sense of being alive. I slumped down to catch my breath for a few moments. I looked down where the rock had hit the ledge only inches from my left foot. There had been a few coils of rope lying on the belay ledge, but now the rope had been sliced to pieces.

It took me a few moments to calm down.

Spiney's head appeared over the edge, looking down the chimney system. He had pulled up a frayed end of the rope with nobody on the end of it. He was looking anxious, expecting to see strawberry jam all the way down the mountain.

Spiney sent down the frayed end of the rope. I tied on and climbed up the chimney to the belay. The belay was on the crest of the spur.

The day had almost disappeared. We were on the crest of the ridge, but still had a long way to go along the spur to get to the ice field. It was going to take us a lot longer than expected to reach the end of the spur. The sun was setting. It was time to bivouac, have a brew and discuss whether to continue or descend with our cut rope.

In the end, we decided to continue climbing with the second rope. It was a fantastic evening sitting on the bivouac ledge watching the sun go down on Aiguille Blaitière. It was starting to get cold. We wrapped up in all our clothes and put our feet into rucksacks for a bit of extra warmth. I heard Spiney snoring and soon I was asleep.

≈

Morning arrived with a shock. A French alpinist climbed over our bivouac, and said, '*Bonjour*,' and quickly moved on. His rope went over us as we lay in our bivouac.

A second French alpinist soon appeared and greeted us with the second, '*Bonjour*,' of the morning and then moved on.

'Shite, let's get goin',' I said, shaking Spiney, trying to encourage some kind of movement.

'Let's get up the hill before the frogs.'

≈ Rock Rock ≈

The two French climbers gave us a real incentive to get moving. There was a sense of urgency. Breakfast was neglected. We packed up as quickly as possible and chased after the two in front. After a couple of pitches it became obvious that there was no way we could keep up with the other two.

Distances are deceptive in the big mountains and after a couple of hours of climbing the end of the spur still seemed a long way away. The serac on the right of the rock spur looked more and more ominous.

By early afternoon we had reached the end of the rock spur and the beginning of the ice. It had taken us about five or six hours of climbing to reach this spot; a lot longer than we had anticipated. There was no sign of the two French, presumably they had continued on up.

Above us lay the ice field. The ice snaked down from the summit of the mountain until it was forced between the rock spur we had just climbed and the Aiguille des Deux Aigles on the right. The ice field above was a total mess of seracs: huge broken ice walls twisted and torn, strange sculptured ice blocks pushed into the air, fissures criss-crossing the ice in all directions. It was like a mountainous sea, frozen in time, cascading down the side of the mountain and coming to an abrupt end with a huge overhanging serac.

Spiney was game to carry on up the ice field, but it was mid-afternoon, and it was warm. I wanted to wait until dawn and climb the ice field above on more stable snow. We had spent the day before watching avalanches coming down the north face of the Midi in the heat of the afternoon sun. Avalanches made me feel nervous. I didn't want to be on the ice field with avalanches coming down.

We had a discussion about what to do, eventually, deciding to bivouac the night at the end of the spur and wait for first light before crossing onto the large overhanging serac. There was

a good bivouac ledge at the end of the rock spur, facing the giant serac, just enough room for two bums and a stove, legs dangling over the edge into eternity. There was a snow patch nearby—perfect for making a brew.
The bivouac was almost at the same height and very close to the huge overhanging serac, but just to the side. We were almost close enough to throw stones at it, but reckoned that if the serac came down it would pass just below the bivouac.

The last few hours of the afternoon were spent making brews and eating the last of our food. We sat on the ledge, feet dangling over the edge, facing the Aiguille du Peigne. There was a lot of air beneath our feet. We dropped a couple of small stones off the edge and counted. One... Two... Three... Four... Five... Six... Seven... Eight seconds before the rock would hit the bottom, and we tried to estimate how far it was to the bottom.
Opposite, the dark, gloomy, ice streaked faces of the Aiguille du Peigne, Aiguille des Pèlerins and the Aiguille des Deux Aigles rose like twisted Gothic spires.

The sun was starting to set over the Aiguille Rouge on the other side of the Chamonix Valley. The last few sunbeams spread a deep red over the horizon, then the colour faded into violet and the enormity of space was apparent overhead. The last golden beams of light illuminated the tops of the twisted spires opposite. A few glitters of streetlight were starting to appear in the valley below. There was comfort in the air, an almost religious feeling of being at one with the mountain.

Bang!!! Suddenly and without warning, there was a very loud and penetrating gunshot sound that shattered the tranquillity. We looked at each other in fear, confusion, and apprehen-

sion. There was a slight movement in the huge serac in front of us, then as if in slow motion the whole serac seemed to slide towards us. It is one of those moments that make you feel very insignificant, very vulnerable. Thousands of tons of ice coming your way and not very much you can do about it. We held on, anticipating the worst. The slow motion became faster as the whole edge of the serac started to peel off. The serac appeared to fall towards us; then slid down into the abyss. There was a feeling of something very big, passing very quickly and very close. Then, there was a gust of wind, a few seconds of silence and an almighty crash as the ice hit the bottom. The rock we were on seemed to shudder under the weight of the crashing serac. Spiney and I did not say anything at first, knowing how close we had come to disaster. We had reckoned that if the serac came down it would miss us: our theory was proved right, but we could not have been closer.
The two of us started laughing as if nothing had happened.

The sun had now set and the horizon was deep blue. Darkness fell all around. Overhead, the stars were brilliant, more numerous than I had ever thought possible. The mountains in front turned grey slowly, then changed into black shadows, becoming part of the night.
Chamonix was glittering down below. The street lights made the town appear close. I thought about the people running about in the town below, leading ordinary lives and questioned myself about where I would rather be. It was a bright starlit night with almost no moon; the only sounds were the occasional creaks and groans of the serac. Looking from our vantage point into humanity down below, one could imagine a little of the emotion of the first man in space looking down on planet earth.

We woke at first light. Our sleep had not been interrupted with other bits of serac falling down overnight. The sharpness of the morning frost made us get quickly organised. There was nothing for breakfast. All the food had been eaten the previous evening, and the gas for our stove was also finished; but there were no thoughts of turning back.

We were very aware of our exposed position and after yesterday's serac fall were anxious to get past the big overhanging serac as quickly as possible in case anymore of it came down. Spiney climbed to the end of the rock spur in one rope length from our bivouac ledge. The rock spur became narrower and narrower until it was not much more than a foot wide. Spiney set up a belay at the end of the rock spur, straddled in a very precarious and exposed position, one leg down the Dent du Crocodile side, the other down the Aiguille des Deux Aigles side and facing the overhanging serac. I went along the spur to Spiney balancing like a tightrope walker. The pitch onto the overhanging serac was going to be my lead. I didn't spend much time worrying about the huge drops on either side. I was more concerned about climbing the serac in front. A large wall of ice blocked direct access to the icefield above. It looked loose, difficult and very exposed. The easiest way onto the icefield was a traverse onto the very edge of the overhanging serac. I moved around Spiney at the belay and carried on to the very end of the rock spur, balanced on the crest, put on my crampons and got my ice axes out.

I leaned out to the right and whacked in both ice axes and kicked in the front points of my crampons into brittle ice. Chunks of ice came flying off at each swing and each kick. I had to make several attempts before each placement felt reasonably secure, since I had no confidence in the ice.

I moved as quickly as I dared. The serac was creaking and

groaning. Every little noise filled me with apprehension. The serac fall the previous night was still very vivid in my mind. The first few steps from rock onto ice were the worst since I had had to move from the relative safety of rock onto the lip of the overhanging serac. The exposure felt mind-blowing, coupled with the fact I was climbing on very fragile, brittle ice that could break off at any second. I knew that if I fell off the traverse I would swing back and hit the rock spur with little hope of getting back up.

There was a sharp bang from inside the serac. I stopped instantly, inert with fear, imagining that a whole sheet of ice was about to break off with me on it. It didn't. I continued climbing.

Once over the initial difficult moves I moved as far up the icefield as I could, put in a "deadman" snow anchor for a belay, and brought Spiney over. He was looking anxious.

We didn't need to say anything. Both of us just wanted to get as far from the serac as possible.

The bottom part of the icefield started at a reasonable angle, but got steeper and steeper further up the mountain. The icefield was broken into a multitude of crevasses and seracs. There was another enormous serac towards the top. From below it looked formidable and the overhanging ice barrier appeared to go across the whole face. It was something to worry about.

We made good progress crossing crevasses and winding through the lower seracs. After some time, we arrived beneath the large serac that blocked further progress up the mountain. There was a deep crevasse guarding access to the overhanging ice wall above. There was no obvious way over or round the serac. This looked as if it could be the crux of the climb. We tried over to the extreme right, but it looked difficult. We then traversed to the extreme left: the serac didn't look as high, but there was a massive drop all the way down to the Blaitière Glacier several thousand feet below.

Climbing the serac on the left looked the easier option. I climbed up and took a belay as close to the serac as I could. The serac overhung about 20-30 feet over my head, but I reckoned if Spiney could move further to the left it would not be so steep and there could be a way forward. I was straddled on a small snow arête, one leg down the iceslope to the Blaitière glacier far below and the other down into the dark crevasse, the ice wall of the serac overhead. I put an ice screw into the deep blue ice to my right and brought Spiney up to the belay. Next pitch was Spiney's lead. Spiney checked out the ice above, stepped onto the overhanging ice wall, traversed round a few steps to the left, then disappeared. There was a shout from above,

'Good bit of ice, just like the Chancer!'
That was what I did not want to hear.
'Just don't start flyin' off doon the hill again!'

The rope moved slowly through my hand. It seemed a long time before all the rope was out. Eventually there was a very faint shout from above to start climbing. I was relieved to move from the belay and get some circulation into my frozen backside.

The step across to the serac was tricky. A couple of moves to the left on bulging, brittle ice was exhausting, then I moved round a corner and up a steep ice wall. The climbing was steep, but the ice was a lot better than I imagined. I appeared at the top of the serac thinking it was the end of the difficulties. However, there was another big serac above which looked difficult, but a "shite shoot" cut through the steepest part of the serac, giving an easier climb. The problem about climbing up a "shite shoot" is that any falling debris from higher up the mountain is channelled down the "shite shoot". I was worried about climbing up the "shite shoot", but it looked the easiest option.

I traversed into the "shite shoot" and started climbing as quickly as I could. I stopped for a quick breather in the thin air. It was a very exposed position, looking down through my legs to see the Blaitière Glacier several thousand feet below.

I made another couple of moves further up the "shite shoot". There was a cry from above. I felt the rope around my waist go tight. I looked up. All I could see was a wall of white coming down towards me. Fuck! This is the end. I am going to die.

Everything happened in a split second. I drove my ice axes and kicked my crampon front points into the ice as hard as I could, and put my face against the snow and held on for dear life.

A fraction of a second is a long time, waiting for an avalanche to hit you. A fraction of a second is long enough for your mind to start playing games. Surely, I should have been hit by now? Maybe it was my imagination? Maybe it was going down a different part of the mountain?

Then... Wham! It felt like six tons of bricks landing on my head. My world went dark. There was a sensation of everything around me moving very fast. Was I falling down the mountain still attached to a piece of ice? It was difficult to tell.

I could feel every muscle in my body straining, holding on, my wrists felt as if they were getting pulled from my arms, my arms felt as if they were being wrenched out of their sockets. Snow filled every gap. It was difficult to breathe so I held my breath. Snow was forcing its way down my nose, into my eyes and ears. There was a constant, "thud, thud, thud" from snow hitting my helmet. My neck was straining to keep my head facing into the snow.

I knew if I let the falling snow get under me I would be lifted straight off. Seconds passed. I was losing hope of holding on. The arm slings attached to my ice axes were cutting into the flesh around my wrists.

Then at last I could feel the strain beginning to ease. A few moments later, the movement had stopped. I started to relax. I was buried under several feet of snow, but the snow was light enough for me to dig myself out.

I was lucky. The avalanche was of light, new snow. Had the snow been harder, or with blocks of ice or stones it would have been a disaster.

I was lucky that Spiney was out of the avalanche fall-line and he had been holding on to me from above. If he had been knocked off his belay, both of us would have been down the mountain.

I climbed up to Spiney as quickly as I could to get out of the "shite shoot" and get warmed up again. I must have looked like a walking snowman; there was snow in every pocket and between every layer of my clothing. The snow was starting to melt from my body heat and I was getting wet.

I got to the belay. Spiney pointed upwards at the grey sky overhead. Our view to the west was blocked by the Aiguille des Deux Aigles and we had been too engrossed in the climbing below to realise there was going to be a change in the weather. There was an ominous change in the atmosphere. The blue sky had disappeared and had been replaced by dark forbidding clouds. The wind had picked up and soon the snow started falling heavily. This was to be our first Alpine storm on the mountains.

I dug out the snow from my rucksack to find my mountain jacket and put it on. Spiney just stood watching. I asked why he was not putting on his own jacket. Spiney announced that he had forgotten it.

The storm moved in with alarming ferocity. Soon we were in a complete white out, the strong wind whipping up freshly fallen snow. We were blinded by white. It was difficult to judge which way was up and which way was down. And what made matters worse was that the fresh snow was starting to avalanche all around us. Every few steps into the newly fallen snow would set off a small avalanche that would slide away beneath our feet. Avalanches came down on us from above. At first the avalanches were quite small, but it was difficult to judge when one would hit in white-out conditions. You could hear a sliding sound just in time to brace against the snow. As the storm grew, the avalanches were becoming big enough to knock us over, so we started to belay each section.

Progress was exhausting and painfully slow, wading through steep snow with a constant fear of being avalanched at any moment.

Our predicament was getting serious. We had not eaten or drunk anything since the previous evening—now there was no food or gas left. We had been climbing since first light and were now very tired. The thin air was taking effect; a few steps were followed by a break and large gulps of air. We were in the middle of a storm, not really knowing where we were on the mountain or how to get back down.

The mountain was constantly avalanching all around us. There was a lot of static, you could hear a buzzing sound in the air, claps of thunder boomed closer and soon lightning flashed across the sky and now it was beginning to get dark.

After some time climbing up steep snow we reached a snow ridge. The two of us looked over the edge, but had to brace ourselves from the wind. My face felt as if it was being sand blasted by ice particles picked up by the hurricane ferocity of the wind. My face was numbed to the bone with cold.

We climbed several pitches up the ridge. It felt as if we were

fairly close to the summit.
We had reached the top of Aiguille du Plan and now the grim reality of getting back down faced us.

There was a bit of a scoop in the snow. I wanted to dig a snow hole and sit out the storm. It was important to find some shelter and get out of the wind. I was concerned about Spiney without a decent windproof jacket. Spiney was concerned about digging a snow whole and being exposed to avalanches and also if the storm were to last for days we would not get back off the mountain. He reckoned that we could drop off the ridge, lose some height, get out of the wind and onto the Vallée Blanche.
It was dark. A quick decision had to be made. It was no place for an argument.

Looking down from the top of the ridge we could just about make out a gully below. Spiney was convinced that we could find some better shelter down in the gully and hopefully get onto the Vallée Blanche.
We climbed down to the top of the gully. I set up a belay at the edge, Spiney got the rope that had been cut by the falling rock out of his rucksack. He cut off the frayed end. I was apprehensive about abseiling down the gully and into the unknown in the middle of a storm. I was also very apprehensive about using a chewed rope, if there were any other cuts or abrasions that we had missed, the rope could snap as one of us abseiled. Spiney clipped in his descendeur, abseiled over the edge and disappeared into the darkness. We both knew what to do. I could feel the rope taut, and presumed that Spiney was still abseiling. After some time the abseil rope went slack, I presumed that Spiney had found a belay and picked up the rope, attached my descendeur and started to abseil down the gully.

I soon was abseiling down a cascade of ice. The ice was very brittle and large pieces would break off every time I used my feet against the ice for balance. I looked down and could not see where the abseil ended. I then abseiled over an overhang and started to spin around in space. I tried to stabilise myself by supporting my feet against large icicles, but the ends of the icicles would break sending me into a spin again. I continued abseiling and went over another overhang. Below I could make out a vague outline of Spiney down below on a steep snow slope off to my right. At least he hadn't abseiled off the end of the rope and into oblivion. There were a few reassuring words from Spiney, 'Yu'll huv tae abseil oaf the end o the rope and drop a wee bit ontae the snow ledge below.'

That was something I didn't want to hear. I came to the end of the rope. I was dangling in free space, slowly rotating in thin air and there was still a good ten feet to go before the snow ledge. I held my ice axes in both hands, then let the short end of the rope pass through the descendeur and held onto the long end of the rope. I watched as the short end of the rope disappeared up. The rope pulled through the belay above. I dropped down and landed on the snow below in a controlled fall with ice axes and crampon front points hitting the snow first, firmly embedded in the snow. The rope came down on my head from above.

I climbed over to Spiney. We didn't say anything. Both of us knew we were in trouble. We were feeling weak with the lack of food and drink and exhausted after climbing all day. We knew it would be very difficult to climb back out from the position we were in and had no idea what was below.

I set up a belay from the point where Spiney had fixed himself to the ice. I went down the gully a bit further to another small ledge. A strong updraft of wind blasted into my face. There was another big drop below. I did not know if we could abseil down. I climbed back up to Spiney.

'We'll huv tae stay here the night.'

Spiney didn't disagree.

There was a slightly overhanging rock face at the top of the steep snow ledge. It looked the best spot to bivouac—out of avalanche danger.

We hacked away at the ice. After some time, we managed to cut a ledge big enough for two backsides to sit on. We coiled a rope each to sit on. Spiney got a large orange polythene bag big enough for two out of his rucksack. This was to be home for the night.

My feet were frozen solid. I was worried about frostbite and decided to take my crampons off and loosen my boots to improve the circulation. Spiney did the same. After a lot of effort, fiddling with frozen leather straps, Spiney got his crampons off and climbed into the polythene bag. Eventually I managed to remove my crampons and got into the polythene bag. The two of us tried to get as comfortable as possible, bums sitting on the coiled ropes, legs hanging down the slope. The polythene bag kept the wind from us, but it didn't stop the snow coming in from the top. Soon we were soaking wet from the condensation inside the polythene bag and the snow getting blown in. The warmth of movement soon turned to the cold of rigidity. We didn't have sleeping bags. Leaving them to save weight now seemed a very bad idea.

My hands and feet were soon very, very cold. Both of us started shivering uncontrollably. The shivering fits went on for hours, through peaks and troughs. I tried to keep some movement in my feet and legs, but they felt like stone and were painful to move. I tried to keep my fingers and toes moving to ward off frostbite.

There was no communication between us. The icy wind had frozen our faces solid. Spiney was fighting his own battle.

≈ Rock Rock ≈

It snowed and hailed continuously all night.
The wind had changed direction and was now blasting straight into our polythene bag, lashing snow and ice at us. The whole sky would light up in an instant and discharges of electricity zig-zagged in all directions. You could feel static running through the air. Thunder boomed overhead, then the sound bounced around the mountain peaks. You could feel the pressure waves rushing past. Big avalanches rumbled down the mountain, like ghost trains in the night.
The cold was seeping through my flesh and into my bones, gnawing at me from all directions. My mind felt as frozen as my feet. I was worried about my toes. I had lost all sensation in my toes some time ago. The shivering went on and on and on.
I started singing "Flying" to myself to take my mind off the cold.

> A'm just hanging ontae a piece o rock
> A'm just holdin' on tae reality
> A'm gripped oot'a ma fuckin' skull
> Nowhere to go but up, what the fuck.

This time the only way to go was down, but neither of us was sure if it was possible. The situation looked desperate.
I continued singing to myself and sang through our repertoire of songs to take my mind off the grim possibilities.

> Again, if tanks run over Poland.
> Divine intervention is the only way,
> I look around in vain,
> To which God can I trust and pray.

Suddenly, I stopped halfway through "Plutonium Child." Some-

thing hit me. Why hadn't I been killed...by the falling stone, the serac fall or avalanche only a few hours before?
Who or what will decide if I am to die or not on the bivouac tonight? Is it all just chance? Is it all just coincidence? Is it a simple roll of the dice of life?
Take a chance in life, roll the dice and see what you get. Is there something more than chance? Or is there a hand that controls the dice? Too many questions without answers were going through my head.

The shivering went on and on and on. Some time in the night, the shivering appeared to lessen and I started to feel faint and drifted into a sleep of exhaustion. For some reason the cold didn't matter so much, and a feeling of contentment, joy, almost happiness started to come over me.
I started to feel afraid that I was dying; a loneliness that lies at the bottom of your stomach; a loneliness, that gnaws relentlessly away at your soul; a loneliness, that leaves you floating about helpless, adrift on an ocean of despair. Death wasn't going to be one second, but more like a slowly ebbing tide draining my life away.
I kept asking myself—should I try and force myself awake or let sleep take over?
The thought "We're not going to get out of this," kept spiralling through my mind. A thought of hopelessness, a mirage of a solution, that appears, then disappears with every gust of wind.
I remember a tunnel of light appeared in my vision, there was a feeling of almost floating away into the storm, a sensation of walking into the clouds and then looking back to say goodbye.

≈

I woke in a massive uncontrolled shiver that would not stop. There was a faint hint of greyness in the darkness. I had survived the night.

My body was in convulsions. My shivering knocked off a layer of snow, which had settled on the polythene bag. The cold had penetrated into every bone. Even though I was shivering so much, I was too lethargic to move. The cold had frozen all thought of moving. Every movement was an extreme effort. I sat there, trying to get my fingers and toes to work again.

Slowly, first light started to appear. The storm was still blowing wild. There was some movement at my side. Spiney had survived the night.

With great effort I got out of the polythene bag. Movement was painfully slow, trying to get the blood flowing around my body again. I went looking for my crampons. All our gear attached to the belay was buried under deep snow. I brushed away the snow.

It was then that I realised that neither of us had tied onto the belay overnight. We had both been sitting on a small ice ledge hacked out of a 60 degree ice slope inside a plastic bag. I couldn't believe it. It was too frightening to think what might have happened if either of us had slipped off the ledge during the night. I clipped into the belay and gave another rope loop to Spiney to clip into. He was still in the poly bag. He took the rope, clipped in and didn't say anything.

I removed my mitts to try and put my crampons on. Frozen fingers trying to adjust frozen buckles and frozen leather straps. My fingers were useless. Frozen flesh sticking to frozen metal. Every few moments I had to put my fingers in my mouth or under an armpit to get some movement. I was aware it would be serious if I dropped a mitt or any other piece of equipment down the mountain. It must have taken well over an hour to put my crampons back on. Toes and fingers numbed with cold. It took us some time to get packed up and get moving again. We had a look at what we abseiled down the previous evening. It looked horrendous to climb back up. I climbed down to look over the edge below. The wind was still blowing vertically up the gully. In the light of day, I could see there was a big drop below into the mist.

Spiney set up an abseil using a "dead-man" as an anchor. This was my abseil. There is always a thought in my mind just before the start of an abseil—what if the protection pulls out? Is it better to fall or be left stranded high on the mountain with no rope and no hope? I double checked the knot and that the 'dead-man' snow anchor had been placed well and asked Spiney to check as well, to make sure there would be no mistakes in our exhausted state.

I threw the rope over the edge, clipped the descendeur onto the rope and put some weight on the "dead-man". It held. I went over the edge and into the cloud. I tried not to think about the rope cutting or the "dead-man" pulling out.

The abseil went on and on, down the narrow gully, over ice bulges, brittle icicles and loose snow on rock. I went over an overhang and came towards the end of the rope. It was too short to reach a snow bay in the gully below. There was no choice but to abseil off the end of the rope and drop a few feet onto the snow below. I let go of the rope, and landed with ice axes and crampon front points firmly planted into the snow slope.

I set up a belay and shouted for Spiney to come down even though he probably could not hear a word. Some time later Spiney appeared out of the mist and came to the end of the rope. He was dangling in free space. He abseiled off the end of the rope, held onto the longer part and dropped down to the belay. The rope came down on us. I didn't want to think what we would have to do if the rope jammed.

Abseil followed abseil. After a number of abseils it became obvious that we hadn't come off the south end of the mountain and onto the Vallée Blanche, but were descending an unknown way down the mountain and had no idea what was below.
I knew the debilitating effect the cold, hunger and exhaustion would have on my reasoning. I tried to force discipline into my head, to check and double-check every abseil point, and got Spiney to double-check my efforts and I his. Both of us knew we were steadily deteriorating, but we didn't speak about our predicament. The only option was down.
I was worried about abseiling off some of the fixed points. A second piece of protection would have given me peace of mind, but I knew that our equipment would quickly run out and we could easily be left stranded high on the mountain. The grim possibilities kept running through my mind, Spiney abseiling off the end of the rope, an abseil point pulling out, the rope cutting, running out of abseil points.
If Spiney fell I would be left abandoned on the mountain with no hope of getting up or getting down. I wondered what the best option was, freezing or falling.

The storm was still blowing for all it was worth. We tried to down climb as much as we could to economise on climbing equipment. Every time we set up an abseil, a piece of equipment had to be left. It became obvious that we were using up all our equipment and it didn't feel as if we were making much progress down the mountain. We had to come up with some ideas.
We rummaged about in the rucksacks for any bits and pieces that could be used as abseiling points. There was a cooking

pot. Spiney punctured two holes in the bottom of the pot with his ice axe and lined the rough edges with insulating tape. A rope was looped through the holes in the pot. The cooking pot could be used as a snow anchor like a "dead-man" if needed. The cooker could be jammed into a big crack and used as an abseil point. The straps were cut off our rucksacks to give some extra slings, and if necessary, one of the rucksacks would have to be cut up.

Abseil followed abseil. We abseiled all day and it was starting to become dark again. We had lost track of how many abseils had been done that day. I stopped counting at 25, Spiney reckoned it was more than 30 abseils. It looked as if we would have to spend another rough night on the mountain. A rock ledge was found for the bivouac. It looked more comfortable and safer than the previous night. I hammered in our last piton, set up a belay and this time made sure that both of us were securely attached. The polythene bag came out of the rucksack again. With a great deal of effort and discomfort we got settled on the ledge. The two of us huddled together inside the polythene bag with feet dangling off the edge ready for another cold night.

As soon as we stopped moving, the shivering started. We settled down in our polythene bag for another grim bivouac. Thoughts of hunger were overtaken by thoughts of survival. The night was endless. The shivering went on and on. My body felt fatigued with the constant shivering. Powerful gusts of wind blasted snow and ice at us, filling up our polythene bag. I tried to empty the bag as best I could. I had lost any sensation in my toes. Dawn seemed an eternity away.

The shivering went on, and on, and on, and on.

I came round in a shivering fit. There was a greyness in the sky, the first sign of dawn. I had survived the night, but the day brought the grim reality of our situation. I was thinking, how many more bivouacs can I survive, how many more abseils to do. There was no incentive to move. My fingertips had gone hard and I had to put them into my mouth to get some circulation back. My toes felt like blocks of ice. I was worried about frostbite again.

It was still bitterly cold and it took all my effort to get moving. Spiney was starting to move. We went through the ritual of getting frozen bodies to move and putting frozen crampons on with frozen hands.

In the process of getting organised Spiney knocked my rucksack off the bivouac ledge and down the mountain. Both of us watched as it disappeared down into the mist. I had forgotten to clip it into the belay. We were lucky that it did not contain any important climbing gear.

We started abseiling again. An hour or two later, the wind started to drop and it stopped snowing. It was the first time in several days I felt our fortunes were changing.

A few more abseils later, the clouds started to part and we could see a bright light appearing as if there was some angelic intervention about to happen. Spiney and I looked at each other wondering where the light was coming from.

More clouds lifted.

It was a light from the *téléphérique* station on top of the Aiguille du Midi. At last we knew where we were. We had descended the west face of Aiguille du Plan!

The clouds broke some more and the glacier could be seen a few hundred feet below, not far to go. There was a great surge of relief, all the doubts disappeared in a flash.

Our last abseil took us onto the glacier. We were off the mountain. We lay on a large boulder on the glacier and soon we were asleep, as the sun appeared between the clouds.

We woke up in the afternoon and had a quick look around for my rucksack, but there was no sign of it. We started to make our way down the glacier. The glacier was fairly flat and there were not too many crevasses around. The two of us started plodding down the glacier navigating round some small crevasses or jumping over them thinking our problems were over. However, we came upon a crevasse that was a bit bigger and thought it better to belay. I forced my ice axe into the snow as far as it would go, wrapped the rope around the head and stood on it to make sure it wouldn't pop out if Spiney fell. Spiney moved to the edge of the crevasse. On the instant he was about to jump, the edge of the crevasse gave way.
Spiney disappeared down the crevasse.
A fraction of a second later, I felt my leg being whipped away from under me and being pulled down to the crevasse foot first. I tried to stop myself with my other ice axe and just managed to come to a halt at the lip of the crevasse.
I shouted down the crevasse to ask Spiney if he was all right.
   'Thought yae wur comin' doon as well,' was the reply.
   'A'm stuck aboot 50 feet doon here. Y'll huv tae jump the crevasse and set up a belay owan the other side.'
I took a run and jump, and landed on the other side of the crevasse. I looked down into the crevasse. Spiney was jammed in a narrowing with a pile of rope around his head. I set up a belay and Spiney front pointed out of the crevasse.

It was getting late in the day, but we were not in a rush; just happy to be down the mountain and off the glacier. On our way back to the boulder doss on the Plan du Aiguille, we met

Reggie, one of the English climbers we had chatted to just before we started the north face of the Aiguille du Plan.
He and his friends were concerned and had been out looking for us. We were as relieved to meet him as he was to meet us.

'Thought you were goners.'

'It's a long story. It took us a wee bit longer than we thought.'

He and his friends made us some food. We were very grateful.

Where's Rep?

The next few days Spiney and I recovered from our ordeal on the north face of the Plan. Our faces were weather beaten and the skin was peeling off, revealing raw pink patches of new flesh underneath. Our lips and noses were all swollen and cracked. Hands were all cut, and bashed black and blue.
We had lost not just all our climbing gear, but a lot of weight as well. A large sack of potatoes was bought and the next couple of days were spent gorging ourselves by cooking up all the possible recipes we could think of with potatoes, cabbage and anything else we had brought along. Boiled potatoes, cabbage and a tin of tuna; fried potatoes, cabbage and baked beans; potatoes, cabbage and corned beef...

Spiney and I were sitting near the tent one night. We had a small fire going to roast potatoes. There was a noise from the bushes behind us.

'Whit the fuck is that noise?'

'Whit noise is that?'

'Shhh, listen...sumboady is cumin' through the bushes.'

'Naw its just the wind...or an animal or sumthin'...its nuthin'.'

'A'm tellin' yae, its sumbudy... Its no an animal.'

A few moments later it was obvious that it wasn't an animal coming through the bushes towards us.

'Quick get those ice axes in case there's trouble.'

Spiney and I stood behind the fire, facing the bushes with an ice axe in hand, wondering who was fighting their way through the dense undergrowth in the middle of the night.

The noise became louder. It was clear the person was having trouble crashing and falling their way through the bushes.

A voice could just about be made out, 'Shite! Fuckin'!'

There was the sound of snapping branches.

'Oh ya! Shite!'

It was a Scottish accent.

'Is that you there, Bish?'

'U've course it's mae, who dae yae think it is, the pope? Oh fuck! Oh ya! Why did yis huv tae camp in the middle o these bushes fur?'

'Cun yae no just walk up the path there like everywan else?'

'Oh Ya! Bastard!!!'

More snapping branches were heard. Spiney and I sat down, carrying on our conversation and turning the potatoes on the fire. Bish was still fighting his way through the bushes.

'Shite! Oh ya...bastard!'

'How yur yae doin' there Bish? Yae hud better hurry up there. Dinner is finishing soon.'

'Oh ya! Shite!'

Bish eventually appears through the bushes, scraped about the face, and clothes in disarry.

'Well done Bish. A thought we wid huv tae leave yae oot there the night.'

Bish skipped the welcoming pleasantries.

'Huv yae seen Rep?'

'Whit dae yae mean huv we see Rep? A thought he wus

cumin' wae yae?'

'A loast him doon near Geneva.'

'Whit dae yae mean, loast him?'

'Well, he went intae this shop fur sum vitols and that wus the last A saw o him. A waited fur fuckin' hoors, but there wus no sign o him. A thought he might be up tae sum high jinx and made it up here by himsel or sumthin.'

'Naw, we huvnae seen him. Is he no owan his machine?'

'His machine packed in and he hud tae stash it in sum fairm. A hud tae gee him a backy awe the way frum somewhere south o Paris. A still huv awe his stuff owan the back o the bike. A dinno where he's ended up.'

'Uch, well yae cunnae dae anythin' aboot it no. A'm sure he'll turn up ra morra.'

The night was spent at the campfire, drinking cheap wine, eating baked potatoes, recalling our epics on the van and the north face of the Plan.

'We wis just tryin tae find oor way aboot, when we wus dun oor by the Frog polis. Bunch o bastards kicked our heids in and slashed open awe ma ma's dried milk and floor thinking it wus drugs or sumthin'.'

'Then there wus this Frog punter tried tae take us oot'a the game—fuckin' nutter—tried tae ram us oaf the road.'

'Nae epics owan the way oot. Jist hud a puncture owan the front, and goat nearly wrapped roon a tree. It wus just Rep's machine blew up. Lucky a wis no far behind when it happened und A picked him up wae awe his gear...'

Spiney was eager to tell the story of the North face of Aiguille du Plan.

'Then we goat lost owan the hill. We did the North face o the Plan and goat stuck in a storm. Hud tae ab off the West face o the Plan—fuckin' nightmare! We wus oawn the hill fur five days wae nuthin' tae eat or drink thought we wus history.'

'Uch well... Yae might make history as the first folk tae climb doon the West face o the Plan, nae other tosser is smart enough tae dae that.'

'Tae top it awe the weather hus been shite, hus been tippin' doon awemost every day.'

'A've tried tae organise a gig, but A cunnae get through tae these locals. We're runnin' low on vitols und we've loast awe oor gear owan the hill. If we dinnae get sum dosh soon we'll huv tae head oaf back hame.'

≈

Next day there was still no Rep. The weather was good and Bish was ready to go up and solo some climb. Rep suddenly appeared at camp.

'Where the fuck huv yae been?'

'Whit, dae yae mean?'

'Where the fuck were yae? Yae fucked off, leavin' mae standin' aboot like a fuckin' plonker. A waited fur hoors fur yae. A wus standin' aboot fur hoors like a fuckin' plonker. A went back tae the shop yae hud been in, und yae were gone... disappeared...vanished. Two minutes yae said. A'll be oot in two minutes yae said. Well a waited fur fuckin' hoors A did.'

'A came oota this wee shop and a must o turned the wrong way or sumthin'...'cos everythin' looked different... A cudnae find ma way back tae the bike. A walked a couple o streets und wus totally loast—A wis. A remembered the name o the hotel yae wur parked opposite, Hotel Francis or sumthin' like that. A asked a taxi driver how tae get there. He told me to get in. The next minute we started driving oota the toon. Fuck knows where we wus goin'. A wus sittin' there watching the meter go roond and roond. Shitten masel a didnae huv any dosh. A showed ma hand wae a few coppers, no enough tae buy a cuppa tea, tae the punter. He wisnae very happy und dumped mae sumwhere in the middle o nowhere. A hud tae start hitchin. A couldnae work oot which wae tae go. A hud nae a map. A wus hitchin' awe yesterday a wus. A got tae this lorry park place somewhere doon the valley here. Naebuddy wid geeus a lift. A stood there fur hoors A did. A stood there fur fuckin' hoors A did, und nae cunt wid geeus a lift. There wus this trucker's café A went fur A seat und a heat up und tae chadge a cuppa tea or sumthin', und a heard these two English drivers say there wur off up the Mont Blanc tunnel. Magic, A sais and followed wan o them oot tae his truck, nipped under the tarpaulin A did and took oaf doon the road in the back o this truck, magic like. A wus hangin' owan there, a wee bit worried A wid faw oaf the back, like, so A tied mesel doon tae this engine that wus under the tarpaulin, so a widnae faw oaf. A sais tae ma sel, he'll huv tae stop fur custums fur a ticket or sumthin at the entrance tae the tunnel und A'll just jump oaf the back, smart like... But the bastard only stops fur a few seconds und A coundnae untie measel frum the fuckin' engine in time. The next thing the truck heads intae the tunnel wae mae oawn the back. Thank Christ he hudtae stop at the other side otherwise A wid o been oaf tae Rome or Sicily or fuck knows.'

'Well yae cood o dun us awe a favour und stayed owan that truck.'

'Well A jumped oaf the back and started headin' back through the tunnel. It's a lang way. A got a mile or two intae the tunnel when the polis stopped und picked mae up. Gave mae sum trouble they did 'cos A didnae huv A passport, but A sais tae them it wus ma birthday und ma pals in Cham got mae drunk und dumped mae in Italy. A'm just try tae get back tae Cham. So A goat A run frum the polis tae just doon the road there. Smashin? Eh?'

'Right...enough o yur lang tales. Get yur gear, let's get goin' in the hill.'

Bish and Rep disappeared to do a climb. Spiney and I went off again to try and arrange a gig. We had only enough money for about a week or two left.
I tried to phone Sophie again. I put a coin into the box and waited patiently for someone to answer. Somebody did. I tried my French again.
'Peu ju parlez a...' but got a familiar reply.
'Allez vous faire foutre! Allez vous faire foutre! Allez vous faire foutre!!! Fuck off! Fuck off! Fuck off!!!'
I let the receiver drop and walked away. I could still hear the punter shouting down the phone some distance away.

It was a depressing day. Sophie seemed our best hope of getting somebody to help organise a gig for the band, but I could not get through. We would have to leave France soon if we could not raise some money.

Afternoon tea with the gentry

The next day on the way into town, I was approached by an old tramp near the train station who said something to me in French.
'Excuse-moi, pouvez-vous me donner un peu d'argent pour une tasse du tée? Excuse me, can you give me some money for a cup of tea?'
'Fuck off! Y'ure askin' the wrong person. A don't huv two bob tae rub taegetheir!' I said, in quick reply.
'Ah, you speak English young man,' the tramp replied in the most incredible posh English aristocratic accent.
You could have blown me over with a feather.

'Could you possibly pass a piece of silver over my hand to buy a cup of tea?'
I was speechless.
'I do not want to trouble you my life story but can you spare something for an old man?'
I was about to walk away wondering what had become of the gentry, then I stopped for a second.
'A'll buy yae a cuppa tea if yae help mae oot wi' a couple o French phrases.'
'Fine, I'll try my best.'
'Right…yur owan! Let's go oor there.'
We went over to a nearby café. I was still coming to terms with having tea with the English gentry. The waiter came over, obviously unhappy dealing with an old tramp and a plukey-faced punk.
'OK whit yur yae wantin'?'
The old tramp ordered a tea and a croissant.
'A'm tryin tae set up a few gigs fur ma band but A cunnae get much promise 'cos a dinnae speak the lingo. A wus in this music shop and the punter thought a wus a total fuckin' heidbanger; he wis just lookin' at mae, like A wis frum another planet. A just cunnae get through tae these frogs cun yae write doon sum French phrases fur mae and A cun try again?'
The old tramp started to write down some words. He stopped in mid-sentence.
'What exactly would you like me to write, young man?'
'Something like, latest punk band frum Scotland ure wanting a gig fur a couple o nights.'
The old tramp started to write down some words.
'I am not sure how to say gig in French, how about show?'
'Aye, that's fine.'
He started writing again, then stopped.
'Hold on a minute. I worked in a bar near Annemasse

down the valley last year. They used to have bands occasionally... Rock bands... Made a lot of noise. I didn't like the noise very much...gave me a headache. I know the owner quite well. What is your band like, The Beatles?'

'Aye, sumthing like that.'

'Are you the Paul MacCartney?'

'Naw, no quite. OK brillant, whit shall we dae, cun yae call him or sumthin'?'

The old man looked at me wanting money.

'Aye, OK here's a few francs.'

I gave him the last of the change in my pocket.

'I am not sure if I can contact him just now. Let's meet here, this time tomorrow.'

'OK magic. Oh, by the way A've been tryin' tae phone this Frog bird, but there's a punter at the other end that just keeps goin' fuckin' mental. Is this phone number alright?'

He looked at the number. There were eight digits.

'Try dialling 16 before the digits; that looks like a Paris number.'

Then he gave me the number back. I was confused. Paris? She didn't say anything about Paris. I had just given my last change to the tramp so I would have to try calling later.

We parted company. I thought that maybe I had been swindled, but something inside me trusted the old tramp.

When I got back to the tent and told Spiney about the old tramp and how he'll help us set a gig, all he could say was, 'Yae been fuckin' dun! Last time it wus sum bird that nicked yur clathes, noo it's sum tramp that's nicked yur money. Yur a fuckin' tosser, sum auld dosser hus taken yae tae the cleaners.'

'Bet yae a beer he'll turn up ra morrra.'

'OK. Yae're on.'

Spiney and I went down to the station the next day at the planned time. The old tramp wasn't there. We went over to the café opposite. I bought Spiney a beer. He was giving me a hard time again for getting ripped off.

'Telt yae were fuckin' dun! Eejit, yur fuckin' bright ideas... Yur alwais loosin' money.'

'Gee us a break, at least A'm tryin'.'

Suddenly our conversation was interrupted.

'Good afternoon, young man,' a posh English aristocratic voice said.

I turned round in disbelief; the old tramp had appeared.

'May I sit down?'

'Aye, sure yae cun pal.'

I offered him a chair.

'This is ma pal.'

We all shake hands.

'Whit's yur name?'

'Just call me Nigel.'

'Right, Nij dae yae huv any news aboot yur pal doon the valley...aboot the gig?'

He paused with a hungry look in his face. I got the waiter over. Nigel ordered himself a cup of tea and a croissant. The tea arrived quickly but all the old tramp could do was complain about the tea.

'The tea here is dreadful, but I don't like coffee. I can never sleep at night if I drink coffee.'

He was a bit dithery. Anxiously, I asked him again.

'Did yae phone yur pal?'

'I phoned the café.'

He replied in a very slow and soft voice.

'Jean-Claude is interested and wants to talk to you. Can you go down sometime soon?'

He mentioned tomorrow afternoon, two o'clock, at his café. Is that alright?'

'Magic, cun yae write doon his phone number and address. We'll be there ra morra.'

The old tramp wrote down the name, address and phone number.

'Cun yur pal speak English?'

'Yes, better than you can young man.'

I wasn't sure how to take the comment.

'Ha! Ha! Good joke there Nij.'

We said thanks, quickly finished our beers, then took off. The old tramp took a nearby newspaper, started reading and continued drinking his tea.

We're rich

Next day Spiney and I drove down to Annemasse to find Jean-Claude. We found the café, not so far from the train station. The two of us went into the café and asked the punter behind the bar for Jean-Claude. It was Jean-Claude. He was expecting us. He gave us a drink and sat us down.

'So, youze have band, yesz?'

'Yes, we play latest punk rock.'

'Ah, yes, Sex Pistols.'

'Something like that, but Sex Pistols ure crap.'

Jean-Claude didn't seem to understand the word crap.

'Rubbish, shite, no good,' I tried again

'Oh, of coursze,' Jean-Claude replied with a confused look.

'Well, cun yae gee us a gig?'

Jean-Claude was a bit confused by the word gig.

'Can we play music? Give show? Concert? Here, at this place?'

After a few thoughts Jean-Claude said, 'D'accord, next Sza-tur-daz, one concer, si good, two more.'
'Magic, how much?'
'Szay 500 francs.' Jean-Claude indicated five fingers.
'800,' Spiney said and put up eight fingers.
'500,' Jean-Claude quickly replied.
'750,' I said with seven and a half fingers.
Jean-Claude wasn't going to add any more fingers.
Spiney tried seven fingers and said, '700.'
Jean-Claude was quite adamant with his five fingers.
'Non 500. Well, OK, 500 it is.'
Everything was over in a few seconds. We shook hands.
'Great. Magic.'
Everyone was happy. We shook hands again.
'I'ze do *affiches*,' Jean-Claude announced.
Spiney and I looked at each other.
'Did he say a fish?'
'Whit the fuck does he want wae a fish?'
'You do a fish?' I asked Jean-Claude.
'*Oui*, I'ze do *affiches*.'
'What the hell is he goin' owan aboot?'
'Mibbe its fur some vitols fur the band? Sandwiches or snacks or sumthin'?'
Spiney keen to keep the conversation going replied.
'Tuna, please. A'll huv tuna.'
Jean-Claude was confused by Spiney's reply.
'Two-Na?'
I was looking through my dictionary to try and find the word for tuna in French or something that resembled the word Jean-Claude had said.
'How d'ya spell that?' I had to ask him.
Jean-Claude took the dictionary, found the word he was looking for and tried to pronounce it.

'Pozsts,' he pointed to the word.

I took the dictionary and read where Jean-Claude was pointing.

'Ah, posters. Yea we need some posters, sorry A mean *affiches*.'

'Wasz you name?' Jean-Claude asked

'Spiney.' Spiney replied

Jean-Claude looked at him in a confused way.

'Non, non, non, the band.'

'We're called BCT – Balls, Cunts and Tits. That's oor name.'

It was obvious that Jean-Claude was confused or didn't like the name.

'BCT. That's the name o the band. It's the new Scotrock band, awe the wae frum bonnie Scotland.'

It was the first time I used the word "Scotrock" but Jean-Claude seemed to latch onto the name and appeared happier.

'*D'accord, d'accord*, Scot Rock. I'ze do something.'

There were smiles and handshakes all round.

'Next Saturday.'

'10 o'clock start.'

I got Jean-Claude to write down the exact time and date of the concert in case there were any mistakes.

'Magic, we'll be here at 6 tae get organised OK?'

'*D'accord.*'

We had only brought one drum. I asked on the off-chance.

'We're a wee bit short o drums, yae dinnae huv an extra owan by any chance?'

Jean-Claude didn't understand what I was talking about so I mimed playing the drums. He seemed to understand and we were led through a set of doors at the back of the café and into a big hall. The place was dark. Jean-Claude put on a light and pointed to a small stage in the distance.

'Yousz play here.'

'Fuckin' grand place yae huv here Jean-Claude.'
He didn't reply and opened the door of a big cupboard. It was stashed full of lights, electrical stuff, a couple of amplifiers and one or two instruments, including a drum.
'Just wait till Bish sees awe this stuff.'
'Fuckin' magic J-C!'
On that note we shook hands again and parted company.

Spiney and I appeared outside the café with big grins on our faces, really chuffed with ourselves, that at last something was beginning to happen. 500 francs would keep us going for at least another couple of weeks in France and the possibility of more gigs meant that we could think about buying some climbing gear to get back into the hills.

We drove back to Chamonix thinking what we would do with the money and what we would need for the gig. Bish and Rep appeared at the campsite late in the afternoon after finishing their climb. An extra large bottle of cheap wine and a chicken were bought and that evening we had a barbecue to celebrate and discuss the forthcoming gig.
'Yu'll no believe the size o the hall. Its huge...'
'Und there's sum extra drums just fur yae, und a cupboard full o lights and music stuff. Amazin' Eh?'
'How much ure they payin'?'
'500 francs.'
Bish wasn't very pleased.
'Only 500 francs!'
'Well we hud tae dae a bit o hagglin'.'
'Well A'll huv tae huv a wee chat wae this Jean-Claude.'
'Its no bad fur a first night...und the promised us more gigs'.'
Bish was still no very convinced.

The next couple of days we got organised for the gig and had a few practice sessions in the woods nearby. Bish and Rep went back into the hill for a short climb. Spiney and I went for a pad in the hills to waste time and not spend any money.

≈ *Rock Rock* ≈

Ze gig

Our big day arrived. Spiney and I set off in the van with all the music gear and Lucy on top. Bish and Rep followed by bike. We drove down to Annemasse for 6 o'clock.
Spiney spied a poster.
  'Hay, look oor there.'
The centre of the poster had big bold letters "Scot Rock", "Punk Rock" with a whole bunch of French words we did not understand.
  'That must be us!'

We arrived at Jean-Claude's café. There were more posters around. A few people were hanging about outside the café. I jumped out of the van and went over to the café. The door was closed. I tapped on the window. Jean-Claude appeared from behind a curtain and opened the door.
  'Is everything OK?'
  '*D'accord*, good, good.'
  'Cun A bring in the music stuff?'
  '*D'ac*...'

All the music stuff was transported in from the van. Jean-Claude gave us a hand and directed us through into the back hall. He turned all the lights on, revealing a large hall, big enough to hold several hundred people. I had not appreciated it was so big from our previous visit.
We carried the gear to the stage. It was raised about a couple of feet off the floor and just big enough for Lucy and the four of us with instruments.
  'Dead good place ya huv here J-C.'
  'D'yae huv the bits o' drums we wanted?'

Jean-Claude didn't understand.

'Drums, bang, bang,' Rep went through the motions of playing the drums.

'*Oui, oui*, all is here.'

Jean-Claude opened up his cupboard to reveal his box of goodies. Rep took a drum and some cymbals. Bish and I helped ourselves to some lights and an amplifier, speaker and mic system.

The next couple of hours were spent getting everything organised and tested. Bish set up the lighting system, Spiney set up the mic and amplifiers, Rep got his drum kit put together, and I assembled Lucy and got the tape recorder tested.

A quick dress rehearsal was in order. The music blasted out of banks of speakers, areas of light flood-lit the stage. Everything worked fine. It actually felt like being on a real stage, unlike the past "joke" concerts.

We were ready for our concert. It was now almost 9 o'clock. Jean-Claude appeared with some beer. He mentioned that the doors would open soon and we were to be ready for 10. He would do a short introduction and that would be the signal for us to come on stage. Bish asked for the lights to be turned off after the introduction, so we could make our entrance. The plan was to sing four songs, have an interval and then the rest in the second half.

We went into a small room behind the stage to get dressed up. Bish pulled out a couple of kilts from a polythene bag. The kilts looked a bit trashed, with torn bits held together with zips and safety pins.

'A've brought sum kilts fur the gig, there's only three so we'll huv tae draw who's wearin' whit.'

I drew the short straw and was relived to be getting the best deal.

'Well, A'm no warin' a kilt tae night.'

'Yes, yae fuckin well ure!'

I couldn't figure out what Bish was going on about. Bish gave me the bin bag the kilts came in.

'Whit the fuck's this?'

'It's yur costum fur the night.'

'A costum...it's just a fuckin' poly bag.'

'That's right, a plastic kilt. That's really punk! Remember this is Scottish punk! And yur no wearin' yur fuckin' keks. Remember yur no a wanker.'

'Fuck off! It's goanty fa oaf in seconds. A'm no running aboot in the scud!'

'Didnae worry, it'll be aweright, a bit o tape roond yur waist and yu'll be just raring tae go.'

'A'm tellin' yae if that poly bag starts cumin' oaf . A'm oaf the stage, pronto.'

'Uch, shoosht yae big fearty.'

'Y'ull just look gallus as fuck wae that poly bag on.'

'Remember, at the end o the last song, it's backs tae the audience and kilts up! Right!'

'Yae, OK Bish.' Everyone agreed reluctantly.

We would all be wearing kilts tonight. Rep appeared with a tin of paint and started writing bits of lyric on Bish. "Coke Can Culture" across his chest, "Plutonium Child" across the back of his shoulders, "Rock, Rock, Rock" down each arm. The can of paint was handed around and soon all our bodies were covered with lyrics.

Spiney spied Rep starting to work on his hair with some cling film and a can of beans.

'Whit the fuck are yae do'in way y'ure hair.'

Rep wrapped the cling film around his head like a turban, started pouring in baked beans then wrapped up the baked beans inside the cling film.

'That looks dead brilliant, but it's an awfay waste o the baked beans.'

'Dinnae worry—A'll eat them afterwards.'

'Fine, just make sure yae dinnae gee mae any.'

Bish had his favourite dark glasses with "X-ray" written on one lens and "Spex" written on the other in big white letters. He also put on a white collar with a bit of the shirt hanging off in tatters and a thin black tie.
We all put on our "EBs", our rock climbing boots, but they were also good for dancing.

The sound of people outside in the hall was building up. I decided to head to the toilet before the start. I put my head out the door for a quick glance to see what was happening. There was a sea of heads in front of me. I quickly reported back

'Fuckin'hell, there must be huners o folk oo't there.'
We all looked nervously at each other. We had never played in front of such a large audience before and, what was worse, we did not know anybody and did not know how the crowd would react to our music.

'Good boy that Jean-Claude...must o done a good job advertising.' Bish tried to reassure everyone.
I could see Rep and Spiney starting to look a bit nervous and began mumbling about bailing out.

'We're no bailin' oot noo. Were goin' oot there tae enjoy oorselves. Think o the dosh jingilin in yur poakit. Think o awe that food yae cun buy after the concert...' Bish jumped in.

I left Bish trying to reassure Spiney and Rep and headed to the toilet wearing my plastic kilt and body paint.
I made my way through the crowd. People were looking at

me as if I just arrived from another world. I stared back at them. There seemed to be a whole collection of the dregs of humanity mixed in with the weird, eccentric and exotic; midgets, drug dealers, prostitutes, convicts, transvestites, bikers, punks, drag queens—a carnival of all weird and wonderful, all shapes and sizes—every combination you could imagine. I wandered through the crowd staring at individuals as if they were like bizarre animals in a circus and wondering where all these people came from. I bumped into this character and nearly got the fright of my life. Standing straight in front was this huge fat bloke with shaved head, all his face and head painted titanium white. He was wearing a leather muzzle mask thing over his face. I turned away suddenly and walked into a couple of women barely dressed in leopard skin outfits and high heels. One of them was holding a chain. I got a glimpse of the character on the end, he was on his knees and didn't look very happy. I continued to move through the crowd pretending to be cool, half-expecting Randy and the Radioheads to be beamed down or to bump into the pair that gave me the hitch in the Citröen Dyanne.

There was a big crowd outside the toilet waiting to get in. The queue wasn't moving, I squeezed past desperate to get in. Each cubicle was open and full of people. With a kilt on (or in this case a polythene bag) I would usually head to a cubicle for a pee, but that didn't seem like an option. I had to squeeze past several girls to get to the urinal. Two of the girls were passionately embracing each other totally unaware that I was there. Another girl was standing beside the urinal watching me. She wasn't going to move and I thought "Well, this is France." I rolled up my polythene bag, started to pee and said, *'Bungjur,'* in my best French. She asked me something in French, which I didn't understand.

'*Avez-vous de la coke?* Do you have any coke?'

'Nice day isn't it?' I replied and smiled.

I finished, then started to work my way through the crowd to get back out. I was wondering if this was Jean-Claude's usual clientele. It was a struggle to get back out of the packed toilet. A punter came over to me and in a low tone of voice offered me some white pills.

'*T'en veux?* Interested in some stuff?'

He forced his hand against my stomach.

'Sorry pal. A don't want any o yur fuckin' shite.'

'*T'en veux?*' He tried again.

I pushed his hand away.

'Fuck off! A told yae. A don't want any o yur fuckin' shite!'

The punter seemed to understand this time and moved on.

I struggled back through the crowd to the changing room and announced,

'This place is hoachin wae werido's. There's fuckin' millions oo't there, junkies, pros the lot awe the nutters o the world. There wis this nutter wandering aboot wae a leather thing strapped tae his face. There wis two birds shaggin' each other in the men's bogs, und there wis this punter bein' dragged aboot wae a dog collar by these two birds... There's folk sellin' drugs too und A huvn'ae seen many bouncers.'

'Nae worries, it awe adds tae the atmosphere,' Bish interrupted.

'Oh fuck, A cunnae go throu wi' this,' Rep was getting worried.

Bish was looking cool.

'Shut yur fuckin' puss! We're goin' oot there, even if A huv tae drag yae oot by the fuckin' balls!'

'A wid check that windae in case things get a bit oot'a hand. There's another wan in the bogs, in case we huv tae bail oot quick like,' I mentioned.

'We're goin' oot there tae enjoy oorselves. We're no runnin' away anywhere, right?' Bish interrupted again.

'Right, Bish.'

I was still not so happy with Bish's idea for the last scene. He hadn't seen our audience yet.

'Bye the way Bish... A'm no sure it's a guid idea exposin' oorselves oot there at the end o the show. There's a whole bunch o weird folk that might get the wrong idea.'

'Dinnae worry. This is France, there awe fuckin' weird here.'

Bish had the last word.

It was almost ten o'clock. All four of us were starting to get nervous, pacing up and down the floor.
Jean-Claude appeared. He was a worried man. He gesticulated that we were on in a few minutes. Bish reminded Jean-Claude to turn off all the lights once he had finished talking. Jean-Claude disappeared out of the room.
Backstage, you could have cut the tension with a knife. Even Bish was starting to look anxious. We all looked at each other in trepidation.
Jean-Claude was out on front saying something in French to the audience. He stopped.
Bish stuck his head out of the door and announced, 'Right we're on.'
We all jumped to attention and went flying through the changing room door and onto the stage. It was dark. We were wearing head torches to find our way around. The audience was jumping up and down, going wild, shouting their heads off. We had not been in such an atmosphere before.

'Let's get goin'.' Bish said.

Rep sat behind his drums. Spiney put his guitar on. I put my guitar on and got the polybag off Lucy.

I looked round to see that everyone was in place and ready to go. There was an "Oh, fuck, what have we done" look on Spiney's face. There were a few seconds fumbling about with Lucy. Bish turned round wondering what was going on. I gave thumbs up for go and nodded the final OK to everyone else. I turned on Lucy and timed 15 seconds of music at half volume. A slow sounding noise came out of the loudspeakers. We turned off our headtorches. The room was in complete darkness. The crowd started to quieten down a bit with the start of the music. I got the spotlight switch and volume control ready then flicked them on simultaneously. The spotlight picked out Lucy and a wall of noise erupted from the loudspeakers.

There was a huge roar from the crowd when they saw Lucy. Lucy was looking great with her ripped tights and her tits going round and round.

There was another 34 seconds of Lucy's solo. I whispered a five second warning to Bish.

'OK, Bish.'

Bish gave thumbs up, turned round and said, 'OK, everyone. One, two, three, four, five, GO!'

Spiney and Rep come in together with the guitar and drums. I simultaneously turn on the full light to the stage. Bish starts shouting into the mike.

> A'm! just hanging ontae a piece o rock
> A'm just holdin on tae re-a-li-tyyy!
> Fuck! Fuck! A'm just holdin' on, on, on tae re-a-li-tyyy!
> A'm gripped oot'a ma fuckin' skuuull.
> Nowhere tae go but up, what the f-u-u-c-k!

Bish shouts out the chorus.

Just wan second tae... Go!

Spiney and I join in on chorus.

Ma body wants tae... Go! Go!

Bish singles solo.
A just wanna be a boring bastard!

Spiney and I join in.
Boring Bastard! Boring Bastard!

The tempo picks up. Rep bashes away on the drums. The baked beans break out of the cling film and start to slide down his face and body. Bish sings on.

Take a Haaappy drug. Whaaa!
tae find a sad taemorrooow uuunder!
It's a fools Parra-dise. Ohooo!
Adams temptation appple fate. Ehhh!
Just wan second tae... Go!
Ma boady wants tae... Go! Go!
A just wanna be a boring bastard!

Boring Bastard! Boring Bastard!

Bish leaves the mic and starts doing a bit of dancing, while Lucy does her solo bit. Bish is looking a bit ridged on the floor.

If...yae don't like the CHIPS
yae cun alwais cum PLAIN!
Owan second tae Pop! A PILL!!!
If...yae think yur in-SAIN!!!

> *Just wan second tae... Go!*
> *Ma boady wants tae... Go! Go!*
> *A just wanna be a boring bastard!*
> *Boring Bastard! Boring Bastard!*

Bish is sounding a bit unsure of himself and nervous, but the sound is working. Rep is bashing away at his drums.

'Careful wae those drum sticks there Rep. There's only the owan set,' I have to whisper over.

Bish is back at the mic.

> *A! quick fix and Fooorget the wooorld,*
> *awe the ills and proooblems that occurrr.*
> *Take a chemical tae delude yur b-raaain,*
> *Try and run but yae cunnae run-run-run away.*
> *Just wan second tae... Go!*
> *Ma boady wants tae... Go! Go!*
> *A just wanna be a boring bastard!*
>
> *Boring Bastard! Boring Bastard!*

Bish is dancing away. Rep jumps over the drums and joins in with Bish.

'Get back tae yur drums fur Christ sake!' Spiney shouts over in a loud whisper.

Rep dashes back, and in the process nearly knocks over the drums and Lucy. He sits down and starts drumming the second Bish starts to sign again.

> *O-nly excitement in LIFE!!!*
> *Jack-O's style was a FRIGHT!!!*
> *Sad bas-tard just a-nother BOADY!!!*
> *on the pile o human SHITE!!!*

> *Just wan second tae... Go!*
> *Ma boady wants tae... Go! Go!*
> *A just wanna be a boring bastard!*
>
> *Boring Bastard! Boring Bastard!*

Bish turns round when he stops singing and gives a wry smile. He is starting to look more relaxed and does a few jigs before starting singing again.

> *Mad-ness or may-be a na-tu-ral state,*
> *gives a fear o living*
> *That dis-turbs the b-raaain,*
> *owan second and it'll be awe a-way!*
> *Just wan second tae... Go!*
> *Ma boady wants tae... Go! Go!*
> *A just wanna be a boring bastard!*
>
> *Boring Bastard! Boring Bastard!*

Bish tries a dance again, does a spin and ends in the crowd. Spiney goes in for the rescue.

'Fuck, Bish is oaf the stage; keep playin' those drums und A'll get him oot.'

I hold onto Lucy's tit to stop the music, while Rep bashes away on the drums. The crowd picks up Bish and holds him in the air. Dozens of hands move him around in the air as he gets passed from person to person. A few moments later he is placed back on stage. Bish gives the nod to continue. I let go of Lucy's tit and the music blasts out as if nothing has happened. Bish picks up the mic and starts singing again.

> *Whit is the CHEM-ICAL,*

> that con-trols yur Miiind?
> Or is it yur miiind,
> That controls yur CHEM-ICAL?
> Just wan second tae... Go!
> Ma boady wants tae... Go! Go!
> A just wanna be a boring bastard!
>
> Boring Bastard! Boring Bastard!

Lucy starts her solo. Bish starts his dance again.

'This time stay owan yur feet!' Spiney shouting over a loud whisper.

There is no reaction from Bish. A couple of girls come on stage and dance along with Bish. He picks up the mic with one hand and puts the other around the girl. Bish starts singing again.

> Need a drug tae con-fuse re-a-lity
> Tae help creative process flooow
> Good idea tae kill ma-sel
> Before A becum a staaar!!!
> Just wan second tae... Go!
> Ma boady wants tae... Go! Go!
> A just wanna be a boring bastard!
>
> Boring Bastard! Boring Bastard!

Lucy plays by herself. The girls are still dancing alongside Bish. Bish is out to impress. He spins round and round, suddenly stops and drops to do the splits, legs splayed apart. It looks painful. Bish gets back on his feet to sing.

> SMILE! And fly through the air,
> Like a bird too close tae the SUN.

> SMILE! For one second o flight,
> And follow the golden path tae HEAVEN!!!
> Just wan second tae... Go!
> Ma boady wants tae... Go! Go!
> A just wanna be a boring bastard!
>
> Boring Bastard! Boring Bastard!

Bish does a spin, then goes onto the floor and starts wriggling about. One of the girls is still on stage looking down at Bish, not sure what is going on. Spiney put his boot on her backside and sets her flying back into the audience. Bish is back on his feet and starts singing again.

> But A'm still here hangin' owan tae a piece o rock
> A'm just holdin on tae re-a-li-tyyy
> Fuck! Fuck! A'm just holdin' on, on, on to re-a-li-tyyy.
> A'm gripped oot'a ma fuckin' skul.
> Nae-where tae go but up, what the F-U-C-K!
> Just wan second tae... Go!
> Ma boady wants tae... Go! Go!
> A just wanna be a boring bastard!
>
> Boring Bastard! Boring Bastard!
> Boring Bastard! Boring Bastard!

The audience is jumping up and down. Some at the front are spilling onto the stage. I push a few back to give us more space. Bish is clapping his hands in the air and shouts out, 'A wanae hear yae sing. Boring Bastard... Boring Bastard.'
A few faint calls come back from the audience. Bish tries again.
　'A wanae hear yae sing... Boring Bastard... Boring Bastard.'

More people from the audience join in. Soon a chorus of 'Boring Bastard, Boring Bastard!' is coming from the crowd. Bish sings the chorus again by himself.

> *Ma boady wants tae... Go! Go!*
> *A just wanna be a boring bastard!*
> *Boring Bastard! Boring Bastard!*

Bish moves out in front and starts to speak to the audience. This bit isn't in the script. I hold Lucy's tit to pause the tape, wondering what is going on; Spiney and Rep look as confused.
   'Hello France!'
There is a big cheer from the crowd.
   'This is The Borrheid Cream Team!'
Another cheer.
   'B!C!T!'
Another cheer.
   'Balls! Cunts! And! Tits!'
Another cheer.
   'It's nice tae be here. We huv cum awe the way frum Scotland tae play a special gig here tae night fur J-C. Let's hear a big hand fur J-C.'
There is no response from the audience.
   'Just start singin' fur Christ sake will yae!' I whisper over to Bish.

Bish gives the nod and I release Lucy's tit. The next song is coming up. Lucy starts a solo sound. I flick the spot on to Bish and dim the back lighting.
Bish jumps into his manic routine, shouting at the top of his voice, *'Rock, Rock, Rock!'* in higher and higher pitch tones, blasting out of the loudspeakers. There is a huge cheer from the crowd.

Spiney plays some cords on the guitar, followed shortly by Rep on the drums. Bish comes in again, shouting into the mic.

> *Rock, Rock, Rock, Rock, Rock, Rock!*
> *Rock the e-sta-blish-ment.*
> *The right huv nae right tae dictate*
> *The revolution hus the right tae rock.*
> *Rock, Rock, Rock, Rock, Rock, Rock!*

Spiney and I come in on chorus.

> *Rock the E-sta-blish-ment.*

Spiney plays alongside Lucy. Bish stands in front of Lucy with hands out, trying to hold Lucy's rotating breasts.
    'Get back yur gontae knacker her.'
Bish turns round and starts singing again.

> *All yae cun dae is s-s-slag mae oaf.*
> *Solve yur owan problem mate.*
> *Dinnae wan a drug tae sedate ma brain.*
> *Need tae get spaced oot owan a rock face.*
> *Rock, Rock, Rock, Rock, Rock, Rock!*
> *Rock the E-sta-blish-ment.*

Bish puts his hand on his groin and starts jumping up and down. He takes the mic again and sings.

> *Don't question ma life, Why?*
> *What's! Yur mis-take, yu've made?*
> *If A lose ma g-r-i-p*
> *Don't remember mae, but*
> *Rock, Rock, Rock, Rock, Rock, Rock!*

Rock the E-sta-blish-ment.

Bish is back in front of Lucy doing some sexy hip rotation movement. I'm signalling Bish to get back in case he knocks Lucy over. Bish gives a wry smile. He takes the mic and starts to sing.

> *People say A'm cazy*
> *A say it's a dead cert*
> *Who am A tae turn the tide*
> *Against the force o Fate!*
> *Rock, Rock, Rock, Rock, Rock, Rock!*
> *Rock the E-sta-blish-ment.*

Bish is about to start his Nazi goose-step routine. I whisper loudly over to Bish, 'Don't do the goose step here fur Christ sake!'
Bish starts goose-stepping across the stage one way, then goose-steps back to the mic to sing.

> *Simply forgotten in a pile o Shite!*
> *A diamond ya cannae Hide.*
> *Look at mae through yur lookin' glass,*
> *Don't like whit yae See!*
> *Rock, Rock, Rock, Rock, Rock, Rock!*
> *Rock the E-sta-blish-ment.*

Bish takes his tie off, swings it about in the air, dances a bit, then launches it into the crowd. He picks up the mic and sings.

> *Don't ask mae why A want tae climb.*
> *In yur fucked up state o mind.*
> *Tell mae that A know nuthin*

> *A tell yae y'ure r-r-right.*
> *Rock, Rock, Rock, Rock, Rock, Rock!*
> *Rock the E-sta-blish-ment.*

Three or four girls come on stage and dance along with Bish.
　'Get those birds oaf the stage, there gontae knock intae Lucy,' I whisper over to Bish.
Bish tries to usher them off the stage, but one of them grabs him and drags him off into the crowd. Spiney and Rep play by themselves, while I hold Lucy's tit.
Bish appears back out of the crowd, gets on the stage and starts singing again.

> *Don't ask mae why A go owan the hill.*
> *Only place tae find peace o mind and will!*
> *Look oot frum ma win-dae.*
> *Dinnae like whit A see!*
> *Rock, Rock, Rock, Rock, Rock, Rock!*
> *Rock the E-sta-blish-ment.*

Someone in the audience starts throwing beer at Bish as he dances. Bish stands in front of the crowd encouraging more beer to be thrown.
I whisper over, 'Start singin' will yae, next time there might be a bottle wae the beer.'
Bish starts singing.

> *Blunt ma Ambition und bottle ma Spirit!*
> *Tae keep mae in ma place.*
> *Don't ask me why A'm a waste o space.*
> *A'm tryin' tae escape the human shite!*
> *Rock, Rock, Rock, Rock, Rock, Rock!*
> *Rock the E-sta-blish-ment.*

Bish starts dancing. Spiney and I join in pogoing. Bish starts singing again.

> *A just wanna be an accountant.*
> *Mr Sensible and huv a hoose.*
> *A wanna live a life o boredom.*
> *und die in ma cuncil estate.*
> *Rock, Rock, Rock, Rock, Rock, Rock!*
> *Rock the E-sta-blish-ment.*

Bish does his dance routine, turns around quickly, slips on the wet floor and falls on his backside.
There is a long piece from Lucy to end the song. I keep close to Lucy in case the tape jams, ready to give her a good kick to get her going again.

The next song is "Plutonium child".
I turn the spotlight off Bish and turn one onto Lucy. There is another huge cheer from the crowd.
Bish is slowly getting to his feet holding his back while Lucy is playing her head off. She comes to an end. Spiney starts with a very fast guitar solo. Bish joins in, singing at a very fast tempo in a staccato style set by Rep bashing away on the drums.

> *There's a nuclear nomb in ma back garden!*

Bish breaks into a short dance.

> *A huv nae shield against a cancer threat!*

Bish dances, arms and legs going in all directions.

> *Whit cun A dae tae protect ma child!*

≈ *Rock Rock* ≈

Bish dances as if he was jogging.

The law is made tae keep me doon!

I join in with the bass guitar, dum, dum, dum… Bish is jumping up and down going mental on the floor, then quickly gets back to the mic and sings.

Disney child pick up a_plutonium toy!

Bish spins around, arms outstretched like a wheel.

Und catch a genetic mutated moose!

Bish goes on his knees and takes the mic with him.

Each handful o earth a radioactive scare!

Bish is still on his knees.

Contamination is the common wurd!

Dum, dum, dum, on the bass guitar. Bish is back on his feet again doing his stuff.

The politician und bigot and xeno-fobe will fail!

Bish starts kicking in the air like kicking a football.

We cun break the chains! Tae gi ther tae pull doon the walls.

Bish kicks in the air again and kicks over the mic. High-pitched feedback is blasted through the sound system. He picks up the mic and sings.

> *Take heart! Let us dance taegither.*

Bish kicks over the mic again. Goes on the ground and starts singing the next line on the ground.

> *A huv a dream where nae budy hus tae fight!*

I come in with a dum, dum, dum on the bass guitar. Bish throws the contents of his beer glass into the crowd, does a spin, lands on the floor, gets back on his feet, and starts singing into the microphone again.

> *This planet a common treasure tae share!*

Bish was flicking sweat from his brow into the audience.

> *But A dinnae owan a handful o Earth!*

Bish starts flicking snots from his nose into the crowd.

> *Expected tae die fur cuntry o birth.*

Bish starts doing some sort of belly dance.

> *Not by sword but a cancer death!*

Dum, dum, dum goes the bass guitar. Bish is back on the floor, wriggling about, doing the worm. He is back at the mic, ready to sing.

> *Owan the Clyde the Polaris Sails!*

Bish is jiggling about.

Frum an Ayr-shire field a ploughman watches.

Bish spins around, hands over his head, his kilt lifting up. He stops suddenly and grabs the mic.

A tourist bus passes everyone looking but see nuthin'!

Bish is shoggling his head about like he had a bee in his hair.

Nuclear bombs pointing naebudy knows where!

I play my bit on the bass guitar: dum, dum, dum... Spiney joins in with Bish, pogoing about. Bish takes the mic.

Ma eastern friend A cannae see!

Bish starts doing some sort of can-can holding onto the bottom of his kilt.

But A dae know nuclear bombs frum heaven
Will hurt ma heid!

Bish is still doing the can-can with his kilt.

Dae they believe the same as mae?

Bish is still doing the can-can turns his back to the crowd and flicks his kilt to slightly expose his bum. There is a cheer from the crowd.
I come in with a dum, dum, dum. Bish faces the crowd, clapping away, encouraging the audience to join in. The crowd starts clapping. He takes the mic.

Again if tanks run oor Poland.

Bish does a quick spin, drops to the floor and then jumps back up almost in one movement.

Divine intervention is the only way!
A look arund in vain!

Bish tries to do the spin and drop with cross leg manoeuvre again. His time he doesn't manage it and ends on the floor. He quickly gets on his feet again to get to the mic.

Tae which Goad can A trust und pray!

I do my one chord on the bass guitar dum, dum, dum. Bish stands still for a change, staring up at the ceiling. He then takes the mic.

The nuclear bomb may solve yur problem,

Bish stands out arms wide open and flicking his tongue in and out.

But the politician owes an ex-planation!

Bish does a twirl and pulls his mouth open with both hands.

A black death disappears beneath the waves.

Bish has his hand by his throat as if choking.

Condition red! Is it practice or is it THE END?!

Bish does one big pogo into the air and lands with a crash. I suddenly switch all the lights off. There is a big cheer from the crowd.

'Ure yae OK?' I whisper over to Bish.

'Yae, nae probs.'

I wait for the audience to quieten down and then bring the spotlight onto Bish. I bring the lights on slowly for the next song, still with the spot on Bish. By this time the sweat is pouring off Bish. The paint on his body is starting to run.

Lucy plays a piece of music, Spiney and Rep join in. I dance along with Bish on stage.

The crowd is really getting in the mood. There are a couple of girls at the front dancing topless, their tits are bouncing all over the place. Another has a shaved head and is wearing a black leather cat-suit thing laced with silver studs and big black leather boots.

The band is playing well and we start to relax and enjoy ourselves.

A girl in front has a chain between her legs, her hips gyrating back and forth along the chain. A couple of girls get on the stage and dance along with us. Bish kicks one in the backside and she falls head first into the crowd. Everyone thinks its part of the act and a big cheer goes up.

'Thank yae! Thank yae!'

Bish is milking the crowd.

'We'll play wan mare song before the interval und we'll back! In fifteen minutes...'

Lucy starts off the next song with Rep tapping out a beat. Bish starts to sing.

A huv every thing

> *but huv nuthing A want!*
> *It's a sad state o affairs,*
> *fur a developed economy!*
> *A sais!*
> *It's a sad state o affairs,*
> *fur a developed economy!*

Bish drops to the floor and starts doing the worm, wriggling about on the ground. Spiney and I are pogoing away, pretending to kick Bish on the ground.
Bish gets back on his feet. Lucy plays a bit by herself. Bish sings into the mic again.

> *Society expects tae cun-form,*
> *Spend und throw away!*
> *Con su mer ism goan wild!*
> *Materialism is the order o taeday!*
> *Chase the dollar,*
> *it's the drug tae swarla.*
> *Hooo ahhh!*
> *A sais!*
> *Hooo ahhh!*
> *Chase the dollar,*
> *it's the drug tae swarla.*
>
> *Ma chines built no tae last!*
> *But buy new every other day!*
> *A dream o fast cars designer clathes,*
> *und don't furget the bimbo in the bikini!*

Bish stretches out both hands towards Lucy's rotating breasts and starts moving his hips as if shagging her. He gets back to the mic.

Only chance in life!
Is tae watch owan ma T.V. set!
The rat race is fur rats!
Und no fur the animal in mae!
It's the konsumer society!
In the kapitalist's paradise!
Huv we furgotten reality?
Chained tae ma T.V.!
Ughhh!
A sais!
Ughhh!
Huv we furgotten reality?
Chained tae ma T.V.!

Bish spins around, arms outstretched, spiralling round like a helicopter; does a bit too much, over balances and goes into the crowd. The crowd push him back on stage. He is back at the mic.

> *Soap opera und game shows,*
> *Stare at a piece o furniture!*
> *Ideal fur the advertiser!*
> *Tae send the message doon the wave.*
>
> *Cum fort frum a semidetached*
> *look oot frum yur cage!*
> *Huv yae realised yur drrream,*
> *Or ure yur afraid o a nightmare?!*
> *A new technology must be alright!*
> *Available fur the jetset.*

Bish pogoes up and down. One foot goes over the edge of the stage and he goes back into the crowd. Trying to get back onto his feet he manages to rip this girl's T-shirt. Her left breast pops out. She disappears back into the crowd.

'Cun yae no stay owan yur feet?' Spiney whispers over to Bish.

Bish carries on singing.

> Fa-mine in Africa is fine!
> Tae watch owan ma T.V. set.
> Plague in Asia won't infect Mae,
> Lying owan ma sofa bed.
> War beamed intae ma living room,
> Nae worries tae dodge the flying Lead!
>
> Slave tae ma machine,
> Pollution is ma right
> An infurmation age,
> But no wan understands.
> Loast in a sea o technology,
> reach oot fur a helping hond.
> Nae hope o a life belt,
> Help less against the force o progress!
>
> Mother nature acting in best interest!
> Against a man made dying planet fate!
> Kill the land und extinct the sea,
> A problem yae cunnae see!
> A slow death o stress,
> or suffocation by car exhaust.
> But the coroner said,
> Death by mis adventure.
>
> Watch Oot!
> It's a polis state!

> *Hooo Ahhh!*
> *A sais!*
> *Hooo Ahhh!*
> *Ughhh!*
> *Ee haw! Ee haw! Ee haw!*
> *It's a polis state!*
> *If yae don't conform!*
> *yu'll be forced tae integrate.*
> *Big brother is watching yae!*
> *owan step oot und yu're deid.*

Bish dances away, stops, puts the mic to his arse and a loud farting sound comes out over the loudspeaker.

'Glad its no me that's singin' intae that mic!' Spiney gives another loud whisper over to Bish.

Bish starts singing again.

> *Society will stoap mae!*
> *Frum ex-pressin myself.*
> *Only escape is ma thought,*
> *bought und sold as a commodity.*
> *A need a psychiatrist help und medicine,*
> *tae be programmed tae follow the Crowd!*

Bish starts his dance again. He stops, spies the big punter with the white face and leather face mask, leads him onto the stage like a dog on lead.

> *Get ma priority right!*
> *Whit A want in life is a dish-washer.*
> *And a life time sub-scrip-tion tae Readers Digest,*
> *package hoaliday in Benidorm,*
> *und don't forget a poodle sham-poo und set!*

At the last word I turn off all the lights and the band goes silent. The crowd are jumping up and down, cheering away. I turn on the hall lights. Bish starts shaking hands with people that are crowding him on the front of the stage.

'Cumoawn let's get back stage... Don't let this pop star stuff get tae yur heid.'

We go off stage and back to the changing room.

'Fuckin' hell, that wis wild oot there.'

'Did'yae see that bird wae her tit's hangin'oot?'

Jean-Claude appears in the dressing room with some beer for us. He appears a bit happier than the last time.

There is banging at the door. Jean-Claude opens the door. Four or five girls try to force their way in. Spiney and I try to help Jean-Claude close the door.

'Tell them tae come back aifter the show,' we all urge Jean-Claude to translate.

Jean-Claude says a few words in French then he closes the door.

'Fuckin' magic, this is whit it's awe aboot, a bit o action the night, boys.'

'There'ze a Germany man want to talk yousz about to do a film.' Jean-Claude says to us turning round with his back to the door.

'A film; he wants us to be in a film?'

'*Oui, oui*, he sesz a film.'

Almost on cue, there is another knock on the door. Jean-Claude opens the door slightly, half expecting to be rushed by a group of girls.

'Come in, mister.'

A tall, well dressed man walks in and introduces himself.

'Hai, I'm Ralf. I work for a film company that makes movies for German T.V..'

He spoke very good English, with a slight American accent.

'I liked your act. I think we could use some of your material. Would you be interested?'

We all look at each other not really knowing what to say.

'Yea, sure we ure,' Bish answers first.

'Do you have a manager?' asks Ralf.

'Manager of whit?' Spiney asks.

'Yea, sure we huv pal, but he's owan holiday the day his maw is ill,' Bish interrupts.

Ralf gives a pitiful look. I not sure if it was out of sympathy or he realised that he was dealing with a bunch of jokers.

There is more banging at the door. The noise outside is growing. Jean-Claude is starting to look nervous again.

'Cun yae come back at the end o the show and we cun discuss business.'

We all look at him seriously as if to say how boring yet another deal. Ralf leaves.

As soon as the door is shut, we all jump up and down in jubilation.

'Fuckin' magic, cun yae believe it. Whit will the boy's back hame think?'

'Owan the box. In a movie.'

'Just think the next time A sign owan, an the brew asks wit wus yur last joob. A cun say, movie star!'

There is more banging at the door. Jean-Claude interrupts our conversation, he is looking more anxious.

'Start soon? OK, OK?'

'No worries, J-C,' replies Bish.

We start to get organised for the second half.

I notice Spiney opening a couple of cans of vegetable soup and pouring the contents into a hot-water-bottle-like flexible plastic container. I ask what the soup was for.

'It's in case A'um a wee bit hungry owan stage!'
Spiney's latest invention was intriguing, but I knew it was best not to ask too many questions. He straps the plastic container to his chest and puts on a T-shirt to conceal the container. Bish is all keyed up ready for the second half.

'Right! Everywan ready? OK. One, two, three, let's go!'

We pile out of the changing room for the second half.

There is a big cheer as we go back onto the stage. Everybody is in good spirits, jumping about. We are all surprised and a bit overwhelmed by the enthusiastic reaction of the crowd. We look at each other and wondered what we are doing right.
Jean-Claude is in the crowd having a shouting match with someone. It looked as if he was trying to stop people stealing drink from the small bar at the other end of the hall. I had a feeling that he was not expecting such a large crowd or such a select group of people.

We start on our next number; it is "Hole in ma heid".
Bish looks around, gives the thumbs up and counts, 'One, two, three, four.'
I start Lucy, but no sound comes out, her tits are stationary. Bish moves forward with the mic and makes a half sound and realises that Lucy isn't working, turns around anxiously, wondering what is going wrong. I fiddle around with the switches to get her going. She won't start. Bish steps out of the spotlight for a second, turns around and whispers with his hand over the mike, 'Get that fuckin' thing goin' fur christ sake!'

'A'm tryin' fur fuck sake—cun yae play that first bit again while a get it goin' again?'
I give Lucy a good whack on the back to get her going, and a few notes come out before I find the pause button. Spiney and

Rep play a bit of a solo to give me time to get organised. I give the thumbs up to Bish.

'One, two, three, four!' Bish tries again.
I release the pause button and the music comes blasting out. Bish goes into song.

> A've go'ta hole in ma heid!
> Nothin tae worry aboot it's quite casual.
> Latest fashion accessory frum the gloassy magazine.
> Quite handy, lets ma brain release the thinkin' process.
> It helps mae see whit's wrong in this world.
> Third World poverty not ma problem, pal.
> Pollution is ma right destroy planet earth.
> A'm stuck oan the point o life.

Lucy does a solo. Bish is spinning round and round. Spiney and I are pogoing up and down in the background. Lucy stops. Rep keeps drumming.

'Get Lucy goin' again fur fuck sake!' Bish whispers across.

'It's awe yur prancin' aboot…its makin' her unhappy.'
I pogo over and give her a few slaps on the back. She still isn't playing.

'Cumoawn, get her playin' again will yae!' Bish gives a louder whisper.

'A'm tryin fur Christ sake!'
I give Lucy another slap on the back. This time her tits start turning again. I hold one, give the thumbs up to Bish, then release Lucy's tit. Bish starts singing.

> A've go'ta hole in ma heid!
> Born working class die working class,
> nowhere tae go no choice, no hope.
> Go fighting, get pissed,

Huv baby grow old find a grave.
Wreck this destroy that,
only identity is ma writing oan the wall.
A'm stuck oan the point o life.

Lucy does her solo. Bish spins around again, trips on something and ends in the audience. He gets back on stage quickly to start the next verse.

A've go'ta hole in ma heid!
People ask why do A climb?
Mental tae dae such things they say.
A say why ure yae livin in such a fucked up state.
The whole world is against mae,
because they do not like whit A say
Be a sheep and follow the state.
A'm stuck oan the point o life.

A funny hissing sound out of Lucy. Spiney joins in with a high-pitched tone on the guitar, then starts making wavey sounds. Rep does a bit on the drums, then Spiney a bit on the guitar, then back to Rep, then to Spiney. The two play around each other. Lucy makes some more strange sounds. Bish comes in.

A've go'ta hole in ma heid!
Take a drug to fix my mind,
chemical illusion clears my vision.
Better than society induced depressive plight.
Only escape from the working class fate
Sniff glue to relax my state.
A nice glass of meths, after dinner taste.
A'm stuck oan the point o life.

Bish is jumping up and down, going into spasms. Spiney and I join in. Bish starts swinging the mic stand round and round, almost hitting the people in the front of the audience.

> A've go'ta hole in ma heid!
> Nae need tae meditate.
> A've found ma piece o mind.
> A've found the point o life
> A'm in a state o ecstasy.
>
> That's right. A'm in a state o ecstasy.
> Ec-sta-sy!
> Ec-sta-sy!

Bish has a few gulps of beer, then carries on. Bish shouts down the mic.

> Huuugh!
> Nuthin's gointae change.
> A sais, Huuugh!
> Nuthin's gointae change.

Bish starts growling and moaning. Lucy starts playing faster and faster. Bish dances faster and faster. Lucy stops. Bish comes in.

> Huuugh!

Lucy plays a bit more.

> A sais, Huuugh!
> Nuthin's gointae change.

Rep does his bit on the drums and Spiney on the guitar. Bish is dancing on the floor. Lucy plays a bit more. Bish comes in.

> Huuugh!

Lucy plays a bit more.

> *A sais,*
> *Nuthin's gointae change.*
> *A sais,*
> *Nuthin's gointae change.*
> *A sais,*
> *Nuthin's gointae change.*

The music dies away slowly and I fade the lights. The crowd are shouting their heads off. A few seconds later I bring the lights back on the stage.
The next song is "Coke Can Culture". I signal across to Bish to be ready. Spiney moves forward towards the microphone, pushing Bish out of the way and signals to me to turn the spot on. Spiney stands silently staring out into the audience. This wasn't in the script. The three of us at the back are looking at each other, wondering what Spiney is up to. The next thing, Spiney starts going into convulsions, holding his stomach and sounding as if he is about to be sick.
 'Eh! Ehhh! Ehhh!' is broadcast at full volume around the hall.
The audience quieten down a bit, wondering what is happening. Spiney is bent double in pain.
Then Spiney gives an almighty, 'Ehhh!!!' and all this vomit is projected out into the audience. The people in front get covered in sick and start to freak out. A girl in front who has been dancing almost topless got a big dollop of vomit in her hair.

She stands there, not knowing whether to cry or scream. Another girl gets a big dollop of vomit in her cleavage. This other punter tries to jump out of the way of the flying wall of sickness, but Spiney manages to vomit in his face and down his T-shirt. Spiney finishes throwing up and wipes his lips clean. The crowd at the front isn't happy. It looks as if there could be trouble. There is an empty beer glass on the ground that Bish had been drinking from. It is now full of vomit. Spiney picks up the glass, casually inspects it carefully in the spot-light for a few seconds, picks out a few vegetable lumps and then starts drinking in big gulps. The crowd at the front don't know how to react: in anger that they have just been covered in sick or in revulsion that Spiney has just drunk his own vomit. It is a great scene.

Bish breaks the tension, 'One, two, three,' and starts into the next song "Coke Can Culture".
Spiney disappears to the back of the stage and takes off the T-shirt and plastic container. Lucy starts playing a stretched sax sound mixed in with some keyboard stuff which Bish and I had mixed together. Spiney reappears, this time with a guitar around his neck playing a high pitched sound.
Bish stands with hands in air at the front of the stage and starts off with a whining sound a bit like a siren.
    'Whoooo! Whooo! Whooo! Whooo! Whooo! Whooo!'
Lucy plays a bit. Bish starts singing.

> *Beams o light frum ma television box,*
> *gees me square eyes,*
> *receptive tae the market hype.*
> *Cellophane wrapped,*
> *pre-packaged, sterilised world,*
> *there's nae where tae escape.*
> *It's a Coke! Can! Culture!*

Lucy does a solo. The three of us are pogoing up and down. Rep leaves his drums and joins in as well.

> *Buy wan and throw away,*
> *it's no an excess, it's a necessity.*
> *Frum Sherpa owan Everest,*
> *tae Eskimo owan the ice flow.*
> *From Masai owan African plain,*
> *tae Indian in Amazon.*
> *They try tae escape,*
> *It's a Coke! Can! Culture!*

Lucy does a solo and all four of us are dancing again. Bish suddenly stops and stares up at the roof until the start of his next line.

> *Yae need tae buy, don't question why,*
> *A'm in a moronic state,*
> *there's nae escape.*
> *It's a Coke! Can! Culture!*

There is a long solo from Lucy. The four of us are dancing away. A couple of girls get on the stage and dance along with us.

> *Feed the starving masses,*
> *gee them a taste o the West.*
> *It's canned and hyped,*
> *and sold as the milk o life.*
> *A don't like the taste,*
> *but A cunnae be right,*
> *The marketing says,*
> *Coke is great.*
> *Cun! Yae! Hear! Me!*
> *Coke! Can! Culture!*

The light on the stage starts to pulsate. Lucy comes out with a telephone sound. Bish starts barking like a dog and comes in with a high-pitched ball-crushing tone.

'Woo, woo, woo.'

It is my turn on the guitar: dum, dum, dum. More telephone sounds from Lucy.

'Woo, woo, woo.'

> A don't like the taste,
> but A cunnae be right,
> The marketing says,
> Coke is great.
> Did yae hear mae?!

Spiney and I shout our heads off.

> A don't like the taste.
> Did yae hear mae?!

Bish puts his ear to the crowd to get them to sing.

> But a cunnae be right.
> Did yae hear mae?!
> The marketing says.
> Coke is great!!!

Bish stops suddenly, but Lucy continues for a bit with a hissing sound.

I shout over to Bish if he wants to try "A view from Stob Dearg" or move onto the next song. Bish is game to continue, so I leave the tape running and indicate to Spiney and Rep that we will be doing "A view".

Rep starts a marching-sound beat on the drums. The audience start to clap along with the beat. Lucy plays some sort of weird pipe music. Spiney jams along with the guitar. Bish is still moving even though he was standing still. He comes in on vocals with a grumpy, vomit-throwing-up sounding voice, almost as if reading each line.

> Buchallie Etive Mor owan guard entrance tae the 'Coe.
> Whit secrets dus the auld shepherd hold?
> A land scoured by glacier and forests scorched by man.
> Rivers o blood treachery deceit and murder.
> Family feud passed frum faither tae son.
> A haunting mist that covers and then exposes the past.
> Tails of horror witches phantoms and ghosts.

Rep plays through with the same beat. Spiney joins in making some weird sounds on the guitar. Bish starts singing again.

> An English army marched north in search o Jacobite.
> Highland soldier marched south tae fight an Empire war.
> The English landlord took the land and slaughtered oor kin.
> Sheep more important than man they died fur profit and gain.
> A stand on Bauchallie Etive Mor wondering where they went.
> Facing an icy wind through silent miles and empty space.
> Way eyes o a child and wonder o a saint.

Bish wanders to the front of the audience blowing kisses in the air. Spiney comes in again with the guitar. Rep is still bashing a slow beat. Bish starts on the next verse.

> Victims o chance and geography yae say.
> There ure many sad periods o history whit a pity.
> When minority culture is viewed as irrelevant a mistake.
> Something tae be conquered replaced moved oota the way.

*As the big boys scheme and play the small cower in fear and fright.
History has taught us nothing except it will happen again.
Cannae they see monoculture is a fright.*

Bish is back facing the crowd giving "V" signs. Spiney does a longer bit on the guitar. Rep keeps the beat slow. Bish starts on the next verse. A girl appears on the stage dancing alongside Bish. She has a series of snake tattoo's running down both arms. She tries to sing something into the mic, but Bish manages to push her back into the crowd in time for the start of the next verse.

*A hear the cry o pipes flowing oor mountain like morning mist.
A cry frum ma brother and memories frum a distant land.
A can see pain in yur tears and hear sorrow in yur song.
A land where yae wur born but never forget,
body and soul as mountain and sea.
Like the wild salmon that leaves these shores,
fights awe nature tae return hame but may die at the hand o fate.*

Spiney starts off slow with the guitar, then after ten seconds or so takes off with a really fast guitar solo. Rep keeps pace with the guitar. Bish moves in for the last verse, shouting down the mic.

*Today A climb these hills in freedom.
A silence golden only tae be broken,
by the sound o a low flying Phantom jet.
An unspoken war declared a new Highland battlefield,
against a distant Soviet threat.
Deceive yursel but ya cannae hide the frost hus settled overnight.
At first dawn light The Buchallie will still be watching.*

Everything came to a sudden end and I turned off all the lights to the stage. The crowd seemed to like it. I was a bit surprised since it was a lot slower and less dancy than the others. I brought the lights slowly up on the stage for our grand finale. There was another fast song that Lucy played mainly by herself, with Rep coming in on the drums on occasions and Spiney giving bits on the guitar. Bish and I were dancing away up front. The crowd were dancing away.
Bish would sing, 'Comply!... Baby... Comply!' every now and then.
The music built up to a crescendo, then suddenly stopped and at the same time I turned off the lights to the stage. There was a big cheer from the crowd.

That was the end of our repertoire.

Everything went well; we were pleased. Bish had put on a great performance. I brought the stage lights back on.
Bish went up front and spoke into the mic.
    'Thank you! Thank you France und good night frum the... B.C.T!'
We all faced the audience and bowed, then turned our backs and bowed again, this time lifting up our kilts exposing our backsides. There was a big cheer from the audience. I switched all the stage lights off.

We started to leave the stage with head torches on. It was the end of our act. It was time to get paid and go home. However, the crowd did not see it that way and there were some people starting to become a bit hostile and soon slow hand-clapping started. Jean-Claude came running over and shouted, 'Plazye, plazye. Plazye more.' He was now looking more manic than ever. The atmosphere started to become more aggressive. We all looked at each other wondering what should happen next. Nobody had thought about an encore.

'Whit the fuck ure wae goin' tae dae?'
I whispered across to Bish, 'Go ontae the stage an' talk tae them for fuck sake, just keep them goin' fur a minute or two. A'll rewind the tape and we'll dae sum o the songs again.'
I went back onto the stage with Bish and started to fiddle around with Lucy in the beam of the headtorch, trying to rewind the tape back to the correct spot. Bish started to speak to the audience, even though most of them probably could not understand a word of English.

'Good evenin' France!' Bish shouted into the mike.
There was a big cheer from the crowd.

'This is oor first concert in France.'
Another big cheer.

'We're playin' here next week.'
Another big cheer.

"cos were getting' paid lots o dosh.'
Another big cheer.
Spiney and Rep reappeared back on the stage.

'Then we're touring Germany.'
Another big cheer.

'Then Italy.'
Rep leaned over and whispered to me, 'Whit the fuck's he goin on aboot?'

'Shhh,' I turned round to Bish and shouted over, 'keep them talkin' while A get organised.'
Bish was still milking the audience.

'Yae cun buy oor latest LP at the door at the end.'
Another big cheer.
Bish was running out of ideas to say. Spiney leaned over to Bish and said, 'Tell them they ure awe a bunch o wankers!'

'Yur awe a bunch o fuckin' wankers!' Bish shouted out.

Another big cheer.

'Bish, A've wound back tae. Hole in ma heid. OK. Bish, music ready,' I shouted over to Bish.

'One, two, three, four,' Bish gave a countdown.

The music blasted off again and Bish started doing his stuff. Nobody seemed to realise that we were repeating the music, may be they didn't care. Everybody started jumping up and down having a good time.

We kept on playing through into the next track "Capitalist Consumer Chaos."

I noticed at the other end of the hall there was some trouble starting. A fight had broken out. We all looked at each other.

'Keep playin' for fuck sake 'cos there'll be a riot here, if we stop,' Bish shouted across to the rest in the band.

We moved quickly onto the next song "Hole in ma heid".

The fight was getting bigger and the crowd started to push tighter towards the stage. We were trying to look cool and casual as if nothing was happening. An anxious sounding Bish shouted over.

'Keep playin fur Christ sake!'

I was trying to push people at the front off the stage. Beer bottles and glasses started flying through the air. Things were starting to get a bit out of hand. The atmosphere was becoming explosive.

The place soon erupted into a total riot. Everybody was fighting somebody. The air was full of flying objects, chairs, bottles, bodies...flying backwards and forwards.

There were a couple of what looked like smoke canisters thrown from the back of the room. The smoke was spilling out everywhere. People were running away from the gas.

'Fuck it's the polis!'

There were men in dark jump suits running around. They had got several punters on the ground and were trying to handcuff them. Another gas canister came in our direction. Spiney kicked it back into the hall. There was an acrid smell in the air. My eyes, nose and throat started to burn.

'Fuck this fur a laugh moan tae fuck oot'a here.'

We dropped everything and headed for the changing room. People were running in panic and confusion in all directions, trying to get out, getting trampled under-foot, trying to get rid of stuff. Lucy was still on stage, illuminated by the spotlight, tits going round and round, playing her head off, oblivious to the chaotic scene.

Our changing room was packed full of people trying to squeeze through a tiny window. We had to wait our turn. Spiney and I helped a couple of girls get out the window, but a big backside was now stuck in the window. Each of us pushed a cheek to get her moving.

The punter who had tried to sell me drugs appeared in the room, and came barging through to the front.

'Haud oawn a minute pal.'

He was looking anxious and tried to push past Spiney and I.

'This boay's no fuckin' real!'

I turned round to Bish and Rep, and said, 'Get this frog tae the back'.

Bish and Rep grabbed him and dragged the punter back. A struggle started. The next thing I heard was, 'He's goat a fuckin' chib!' and the punter started slashing the air in front of Bish. Bish and Rep backed off.

Spiney picked up a nearby fire extinguisher and shouted over, 'Hay, ARSEHOLE!'

The punter turned round. Spiney directed the extinguisher into the punter's face and pressed the trigger. For a split second the punter braced, expecting a jet of water or foam to hit his face. Instead, a little dribble of foam came out, Spiney

looked a bit distraught, and gave the punter a wry smile. Bish and Rep jumped on him from behind, put a T-shirt over his head and got him to the ground. The knife was still in the punter's hand. Spiney belted his hand with the end of the fire extinguisher. There was a shout of pain from the punter. The knife was free. I kicked it into the corner. The punter got up and disappeared out of the room.
It was all over in seconds. All Spiney had to say about the situation was, 'Fuckin' useless frog fire extinguisher!'
He threw it to the side and went back to helping the girl get out of the window. Her bum was still stuck.

Soon we were out in the night air. I could see across to where the toilet was; there was a fight. It looked as if a couple of police were trying to arrest someone, but then more characters arrived and started to beat up the police.

We headed over to a small nearby hill to watch the unfolding scene. Several handcuffed people were put into the back of a police Citröen van. There were people running about in all directions. Some others joined us on the hill. A couple of bikers disappeared down the road. A cop went over to our van and Bish's bike. From a distance it looked as if he was taking down our registration plates.

It was a chilly night. We weren't wearing very much and soon were shivering in the night air. Eventually, the police disappeared. The café was quiet. We went closer to investigate. There was an eerie silence about the place. The door at the front of the café was locked. I banged on the window a couple of times. Nobody came. The four of us went round to the back. The changing room window was locked. We went round to the toilet window, it was broken, so we went in to find our music gear.

Spiney went first through the window. I followed. I landed on broken glass on the floor. There was just about enough light from a nearby street light to see inside.
The wash hand basin was smashed to pieces. The toilet door had been broken down from the outside in, and was hanging from one hinge. There were used syringes lying about in one corner.
We moved into the main hall. Broken glass crunched underfoot as we walked. It was dark and spooky. There was a strong smell of stale beer and cigarette smoke mixed in with an acrid smell of gas. The smell of gas was overwhelming and my eyes were soon pouring with tears. Spiney appeared in the main hall, with tears running down his face. I managed to find a light switch for the main room and turned it on. We stood there and scanned around. It was a scene of devastation.

Lucy was gone! The stage had been cleared. All the music stuff had disappeared! The police had lifted the lot.
I went back into the toilet and told Bish and Rep that everything had gone including Lucy. We all came back into the hall and spread out looking everywhere for Lucy and any of our musical stuff in case it had been stashed somewhere, but I knew at the back of my mind it was all gone.
I checked out the cupboard Jean-Claude used for his electrical stuff, it was half full of empty beer bottles. Spiney checked out our changing room there was nothing there except some of the clothes we had forgotten to pick up in our rush to leave. There was a pile of stuff in the corner of the hall. Bish and Rep went over to investigate; nothing. Then they checked behind the bar, there was some blood on the floor, but no Lucy.

We all reported back that there was nothing to be found. With heads low we headed back out. We crawled out of the toilet window and sat down on the tarmac outside contemplating what had just happened. There were almost tears in our eyes.

'It's awe gone. Lucy, ma guitar, awe the music, the drums the fuckin' lot.'

'The fuckin' frog polis huv taken the lot.'
Rep tried to be optimistic.

'We could always go and ask the frog cops fur it back.'

'Don't be fuckin' stupid, we would end up gettin' charged wae drug dealing or beating up the polis or sumthin'.'

'Dae'yae fancy the next couple o years in the frog nick?'

'We've already been dun over by the frog polis fur drug runnin'. A cunnae see them understonin' oor side o the story.'

We started to feel the chill in the night air again. There was no other option, but to go back to Chamonix.
Bish and Rep got on the bike. Spiney and I got into an empty van. We didn't say anything. There was nothing to say. All the climbing gear had been lost on Aiguille du Plan and now all the music gear had been lost to the French police.
Lucy was gone. She was irreplaceable. All the months of hard work, writing the songs, putting sounds together on tape, all the practise sessions were wasted.
All the instruments were gone. It would cost a lot of money to replace them. Hard earned money that was for climbing gear and trips.
Our movie debut with Ralf went up in a puff of smoke. The girls that were after us had disappeared into the night.
We hadn't got paid for the gig and were now broke. It had been a bad night.

≈

Next day we woke in a very sombre mood. Nobody was saying

very much. I went down to the train station, hoping to meet the old tramp and ask for advice. I waited all day. He didn't appear.

Back at camp, the four of us sat miserably around an evening fire, heads low, staring into the flames.

'A wannae go hame,' Rep pipes out.
Everyone looks at Rep.
'A wannae go hame.'
'Stop moanin' will yis.'
'A wannae go hame.'
'Will yis just fuck oaf then?' came a blunt reply from Spiney.
'It's awe gone. Lucy, the guitar, awe the music...' Bish mumbled out emotionally.
'It's the end o the band...' said Spiney.
We stared into the evening fire.

Last night's lyrics were going around my head. The words seemed to have extra resonance. MacTin's prophecy seemed to have come true.

> *Born working class, die working class.*
> *Nowhere to go, no choice, no hope.*
> *Who am I to turn the tide,*
> *Against the force of fate.*

I could feel tears building up in my eyes. Just when things were starting to look up, the police ruined everything.

> *Watch out*
> *it's a police state.*
> *If you do not conform*
> *You'll be forced to integrate.*

The words were going round and round my head. I could picture Bish jumping up and down, singing away to last night's audience.

> Big Brother is watching you
> one step out and you're dead.
> Society will stop me,
> from expressing myself.

How true the words appeared to be. Somehow the concert seemed a long way away and the band just a dream. I sat looking at the flames and feeling totally depressed. I had a headache all day that wouldn't go away.

> Blunt my ambition, bottle my spirit
> To keep me in my place.
> Don't ask me why I'm a waste of space.
> I'm tryin' to escape the human shite.

The words echoed around in my mind, wondering what we had done wrong.

> The whole world is against me,
> Because they do not like what I say.
> Be a sheep and follow the state.

All the hard work, setting up the band; all the trouble, getting the music together; all the time, money and effort to get to France for the summer. The whole lot came tumbling down like a house of cards. I just wanted the ground to open and swallow me up.

Bish broke the silence.

'Uch well... At least yae goat sumthin' oota Jacko.'
'Eh? Whit wus that Bish?'
'Yur songs... Jacko gave yae the inspiration tae write yur songs, didn't he?'
'Eh? Oh aye, a big help that is noo. Its awe been flushed doon the fuckin' pan.'
'A wanna go hame,' Rep pipped out.
Spiney glared at him.

The conversation quickly died and the atmosphere went glum again.
I stared into the fire and started to think about what Bish had just said. It had never really dawned on me before that Jacko was the source of the songs and in an in-direct way had lead to the concert last night. After all, if there had been no songs, there would have been no band and no concert...and we wouldn't be feeling so depressed.
Bish started me thinking about Jacko again. May be there was some connection between Jacko and ourselves after all.
I sat looking at the flames and remembered the misery of the bivouac on the North face of Aiguille du Plan and how close it was to the end. The lyrics came into my head.

> What is the chemical that controls your mind?
> Or is it your mind that controls your chemical.

I remembered the weird sensation of happiness and warmth at the back of my head as I shivered away on that ice ledge and tried to make sense of it. What was happening in my head?
Maybe there is some commonality between the adrenaline and addiction. Maybe there is some commonality between pleasure and self-destruction. Maybe there is a commonality between ourselves and Jacko. This kind of triangular paradox bothered me.

A few words came into my head. There was a piece of scrap paper nearby. I started to scribble down a few words.

> *A lust for danger makes me human,*
> *gives my brain adrenaline fix to keep me right.*
> *Otherwise I'll need a drug to blow my mind,*
> *and help me look after myself in modern life.*
> *I'm so happy I could kill myself,*
> *on search for the fountain of inspiration.*
> *A Holy Grail with no beginning or end,*
> *a paradox that never makes sense.*

A title for the song came into my head, "Adrenaline Punk Junky". I wrote down the title and stuffed the paper into my pocket.

'Whit ure yis writin' those songs fur? That's the band flushed doon the lavvy.'
'Uch well, A kinda like writin' them.'
'A wannae go hame,' Rep pipes out again.
'Well yis cun fuckin' walk hame eh?'
'Cunnae believe we've loast everythin'.'

Silence. Then came a big argument.
'Cunnae believe we've loast Lucy.'
'It wus yur fault fur leaving her there.'
'It's awe yur fault fur bringin' us oot here.'
'Naw it wusnae.'
'Aye it wus.'
'A wannae go hame.'
'Look who's fuckin' whingin' noo.'
'Fuck oaf, cunt!'
'Will yis stop fuckin' moanin' will yis!'

'A wannae go fuckin' hame!'
'Fuck oaf will yis, just fuck oaf!'
'Fuck yis oaf yurself.'
'No, yous fuck oaf!'
'No, yous fuck oaf!'
'No, yous fuck oaf!'
'No, yous fuck oaf!!!'

The shouting match between Rep and Spiney was getting louder and louder.
Bish storms off, quickly collects his stuff and get's on his bike.
'See yis back hame ya bunch o loosers.'
Bish kick starts his machine, rev's up the engine and disappears into the night driving like a madman. Rep runs after Bish.
'Looks like your hitchin' back hame Rep! Fuck oaf! Und don't cum back!' Spiney shouts out.

≈

The following day I went back to the train station and hung around all day to see if Nigel would appear. He didn't.
Back at the camp site it was the same as the day before, two depressed and miserable faces staring into the camp fire, and the headache was still there.
'A wonder where Bish and Rep ure noo? A thought they would cum crawllin' back.'
'Fuck knows, Bish wus in sum mood last night... A've never seen him in such a strop...'
'Did yis see Rep's face, when Bish took oaf without him. A'm more worried aboot us gettin' back hame ourselves in the van. Lucky A brought a siphon tube in case we need sum extra petrol.'
Our options were running out fast. We sat around the camp

fire looking at each other, close to tears, not saying very much, feeling miserable and totally depressed. The world seemed an empty place. I wanted to be back on the mountain and escape our depressed state, but there was no money and no climbing gear.
I wanted to feel the exhilaration of the climb again, but then I remembered the bad bivouac, the avalanche, the serac fall and the rock cutting the rope. Would I have survived if it had been colder on the bivouac? If the avalanche had been bigger? If the serac fall had been closer? Or the falling rock a few more inches to the right? How does Nature determine if I live or die? Is it all just chance? It's like a game, a lottery. Jacko played the game and lost. We played the game and survived. Who or what determines the outcome? I sat looking at the flames with that question rolling about in my mind.

I took out the piece of paper from my pocket. "Adenaline punk junkie" was scribbled on one side. I turned the paper over and started to write.

> Does the hand of God roll a dice?
> To determine if I live or die.
> Or in our messed-up, chaotic world,
> Is there a deeper order we don't understand?
> It's the question of life.
> As the Grand Plan unfolds.
> An unseen nature is exposed.

I stopped writing, crumpled the piece of paper into a tight ball, threw it into the fire and watched it burn.

≈

≈ Rock Rock ≈

This was our last day in Chamonix. We got into an empty van and drove off down the Chamonix Valley, through Annemasse and stopped at Jean-Claude's café, hoping he would be there and give us our 500 francs. I knew the cause was hopeless, but had to try anyway.

I jumped out of the van and tried the front door. The café was locked. There was a fermé sign on the door. I knocked on the door several times, there was no reply. I looked through several windows for any sign of life. The place looked deserted.

I turned around, walked away from the café, got into the van and we drove away.

"My way" by Bish

'Eh... Hello Bish cun yis hear us?'
'Ehhh...' a few groans from Bish.
'How ure yis feelin'?'
'Ehhh...fuckin' magic...whit dae yis think?'
'Yis look a bit o a state.'
A few grunts from Bish.
'A mean, yis look a bit mangled. Like mince. A mean, like real mince.'
A few more grunts from Bish.
'Cun yis talk OK, through awe those bits o tubes und other stuff stickin' in yis?'
Bish nodded ever so slightly.
'So whit happened?'
'Naw sure...like A kinda cunnae...A kinda cunnae...quite remember...the last... The last A remember wus...beltin' roon this road...und that's it...und that's it.'
'Well, the doc sais that yis ure lucky tae be alive. The doc sais that, yis wur cut ootae a mangled mess o cars. Yis must huv being givin' it laldy. It must o been a spectacular! Whit the fuck were yis doin'? The doc sais the fire bridge wus there, und they thought yis wur deid, und started makin' a video o the crash fur trainin' purposes, but the ambulance came along, und found oot that yis wurnae quite yet deid.'
Bish gave a wry smile.
'The doc's here...ure the big chief's...it's awe yes sir, yes sir, three bags full sir...yis cunnae tell them anythin'...bossin' yis around awe the time...they hate climbers...they hate bikers... so they really hate me...fuckin' nazi's they ure... A keep tellin' them A'm wanting oota here pronto...und a mean pronto... Fuckers keep tellin' me... A could be in a wheelchair... A keep

tellin' them... Nae fuckin' way... A cunnae climb in a wheel chair... A need tae get oota here pronto!'

'Eh...well Bish, it's like this, cun yis hear me, it's Steevie. The doc came oot wae a big list o stuff that's wrang with yis, wit wus it he said again...multiple compound fractures o yur legs, skull, pelvis, spine...und grafts, A cunnae remember if he said it wus skin grafts, bone grafts or muscle grafts frum sumwhere tae sumwhere else... A cunnae understand holf the things these doc's ure talkin' aboot, it's another language tae mae, but A don't think yis will be doin' much dancin' up the rock soon... The doc sais yis major organs ure OK, but they wur worried aboot brain swellin' und damage... Dae yis know yis huv been in a coma fur ages?'

'Hello Bish, cun yis hear me, it's Rep. The doc wus saying yis wur gontae become a vegetable, like a turnip or maybe even a cabbage, but A told him, that yur normally like that, so yis will be just fine.'

Bish gave another wry smile.

'A'm fuckin' oota here pronto a tell yis...'

'A Bish yur layin' in bed, pegged oot in a steel frame with tubes sticking oot o yis. Yis ure like a construction site, don't think yis yur goin' anywhere pronto.'

'A'm fuckin' oota here A.S.A.P. und back owan the hill A.S.A. fuckin' P. A'm tellin' yis!'

'Yis still huv tae get unplugged from awe these machines first.'

'Nae fuckin' bother, nae fuckin' pain, nae fuckin' gain... A'm oota here A.S.A.P., understand A.S.A. fuckin' P!'

'The anti-social rebel. The doc's here must luv yis.'

'A'm tellin' yis...they hate bikers...they hate climbers...so they hate me the most...A sais tae them...we're keepin' yis in a joab whit ure yis complainin' aboot?'

'Ah, Bish yis ure just a Punk Rock hero, tae old tae Rock &

Roll und too young tae die.'

'A'm tellin' yis... A'm ootae here pronto... A.S.A. fuckin'P. Fuckin' hate this place. A do... A'm back in the hill... A.S.A. fuckin'P.!'

Back on the Hill

After discharging himself early from hospital and months of physiotherapy, Bish was determined to get back on the hill. Soon Bish was crawling on hands and knees to get up the local hills—no fuckin' pain, no fuckin' gain. Then it was small painful step by small painful step walking up bigger hills—no fuckin' pain, no fuckin' gain! Soon, Bish started running up the higher hills—no fuckin' pain, no fuckin' gain.
Bish was back on the rock, simple stuff at first, but getting up harder and harder climbs. Bish was determined to get fitter, stronger, leaner and meaner on the hill.
Sometime later, Bish was soloing ice climbs in Glencoe. At the end of the day, walking back down the hill wasn't an option. Bish ran down the hill and in the darkness ran off the end of a cliff. DEAD!

"My Way" by Bish

'This time Rep yis say fuck all! Understand fuck all!' Spiney whispered loudly into Rep's ear.

'Today we are gathered to celebrate the life of Bish. Humanists accept death as part of the natural order. We bring people together to express sadness at the loss, pay tribute to the connections they made and left behind, but also to celebrate the life lived.'
Rep, Spiney and Steevie are sitting at the back of a crowded crematorium full of mourners.

The Humanist minister continues, 'I ask you to stand for a moment of silent reflection. Before we return Bish to the earth, there will be a short piece of music to reflect the character of Bish and the life he lived. I ask you to exit after the music. There'll be no closing words.'

The room was silent except for a few sniffs and snobs from the crowd.

A dark velvet cloth draped over Bish's coffin moved slightly. Rep looked up. Spiney glared at him. A few noises came over the crematorium PA system.

The room is silent again. Suddenly, the sound of a squeaky male voice gurgles out over the PA system.

> *And now, the end is near.*
> *And so A face the final curtain.*

People in the crowd started to look around wondering what was going on. The Humanist minister bows his head.

Rep whispers out loudly, 'Fuck me! Is that Jacko singin'?'

'Naw, it's Bish singin'. Now shut the fuck up!'

'Whit!'

'Shut it!'

'Bish wus plannin' tae get the band up und runnin' again, und we started recording a few songs for the next BCT World Tour.' Steevie whispered over.

The vocals continue, 'Rock Rock Rock!!' Bish's voice ringed out.

Eyebrows raised and faces turned in the crematorium, wondering what was going on. The music continues.

> *A've lived a life that's full o'shite.*
> *Travelled each and every nowhere.*
> *And more, much more than this*
> *A did it my way.*

'Fuck me! That's spooky eh!' Rep butts in.
'Shut it will yis!'

Bish's rendition of "My Way" continues in a slow methodical tone.

> Regrets, A 've had a few
> Too many to tell yis.
> A did, what A had tae do, just tae fuck yis.
> A've tried tae climb und drive like fuck
> A planned each careful step along the shiteway
> And more, much more than this
> A did it my FUCKING WAY!
> A wanna climb, don't tell me no.
> A wanna drive my bike, don't tell me no.
> Don't tell me to socialise
> Don't tell me I'm shite
> Fuck the establishment.
> Fuck this and fuck that.
> A did it my way.
>
> Born working class, die working class.
> Nowhere to go, no choice, no hope.
> Who am I to turn the tide,
> Against the force of fate.
> Watch out, it's a police state
> If you do not conform
> You'll be forced to integrate
> Big Brother is watching you
> one step out and you're dead.
> Society will not stop me,
> from expressing myself.
> A did it my way!

≈ Rock Rock ≈

Blunt my ambition, bottle my spirit
To keep me in my place.
Don't ask me why I'm a waste of space.
I'm tryin' to escape the human shite.
The whole world is against me,
Because they do not like what I say.
Be a sheep and follow the state.
A did it my FUCKING WAY!

≈ Rock Rock ≈

The Songs

Flying

I'm just hanging onto a piece of rock.
I'm just holdin' on to reality.
I'm gripped oot'a m'a fuckin' skull.
Nowhere to go but up, what the fuck.

Chorus:
Just one second to go
My body wants to Go! Go!
I just wanna be a boring bastard.
Boring Bastard! Boring Bastard!

Take a happy drug,
to find a sad tomorrow.
It's a fool's paradise
Adam's temptation apple fate.

If you don't like the chips,
you can always complain.
One second to pop a pill,
if you think you are insane.

A quick fix and forget the world,
all the ills and problems that occur.
Take a chemical to delude your brain,
try and hide but you cannot runaway.

Only excitement in life,
Jacko's style was a fright.
Sad bastard, just another body
on the pile of human shite.

Madness or may be a natural state,
gives a fear of living.
That disturbs the brain,
one second and it will be away.

What is the chemical,
that controls your mind?
Or is it your mind,
that controls your chemical?

Need a drug to confuse reality
To help the creative process flow
Good idea to kill myself
Before I become a star.

Smile, and fly through the air,
like a bird too close to the sun.
Smile, for one second of flight,
and follow the golden path to heaven.

But, I'm still here, hanging onto a piece o rock,
I'm just holdin' on to reality.
I'm gripped oot'a m'a fuckin skull.
Nowhere to go but up.

Rock, Rock

The right have no right to dictate,
the revolution has the right to rock
Rock, rock, rock, rock
Rock the establishment.

All you can do is slag me off.
Solve your own problems, mate.
Don't wanna drug to sedate my brain.
Need to get spaced out on a rock face.
Don't question my life, why?
What is your mistake, you hide?
If I lose my grip and die,
Don't remember me, but party.
People say I'm crazy,
I say it's a dead cert.
Who am I to turn the tide,
against the force of fate.
Simply forgotten in a pile of shite,
a diamond you cannot hide.
Look at me through your looking glass,
Don't like what you see.
Don't ask me why I want to climb.
In your fucked up state of mind.
Tell me I know nothing,
I tell you – you are right.
Don't ask me why I go on the hill.
Only place to find peace of mind and will.
Look out from my window,
Don't like the world that I see.
Blunt my ambition, bottle my spirit,
to keep me in my place.
Don't ask me why I'm a waste of space,
I'm trying to escape the human shite.
I just wanna be an accountant,

≈ Stephen Najda ≈

Mr Sensible and have a house.
I wanna live a life of boredom,
and die in my council estate.

Plutonium child

There's a nuclear bomb in my back garden.
I have no shield against a cancer threat.
What can I do to protect my child?
The law is made to keep me down.

Disney child, pick up a plutonium toy,
and catch a genetic mutated mouse.
Each handful of earth, a radioactive scare.
Contamination is the common word.

The politician and bigot and xenophobe will fail.
Break the chains together and pull down the wall.
Take heart, let us dance together,
I have a dream, where no one has to fight.

This planet, a common treasure to share,
but I do not own a handful of earth.
Expected to die for country of birth,
not by sword but a cancer death.

On the Clyde the Polaris sails.
From an Ayrshire field, a ploughman watches.
A tourist bus passes, everyone looking, but see nothing.
Nuclear bombs pointing, nobody knows where.

My eastern friend, I cannot see.
But I know nuclear bombs from heaven,
will land on my head.
Do they believe the same as me?

Again, if tanks run over Poland
Divine intervention is the only way,
I look around in vain,
to which God can I trust and pray.

≈ *Stephen Najda* ≈

The nuclear bomb may solve your problem,
but the politician owes an explanation.
A black death disappears beneath the waves.
Condition red. Is it practice or is it the end?

Capitalist Consumer Chaos

I have every thing,
but have nothing I want.
It's a sad state of affairs,
for a developed economy.
Society expects us to conform,
spend and throw away.
Consumerism gone wild,
materialism is the order of today.
We are living in a soft age,
in a protected state.
Chase the dollar,
it's a drug to swallow.
Machines built not to last,
but buy new every other day.
A dream of fast cars, designer clothes,
don't forget the bimbo in the bikini.
Only chance of life,
is to watch on my T.V. set.
Rat race is for rats,
and not for the animal in me.
It's the consumer society,
in the capitalist's paradise.
Have we forgotten reality?
Chained to my T.V.
Soap opera and game shows,
stare at a piece of furniture.
Ideal for the advertiser,
to send the message down the wave.
Comfort from a semi-detached,
look out from your cage.
Have you realised your dream,
or are you afraid of a nightmare.
A new technology must be alright,
available only for the jet-set.

≈ Stephen Najda ≈

Famine in Africa is fine,
to watch on my T.V. set.
Plague in Asia won't infect me,
lying on my sofa bed.
War beamed into my living room,
no worries to dodge the flying lead.
Slave to my machine,
pollution is my right
An information age,
but no one understands.
Lost in a sea of technology,
reach out for a helping hand.
No hope of a life belt,
helpless against the force of progress.
Mother nature acting in best interest,
against a man-made dying planet fate.
Kill the land and extinct the sea,
A problem I cannot see.
A slow death of stress,
or was it suffocation by car exhaust.
But the coroner said,
death by misadventure.
Watch out!
It's a police state.
If you do not conform,
you will be forced to integrate.
Big brother is watching you,
one step out and you're dead.
Society will stop me,
from expressing myself.
Only escape is my thought,
bought and sold as a commodity.
Need a psychiatrist help, and medicine,
to be programmed to follow the crowd.
Get my priority right,
what I want in life is a dish-washer.

≈ Rock Rock ≈

And a life-time subscription to Reader's Digest,
package holiday in Benidorm,
and don't forget, a poodle shampoo and set.

≈ *Stephen Najda* ≈

Hole in ma heid

I've go'ta hole in m'a heid.
Nothing to worry aboot, it's quite casual.
Latest fashion accessory from the glossy magazine.
Quite handy, lets my brain release the thinkin' process.
It helps me see, what's wrong in this world.
Third World poverty, not my problem, mate.
Pollution is my right, destroy planet earth.
I'm stuck on the Point of Life.

I've go'ta hole in m'a heid.
Born working class, die working class,
nowhere to go, no choice, no hope.
Go fighting, get pissed,
have baby, grow old, find a grave.
Wreck this, destroy that,
only identity, is my writing on the wall.
I'm stuck on the Point of Life.

I've go'ta hole in m'a heid.
People ask, why do I climb?
Mental to do such things, they say.
I say, why are you living in such a fucked up state
The whole world is against me,
because they do not like what I say.
Be a sheep and follow the state.
I'm stuck on the Point of Life.

I've go'ta hole in m'a heid.
Take a drug to fix my mind,
chemical illusion clears my vision.
Better than society induced depressive plight.
Only escape from the working class fate.
Sniff glue to relax my state.
A nice glass of meths, after dinner taste.

≈ Rock Rock ≈

I'm stuck on the Point of Life.

I've go'ta hole in m'a heid.
No need to meditate.
I've found my piece of mind.
I've found the Point of Life.
I'm in a state of ecstasy.

≈ Stephen Najda ≈

Coke Can Culture

Beams of light from my television box,
gives me square eyes,
receptive to the market hype.
Cellophane wrapped,
pre-packaged, sterilised world,
there's nowhere to escape.
Its a Coke can culture.
Buy one and throw away,
its not an excess, it's a necessity.
From Sherpa on Everest,
to Eskimo on the ice flow.
From Masai on African plain,
to Indian in Amazon.
They try to escape,
the Coke can culture.
You need to buy, don't question why,
I'm in a moronic state,
there's no escape.
It's a Coke can culture.
Feed the starving masses,
give them a taste of the West.
It's canned and hyped,
and sold as the milk of life.
I don't like the taste,
but I cannot be right,
The marketing says,
Coke is great.

≈ Rock Rock ≈

A view from Stob Dearg

Buachaille Etive Mor, on guard, entrance to the 'Coe'.
What secrets does the old shepherd hold?
A land scoured by glacier and forests scorched by man.
Rivers of blood, treachery, deceit and murder.
Family feud, passed from father to son.
A haunting mist, that covers, and then exposes the past.
Tails of horror, witches, phantoms and ghosts.

An English army marched north in search of Jacobite.
Highland soldier marched south, to fight an Empire war.
The English landlord took the land, and slaughtered our kin.
Sheep more important than man, they died for profit and gain.
I stand on Bauchallie Etive Mor, wondering where they went.
Facing an icy wind, through silent miles and empty space.
With eyes of a child, and wonder of a saint.

Victims of chance and geography, you say.
There are many sad periods of history—what a pity.
When the minority is viewed as irrelevant, a mistake.
Something to be conquered, replaced, moved out of the way.
As the big boys scheme and play, the small cower in fear and fright.
History has taught us nothing, except it will happen again.
Cannot they see, monoculture is a fright.

I hear the cry of pipes, flowing over mountain like morning mist.
A cry from my brother, and memories from a distant land.
I can see pain in your tears, and hear sorrow in your song.
A land where you were born but never forget,
body and soul, as mountain and sea.
Like the wild salmon that leaves these shores,
fights all nature to return home, but may die at the hand of fate.

Today, I climb these hills in freedom.
A silence golden, only to be broken,

by the sound of a low flying phantom jet.
An unspoken war declared, a new Highland battlefield,
against a distant Soviet threat.
Deceive yourself, but you cannot hide, the frost has settled overnight.
At first dawn light, The Bauchallie will still be watching.

Rock Rock

"My Way" by Jacko	p.9
Pure Fuckin' Mental	p.18
Devil's Delight	p.58
Lucy	p.108
The Old Man	p.155
Devil's Delight (part 2)	p.189
The van	p.210
The BCT World Tour	p.226
Aiguille du Plan - Up the North face and down the West face.	p.255
Ze gig	p.294
"My Way" by Bish	p.347
The songs	p.356

ISBN : 978-1-913964-15-3

All Rights Reserved. No part of this book can be used or reproduced in any manner whatsoever without written permission from the publisher, except in the case of brief quotations embodied in critical articles or reviews.
A catalogue record for this book is available from the British Library.
Editor: Charlotte J. March
Cover: Wolf Graham
Book Design: Wolf Graham

Publishing Company: Black Wolf Edition & Publishing Ltd.
Scotland
www.blackwolfedition.co.uk

Copyright © 2022 by Black Wolf Edition & Publishing Ltd. and other respective owners identified in this work. Designs and Patents Act 1988 All rights reserved. First Edition 2022

www.ingramcontent.com/pod-product-compliance
Lightning Source LLC
Chambersburg PA
CBHW030047100526
44590CB00011B/354